DISCOURSES COMPLETE

BOOKS 1 - 4

EPICTETUS

ADAPTED FOR THE CONTEMPORARY READER BY
JAMES HARRIS

ISBN: 9798480408133

CHAPTER 1 - THINGS IN OUR POWER AND NOT IN OUR POWER

Out of all the mental faculties, you can't find one which is capable of contemplating itself; and, consequently, it's not capable either of approving or disapproving what it does. How far does contemplating power go? As far as forming a judgement about what is written and spoken. And how far in music? As far as judging if a melody sounds good or not. Could either of them contemplate itself? Not at all. When you want to write something to your friend, grammar can tell you what words to use; but it can't tell you whether you should write or not. And it's the same with music to musical sounds; but whether you sing or play the guitar, or do neither, music can't tell you that. What faculty then can tell you? The faculty which contemplates both itself and all other things. And what faculty is that? The rational faculty; because this is the only faculty we possess which examines itself, and what power it has, how much value there is in this great gift, as it examines all other faculties: and what else is there which tells us that things made of gold are beautiful, because they can't tell us themselves? Evidently it is the faculty which is capable of judging appearances. What else judges' music, grammar, and the other faculties, proves their use and points out the correct occasions for using them? Nothing else but reasoning.

And so, it should be, the best of all, and supreme, as it is the only thing which the gods have placed in our power, the right use of appearances; everything else was not given to us to possess and control. Was it because they chose not to? I think if they had been able to, they would have given us power over the rest, but they couldn't. Because as we exist on the earth, and are contained in a body, how was it possible for us not to be hindered by these external things?

The gods might say "Epictetus, if it were possible, I would have made the body free and not exposed. But please don't be ignorant: the body is not yours, it is fine suit for you to wear. And since I wasn't able to do what I mentioned, I gave you a small portion of the gods abilities, the faculty of pursuing an object and avoiding it, of desire and aversion, and, in summary, the faculty of using the appearances of things; and if you take care of this faculty and consider it your only possession, you will never be hindered, never impeded; you will never feel sad, you won't blame anything or anyone, and you won't flatter any person."

"Does this seem insignificant to you?" I hope not. "Be content with this then and thank the gods." When something is in our power we should look after it, and stick to it, but we tend to look after many things which are not our true possession and become bound to them, we become bound to the body and to property, to family and friends, and to our children. When we are bound to many things, we are depressed by them and dragged down. For example, when the weather isn't very good for sailing, we sit down and feel discouraged, continually on the lookout to see which way the wind is blowing. "North." What does that really mean to us? "When will it blow to the west?" Whenever it decides to, my good friend, because God has not made you the manager of the wind. So then, we have to make the best use of the things which are actually in our power, and use everything else according to their nature. What is their nature? Whatever God decided.

So, if you faced having your head cut off, would you feel sad? Wouldn't you stretch out your neck, like Lateranus did in Rome when Nero ordered him to be beheaded? He stretched out his neck and received a weak blow, which made him tuck it in for a moment, then he stretched it out again. Earlier, when he was visited by Epaphroditus, Nero's helper, who asked him about the cause of the offense he was accused of, he said, "If I decide to say anything, I will tell your master."

So how should a man behave in these circumstances? The only thoughts required are "What is mine is mine, and what is not is not." If I have to die, should I face death and feel sad? If I have to be put in chains, should I feel sad? If I face exile does that mean I can't go with a smile, cheerfulness and contentment? So, it was put to Lateranus "Tell me the secret which you possess." And he didn't reply, because that was in his power. "But I will put you in chains." Man, what are you talking about? Me in chains? You could cut off my leg, but my willpower not even God himself can overpower. "I will put you into prison." My poor body, you mean. "I will cut your head off." When? Have I told you that my head can't be cut off? These are the things which philosophers should meditate on, which they should write about daily, and in which they should exercise themselves.

Thrasea used to say, "I would rather be killed today than banished tomorrow." But what did Rufus say to him? "If you think you choose death as your preference, isn't that a fallacy? Who has given you the choice? Shouldn't you be content with what has really been given to you?"

What did Agrippinus say? He said, "I'm not trying to hinder myself." When it was reported that his trial was taking place in the Senate, he said, "I hope it turns out well; but it's the fifth hour of the day"- this was the time when he was used to exercise and then take the cold shower- "let's go exercise." After his exercise, someone came and told him, "You were convicted." "To banishment," he replied, "or to death?" "To banishment." "What about my property?" "It's hasn't been seized." "Let's go to Aricia then for dinner," he said.

This is a man who has studied what a man should study. To have made desire and aversion free from hindrance, and free from all that a man would usually try to avoid. If I must die now, I am ready to die. If later, I will go to dinner because it's dinner time. And when I do die, how will I die? Like a man who gives up everything that belongs to someone else

CHAPTER 2 – HOW A MAN ON EVERY OCCASION CAN MAINTAIN HIS PROPER CHARACTER

To a rational being, the irrational is intolerable; only the rational can be tolerated. Blows to the body are not always intolerable. "Why is that?" Some endure blows to the body when they learn that it is consistent with their reason. "To hang yourself is not intolerable." When it becomes rational, you would go and hang yourself. In short, if we observe, we find that man cannot feel more pain than that which is irrational; and, on the contrary, attracted to nothing more than that which is rational.

But the rational and irrational appear different to different people, just like good and the bad, profitable and unprofitable. For this reason, particularly, we need discipline, in order to learn how to adapt the preconception of the rational and the irrational to the things which conform to nature. But in order to determine the rational and the irrational, we don't only judge external things, we also consider what is appropriate for each person. Because to one man it is consistent with his reason to hold a begging bowl, but for another, it isn't. This man will not have any food if he doesn't hold the begging bowl, but if he does he ends his hunger. To another man not only would holding the bowl be intolerable, but also to allow another person to acquire his food for him. So, if you asked me if you should hold the bowl or not, I would say receiving the food is worth more than not receiving it, and being hungry is a greater indignity than being fed; so, if you measure your interests in this way, you would go and hold the bowl. "But," you say, "this wouldn't be worthy of me." Well, then, it's up to you to introduce this consideration into the inquiry, not me; because it is you who knows yourself, how much you are worth to yourself, and at what price you sell yourself; because men sell themselves at various prices.

Because of this, when Florus was deliberating whether he should attend Nero's spectacles and perform in them, Agrippinus said, "Attend": and when Florus asked Agrippinus, "Why don't you attend?" Agrippinus replied, "Because I don't even deliberate about the matter." Because once a man brings himself to deliberate about such matters, and to calculate the value of external things like this, he is very close to forgetting his own character. Ask me, whether death is preferable or life? An I will say "life." "Pleasure or pain?" I will say "pleasure." But if I don't take a part in this, I will have my head cut off. Go and take part then, but I won't. "Why?" Because you considering yourself to be like one thread of a garment. Then it makes sense for you to be like the rest of men, just as the thread has no design to be anything superior to the other threads. I want to be purple, the small part which is bright on the garment, and makes all the rest appear graceful and beautiful. So why would you ask me to be like everyone else? If I did that how would I be different?

Priscus also knew this, because when Ceasar commanded him not to go into the senate, he replied, "It's in your power not to allow me to enter the senate, but as long as I am a member, I have to go in." "Well, go in then," said the emperor, "but don't say anything." "But if I am asked for my opinion – you expect me to be silent? I have to say what I think is right." "I you do, I will arrange for your death." Didn't I tell you that I'm immortal? You will do your part, and I will do mine: it is your part to kill; it is mine to die, but not in fear: your part to banish me; mine to depart without sorrow."

But what good could this do, as Priscus was only a single person? The same good that purple can do for the white robe? It is clearly visible like purple on the gown, and is displayed as a fine example in contrast to everything else? But under different circumstances, another man would have replied to Caesar who told him to not to enter the senate, "I thank you for allowing me to live." But any man like this Ceasar wouldn't have even forbid to enter, because he would know that a man like this would sit there like an empty bottle, or, if he did speak, he would say whatever Caesar wanted him to.

So, if someone said Epictetus, shave yourself." "If I am a philosopher," I answer, "I won't shave myself." "But I will cut your head off" Well, if that will do you some good, take it off then.

Someone once asked, "How can each man perceive what is suitable for his character?" Does the bull, when the lion has attacked, discover his own powers and put himself forward in defence of the whole herd? It is clear, that with any power, the perception of having it is immediately conjoined; and, therefore, whoever has such power will not be ignorant of it. A bull is not made suddenly, neither is a brave man; but we must discipline ourselves in the winter for the summer, and not carelessly run toward anything which doesn't concern us.

Always consider at what price you are selling your own will; if for no other reason than this: you shouldn't sell it cheaply, but only for that which is great and superior, perhaps something which belongs to Socrates and others like him. "You may say, if we are naturally like this, why aren't there many of us like him?" Is it true that all horses run fast? That all dogs are highly skilled in tracking footprints? Not at all, so, since I am naturally dull, for that reason shouldn't I strive for excellence?" Of course not. Epictetus isn't superior to Socrates; but if I'm not inferior, that would be enough for me; I will not obsess over the body; but I won't neglect it, I will not obsess over property, but I will not neglect it, and I will not neglect looking after anything because due to fear of reaching the highest degree.

CHAPTER 3 – HOW A MAN SHOULD PROCEED FROM THE PRINCIPLE OF GOD BEING THE FATHER OF ALL MEN

If a man is able to accept this as he should, that we all originate from God in a very special manner, and that God is the father both men and any other gods, I think he would cease to have any mean thoughts about himself. But if Caesar employed him, perhaps no would endure his arrogance; but if he knew he was a son of God, wouldn't he be joyous? Yet many don't follow this; some view the generation of man, and his body in common with the animals, and reason and intelligence in common with the gods. This is sad, as he doesn't view the entirety of himself as having originated from God. It is of great necessity that every man uses everything according to the opinion which he has about it, those, the few, who think that they are formed for righteousness and modesty and a sure use of appearances have no mean thoughts about themselves; but for many others it is quite the contrary. Because they look at themselves and say, "What am I? A poor, miserable man, with an unhealthy body." Yes, this person is poor indeed; because they fail to realise they're more than a body." Why do they neglect that which is better, and attach themselves to this solely?

To view ourselves as only a body, is inclining us become like wolves, faithless, treacherous and mischievous: some become like lions, savage and untamed; but the greater number of people become like foxes and other animals. Because what else is a man who creates false stories about others and has evil thoughts and intentions than a fox, or some other more disgusting and mean animal? So, realise you are more than a body so that you do not become one of these miserable animals.

CHAPTER 4 – PROGRESS OR IMPROVEMENT

A man is making progress, if he has learned from philosophers that desire means to desire good things, and aversion means aversion from bad things; having learned too that happiness and tranquillity are not attainable by a man if he doesn't obtain what he desires, and avoids falling into that which he should avoid. A man that doesn't do this takes away from himself desire altogether and defers it, but instead his aversion is applied to things which he wills for. Because if he attempts to avoid anything independent of his will, he knows that sometimes he will fall into the very thing he wants to avoid, and he will be unhappy. But if virtue promises us good fortune, tranquillity and happiness, certainly the progress toward virtue is progress toward each of these things as well. Because it is always true that whatever point the perfecting of anything leads us to, progress is an approach toward this point.

If virtue provides what I say, why do we seek progress in other things and make a display those instead? What is the product of virtue? Tranquillity. Who is improving then? Is it the man who has read many books written Chrysippus? Does virtue really consist in having understood Chrysippus? If this is so, progress is clearly nothing else than knowing a great deal of Chrysippus. But now we are saying that virtue produces one thing. and we declare that approaching it through reading is another thing, namely, progress or improvement. " Someone might say, "well, the man is able to read Chrysippus by himself. He must be making great progress, so we shouldn't mock the man." But without knowing the effect of virtue the progress is unknown. So, our work first lies in our desire and in our aversion, it must be perfected so you are not disappointed by your desire, and so you don't fall into that which you want to avoid; in your pursuit and avoiding, that you make no error; in accepting this, or suspending your acceptance. The first things, and the most necessary, are those which I've mentioned. If you cannot tell me that which you desire or wish to avoid, how can you tell me you are improving?

Show me your improvement. If I were talking to an athlete, I would say, "show me your shoulders"; and he might say, "here are my dumbbells." Your dumbbells are not the result. "I want to see the effect of the dumbbells." With you I am not inquiring about this, but how you exercise pursuit and avoidance, desire and aversion, how you design your purpose and prepare yourself, whether conformably to nature or not. If conformably, give me evidence of it, and I will say that you are making progress: but if not conformably, leave my presence and don't tell me about your books. Write the books yourself; and what will you gain from it? Don't you know that one book costs only five denarii? But doesn't the publisher seem to be worth more than five denarii? Never, then, look at the matter itself in one place, and progress toward it in another."

When is there progress then? When any man, withdraws from the external, turns to his own will to exercise it and to improve it by labour, to make it conformable to nature, elevated, free, unrestrained, unimpeded, faithful, modest; and if he has learned that he who desires or avoids the things which are not in his power cannot be faithful or free, but of necessity he must change with them and be tossed about with them as if he was in a storm, and of necessity must subject himself to others who have the power to procure or prevent what he desires or wants to avoid; finally, when he rises in the morning, if he remembers and keeps these rules, cleans his body like a man of faithfulness, eats like a modest man; and if in every matter that occurs he works out his main principles, like the runner does with reference to running, and the vocal coach with reference to the voice - this is the man who truly makes progress, and this is the man who has not travelled aimlessly. If he has strained his effort to the practice of reading books, and works only at this, and has travelled for this, I would tell him to return home immediately, and not to neglect his affairs there; because he has travelled for nothing. But his is something: to study how a man can remove from his life sorrow and complaining, "poor me" and "how poor I am," and to also remove misfortune and disappointment and to learn what death is, exile, prison, and poison, so he is able to say when he faces these, "Dear Crito, if this is what the gods will, then let it be"; and not to say, "I'm such a poor man, so old that I now have grey hairs" Who speaks like this? Do you think that I can name a reputable man with such a low condition? What else is it but a tragedy, the perturbations of men who value the external? If a man can learn by fiction that no external things which are independent of the will concern us, he should like this fiction, and by the aid of it should live happily and undisturbed. But you must consider for yourselves what you wish.

What does Chrysippus teach us? The reply is, "to know that these things are not made up, that happiness comes and tranquillity arises. You will learn how true and conformable to nature things are which make us free from inner disturbance." Should he be praised then for showing the way. For Triptolemus men have built temples and altars, because he gave us the means to cultivate food; but for the man who discovered truth and brought it to light and communicated it to all, not the truth which shows us how to live, but how to live well, who for this reason has built an altar, or a temple, or has dedicated a statue? Well there is no need, because the gods have given us the vine, and wheat, we offer them thanks: and as they have produced in the human mind, that which they designed to show us the truth, which relates to happiness, we can thank God for this.

CHAPTER 5 – AGAINST THE ACADEMICS

If a man said Epictetus is in opposition to truth which is evident, it wouldn't be hard to find an argument which would make him change his opinion. But this wouldn't arise from either that man's strength or the teacher's weakness; because when the man, though he has been proven wrong, is hardened like a stone, how could we then be able to deal with him by argument alone?

There are two kinds of hardening, one is the understanding, the other is the sense of shame, when a man has resolved not to agree to what is clear and will not stop contradicting what is apparent. Most of us are afraid about harm to the body, and would try our hardest to avoid such a thing, but as mentioned above these people care less about damage to the soul. And with regards to the soul, if a man is in such a state as to not comprehend, or understand at all, we would think that he's in a bad condition: but if the sense of shame and modesty are fully removed from him, we might call this power.

Do you comprehend that you are awake? "I don't," one man replies, "because I don't even comprehend when during my sleep I imagine that I'm awake." Should I still argue with this man? And what fire needs to be lit to make him realise? He can perceive, but he pretends that he doesn't. He's even worse than a dead man. What he doesn't see is the contradiction: he's in a bad state. Another sees it, but he doesn't change the opinion he expresses, and so, makes no improvement: he's in a worse condition. His modesty is damaged, and his sense of shame; and the rational faculty hasn't been fully removed from him, but it is in a bad condition.

CHAPTER 6 - PROVIDENCE

For everything which happens in the world, it's easy to praise God, if a man possesses these two qualities, the ability to see what belongs and happens to all people and things, and a grateful attitude. If he doesn't possess those qualities, a man won't be able to see the clearly the correct use of things; he will not be thankful for them, even if he has them in his possession. If God had made colours, but hadn't made the faculty of to interpret them, what would be their use? None at all. On the other hand, if God had made the faculty of vision, but hadn't made objects which the vision could recognise, what would be the purpose of vision? None at all. Well, suppose that God had made both, but had not made light? In that case, also, there would have been of no use. Similarly, we have the knife for cutting, and from the very structure of things which have been created, we are accustomed to notice that the creation was made by someone, and that it hasn't been constructed without a purpose. Don't then each of these creations prove the workman exists, and don't visible things and the faculty of seeing and light demonstrate God? And the existence of male and female, and the desire of both to join, doesn't this demonstrate God?

If they don't, let us consider the constitution of our understanding that when we encounter objects in reality, we receive impressions from them, but we also subtract something, or add something, and, in fact, pass from person to person something else which in a manner resembles the initial object: isn't this sufficient evidence to induce some men not to forget the workman? If not so, let that man explain to us what it is then, that makes each thing, or how it is possible that such wonderful things like art could exist by chance?

What do we find which exists in us? Many things of course, reside inside us as rational animals; however, we will also find many in common with irrational animals. Do irrational animals understand why things are done? Of course not. Because to act is one thing, but understanding why is another: God designed irrational animals to act in accordance with the present moment, but gave us the ability to understand the use of action. It is enough for them to eat and to drink, and to sleep and to procreate, and to do all the other things which they do. But for us, to who God has given also the faculty of understanding, these things are not sufficient; because unless we act in a proper and orderly manner, and conformably to the nature and constitution of ourselves, we could never attain our true status. Our constitutions are different, and also the actions and results are different. In those animals, then, which has been adapted for action only, action alone is enough: but in an animal which has the power to understand the actions, unless he exercises that understanding, he will never attain his proper state. Well then, God created every animal, one to be eaten, another to serve for agriculture, another to supply cheese, and another for some similar use. But God has introduced man to be a spectator of God and of His work; and not only a spectator of them, but an interpreter. For this reason, it is shameful for a man to begin and to end where irrational animals do, but rather he should begin where they begin, and end where true nature ends in us; and nature ends in contemplation and understanding, in a way of life conformable to nature. So, take care then not to die without having been a spectator of these things.

Everyone travels to Olympia to see the work of Phidias, and they all think it's such a shame to live a life without seeing such great work. However, when there is no need to take a trip, we can find the work of God before us, wouldn't you desire to see and understand that work? Can't you perceive what you are, or what you were born for, or what you have been given the ability to see for? But you say, "There are some things which are bad and troublesome in life." Do you think there are none in Olympia? Aren't people burnt to death? Don't people get wet by the rain? Do you not hear the noise? But I suppose that offsetting all of these things against the magnificence, you will endure these problems. So, do you can't you comprehend that you have been given the ability to bear anything that happens? Haven't you received greatness of soul? Haven't you received manliness? Haven't you received endurance? So why should we concern ourselves with anything that can happen if we possess greatness of soul? What can distract my mind or disturb me, or appear painful? Shouldn't I use my power for the purposes for which I was given it, or should I be upset and fear over what could happen?

"Yes, but my nose runs, what's the purpose of that?" Don't you have hands? Don't you think it's so you can wipe your nose? " That would then be consistent with reason that there should be running of noses in the world?" Actually, how much better is it to wipe your nose than to find fault a fault with it. What do you think Hercules would have become if there wasn't lions, stags and boars, and certain unjust, immoral and wild men, which Hercules used to drive away and clear out? What would he be doing if nothing of this kind existed? Isn't is obvious he would have wrapped himself up and slept? First of all, he wouldn't have become Hercules, if he was dreaming away his life in such luxury and ease. Even if he was as strong as he became, what would have been his use? How would he have obtained his arms, the strength of his body, his endurance and noble spirit, if such circumstances and occasions had not roused him to exercise? "Doesn't if become clear, that a man must provide for himself the means to exercise, and to introduce a lion from some place into his reality?" This may appear as madness: I don't literally mean a real lion, but, they were useful for demonstrating what Hercules was and for exercising him. So, having observed these things, can you observe the faculties which you have, and when you have looked at them, say: "God, bring to me any difficulty that you decide, because I have faculties given to me by you to strengthen myself through anything that happens." You won't do it, you sit still, trembling in fear that some things are going to happen, and crying over what does happen: and then you blame God. What is the consequence of such a weak spirit but disrespect to God? And yet God has not only given us these faculties; by which we are able to tolerate anything that happens without being depressed or broken by it; but, like a good king and a true father, God has given us these faculties subject to no compulsion, and has put them entirely in our own power, without reserving any of the power to be able to hinder you. You, who have received these powers free and as your own, use don't use them: you can't even see what you've received, and from where; some of are blind to the giver, and never acknowledge God, due to the meanness of your spirit, only ever finding fault and being angry toward God. However, I will show to you that you have the power and means to possess greatness of soul and manliness but the power you have for finding fault and making accusations, please don't show me.

CHAPTER 7 – THE USE OF HYPOTHETICAL ARGUMENTS

The handling hypothetical arguments, and those of which derive their conclusions from questioning, and in actuality all arguments, relate to the duty of life, though many don't realise this truth. Because in every matter we inquire how the wise and good man can discover the correct path and the correct method of dealing with these issues. In contrast, the bad man takes no care about conducting himself rashly or carelessly in questioning and answering. However, he should realise that inquiry should be made into those topics on which in particularly questioning and answering are needed in argument. What is the purpose? To establish true propositions, to remove the false, and to withhold confusion from that which is not plain. Is it enough to learn only this? "It's enough," a man may reply. Is it, then, also enough for a man, to believe, in the use of coined money, what is genuine and what is counterfeit? "It is not enough." What, then, should be added to this? None other than the faculty which proves and distinguishes the genuine from the fake. Consequently, also in reasoning what has been said is not enough; but is it necessary that a man should acquire the faculty of examining and distinguishing the true and the false. Besides this, what is proposed in reasoning? "That you should accept what follows from that which you have properly understood." Well, is it enough in this case? It isn't enough; but a man must learn how one thing is a consequence of other things, and when one thing follows from one thing, and when it follows from several collectively. Consider carefully, that it is necessary, that the following power should also be acquired by him who wishes to conduct himself skilfully in reasoning, the power of demonstrating to himself several things which he proposes, and the power of understanding the demonstrations of other people, including not to be deceived by hypothetical arguments, as if they were demonstrating pure reason.

In fact, in some cases we have granted the hypothetic arguments or assumptions, and form that are compelled to action; although it isn't true. What should I do? Should I say that I didn't grant these things? "No, you shouldn't do this." Should I say that the consequence didn't arise due to what has been accept? "This isn't allowed either." What should I do then? Imagine this: to borrow money isn't enough to make a man a debtor, but add to this fact that that he continues to owe the money and that the debt is not paid, so it is not enough for you to admit that you have granted the hypothetical, if you still abide by what you have granted. Indeed, if the hypothetical still exists in the mind in the same manner as when it was granted, we must accept the consequences: but having realised, if it doesn't remain, it is necessary for us withdraw from what we granted, and through this we avoid the consequences of that which isn't true. Now the inference is not our inference, neither does it result with our downfall, since we have removed the false which we once believed. We have to carefully examine such premises in the course of questioning or answering, or by making the reasonable conclusion, however, premises undergo variations, and occasionally cause the foolish man to be confused, if they are unable to draw a reasonable conclusion. So why should we carefully examine? So, we don't take inappropriate actions and become confused in any way.

Sometimes it may become necessary to grant some hypothesis as a kind of passage to an argument which follows. Should we then allow every hypothesis that is proposed, or refuse all? And if some, which should we allow? And if a man has allowed a hypothesis, should he in every case abide by it? or must he sometimes remove it, but admit the consequences and not make excuses for it? Yes; but suppose that a man says, "If you admit the hypothesis of a possibility, I will lure you into an impossibility." With a person like this should a man of sense refuse to enter into an argument, and avoid discussion and conversation with him? How can a man of sense, use careful argumentation, be so skilful in questioning and answering, be protected by false reasoning? Should a man like this enter into the argument, and due to his level of skill allow himself to relax? And if he doesn't take care, how could he be the man we consider him to be? Is it possible without preparation, that he could maintain a continuous and consistent argument?

There can be no negligence and sluggishness, why do we seek easy methods for not being diligent and watchful when cultivating our reason? "What if I make a mistake which causes the death of my father?" Where was the father in this matter that you could kill him? What have you done? If the father was not in the vicinity, then the only fault that was possible here is the fault which you have committed, for the father to have died he would have had to have committed his own fault. This is the same as what I told Rufus when he blamed me for not discovering one thing in a certain form of reasoning: "I suppose," I said, "that I have burnt the capital." "He replied, "Capitol?" Are these your only crimes, to burn the capital and to kill your father? For a man to act so foolishly and carelessly, not to understand argument, or demonstration, or hypothetical reasoning, or to see in questioning and answering what is consistent with that which we have granted or is inconsistent; don't you see the error in this?

CHAPTER 8 – THE FACULTIES ARE NOT SAFE FOR THE UNINSTRUCTED

In many ways, we can change things which are equivalent to one another, and in just as many ways, we can change the forms of arguments in argumentation. This is an instance: "If you have borrowed and not repaid, you owe me the money: you have not borrowed and you have not repaid; then you do not owe me the money." This skill suits the philosopher more than any man; because the hypothesis contains imperfect reasoning. it is clear to see that a man understands perfect reasoning must equally be an expert in the imperfect also.

"Why don't we exercise ourselves and one another in this manner?" Because at the moment, although we are not exercising in these things and not distracted from the study of morality, by me at least, we will be making no progress in virtue. What can we expect if we add the study of reasoning? Especially as this wouldn't be the only occupation which would hinder our progress in more necessary pursuits. There is great power in arguing and persuasion, and in particularly if it is exercised regularly, however every faculty acquired by the uninstructed and weak brings with it the danger being elated and inflated by it. Because how could someone persuade a man, who believes he's the master of persuasion, that he shouldn't become attached to this, but to attach it to himself? Wouldn't he disregard your reasoning, and walk inflated – puffed up, not listening to the reasoning of any man around him?

"Wasn't Plato a philosopher?" I reply, "And was Hippocrates a physician? You see how Hippocrates speaks." Does Hippocrates, speak in the manner of physician? Why do you compare things which have been accidentally united in the same men? If Plato was handsome and strong, should I also work and endeavour to become handsome or strong, as if this was necessary for philosophy, because a certain philosopher was at the same time handsome and a philosopher? Can't you see and distinguish in respect to men who become philosophers, what things belong to belong to them in this regard and what in other respects? And if I were a philosopher, do you also have to become one? Is it up to me what faculties you possess? Not at all; as surely as I don't take away your ability to see. But if you ask me what's the good for a man, I can't tell you anything else other than there is a certain disposition of the will with respect to the appearance of everything.

CHAPTER 9 – HOW TO FORM THE FACT THE WE ARE LIKE GOD AND MAY ENJOY THE CONSEQUENCES OF THIS

If all that has been said by philosophers about the relationship between God and man is true, what else is left for men to do than what Socrates did? Never reply to the question of what country you are from, saying you are an Athenian or a Corinthian, reply saying that you are a citizen of the world. Because why would you say that you are from a small part of the world only where your body was generated? Because by being a citizen of the world, now you are not only calling yourself Athenian or Corinthian, but that which comprises the small place itself, the whole country and wherever the originators of your family line came from? A true man has observed with intelligence the administration of the world, and has learned that the greatest, supreme and the most comprehensive community is that which is composed of men and God, and that from God have descended the seeds not only to my father and grandfather, but to all beings which are generated on earth, and in particularly logical men – because these are, by their nature formed to have communion with God, by means of reason joined with Him- why shouldn't a man like this call himself a citizen of the world, why not a son of God, and why should he be afraid of anything which might happen for doing so? Is a relationship with Caesar or with any other powerful man in Rome sufficient enough to enable us to live in safety, without any fear at all? Not at all, however, to have God as your maker, father and guardian, releases us from these fears. But a man might say, "When will I be able to eat some bread, I have nothing?" What about people who escape prison and runaway? Do they rely on their land or stores of silver? They rely on nothing but themselves, with or without food. Do you think it is necessary for a philosopher who travels to foreign regions, to trust and rely on other people, and not be able to take care of himself? Would he be inferior to irrational animals which by the way, are capable of being self-sufficient, neither failing to get their food, or to find a suitable way of living, which is also conformable to nature?

I think that the old men amongst us, shouldn't only sit discussing having no mean thoughts, but to take care that there are no young men with a mind like that, and that when they have recognized their relationship to God, and that we are chained by these bonds, the body, I mean, and whatever else is necessary to us for the economy and commerce of life, they should intend to shake off these things as if they were painful burdens which have become intolerable. This is the work that your teacher should be employed for, if he really were to teach what is truly meaningful. You could say to him, "Epictetus, we can't endure for any longer being bound to this body, feeding it, resting it, cleaning it, and complying to the wishes of society. Shouldn't we be indifferent to these things and understand that death is not an evil thing? And aren't we related to God, and didn't we come from Him? We should be allowed to leave and return to the place which we came from; and allowed to be released at last from these bonds which we are weighed down with. In this reality there are evil people, thieves and courts of justice, and those who are named tyrants, who think they have power over us through the body and its material possessions. Allow us to show them that they have no power over any man." And I would say in reply, "Friends, wait for God; soon he will give you the signal and release you from this service, then go to Him; but for the present endure this plane where he has placed you: your time here will be short, and easy to bear, because what tyrant or thief, or what court of justice, are formidable to those who have considered the body to be of no value? Wait then, don't leave without a reason."

Something like this should be said by the teachers to the youth of today. But now what is happening? The teacher is a lifeless body, and you are lifeless bodies. When you have been filled yourself today, you sit down and think about tomorrow, how you'll get something to eat. Listen it's simple, if you have it, you will have it; if you don't, you will leave life. The door is open. Why do you worry? There should be no room for tears. Why should anyone envy another? Why should a man admire the rich or the powerful, even if they may have a violent temper? What benefit is this to us? We shouldn't care about what they can and cannot do. How did

Socrates behave in respect to these matters? In no other way than a man should, who is convinced that he is related to God? "If you say to me now," said Socrates to his judges, "'We will acquit you on the condition that you no longer talk in the way you have up until now, do not bother the young or the old,' I would say to you, 'you know if one of our commanders appointed me to a post, it is my duty to keep and maintain it, and possess the will to die a thousand times rather than leave it; so you are absolutely absurd if you can see that God has given me a post and you think I am going to vacate it.'" Socrates speaks like a man who communicates with God. But we think about ourselves as if we were only a body.

A man once wrote to me asking for my advice. This was a man most people thought, had been unfortunate, because formerly he was a man with a high rank and very rich, but he was stripped of everything. I wrote to him in a consoling manner; but when he read the letter, he sent it back to me and said, "I asked for your advice, not your pity: no evil has happened to me."

In order to test me, Rufus used to say: "one day you will inherit this or that from your master"; and I replied that these things happen in the ordinary course of life. However, there are greater things which I am able to obtain for myself. Because, in fact, what a man has within himself, is foolish to wait and receive from another. So, I am able to receive from myself greatness of soul and a generous spirit, I do not need to receive from my master - land, money or a prestigious job? Should I wait for these and be ignorant about my own possessions? When a man is so cowardly, not to give himself these great riches – he becomes just a body of bad blood. If he were to become more, he would realise no one remains poor through other people.

CHAPTER 10 – THOSE WHO SEEK PROMOTION IN ROME

If we apply ourselves to our work with as much effort as the old men in Rome do, perhaps we can also accomplish something. I am acquainted with a man, older than myself, who has now become the superintendent of corn in Rome, and I remember the time when he came here after having been exiled from his native land, what he said as he relayed the events of his former life, and how he declared that with respect to the future, he would look after nothing else than living the rest of his life in peace and tranquillity. "Because only a little of life," he said, remains for me." I replied, "You won't do that, because as soon as you smell Rome, you will forget everything you've said; and you are admitted into the imperial palace, you will rush in and thank God." "If you find me, Epictetus," he answered, "setting even one foot inside the palace, you can think whatever you want of me." Well, what did he do? Before he entered the city, he received letters from Caesar, and as soon as he received them he forgot everything, and since has added one piece of business to another. I wish I was there now to remind him of what he said when he was passing this way and to tell him about how much better of a seer I am than him.

Do I think that man is an animal made for doing nothing? Of course not. But why aren't we active? Myself for example, as soon as day comes, I remind myself of what I must read to my pupils; then I say to myself, "why should I plan what I read today, when all of my material is good material? The first thing for me to do is sleep." What is the resemblance between what people plan to do, and actually do? If you observe what they do, you will see. What do some people do all day long than make up stories, inquire among each other, give and take advice about small quantities of grain, a bit of land, and similar talk of profit? Isn't it the same thing to receive a petition and to read in it: "I ask you to permit me to export a small quantity of corn"; or something like this: "I ask that you learn from Chrysippus what is the administration of the world, and what place in it the rational animal takes; consider also who you are, and what is the nature of your good and bad." Are these things like the other, do they require equal care, and is it equally bad to neglect this or that? Are we the only people who are lazy and love sleep? No; usually the younger men are. But when old men see the young men amusing themselves, they are eager to join them; but if I saw an active and zealous old man, I would be much more eager to join him in serious pursuits.

CHAPTER 11 - ON NATURAL AFFECTION

When he was visited by one of the magistrates, Epictetus had a few questions to ask him. First, he asked if he had a wife and children. The man replied said he did; and Epictetus asked, how he felt under the circumstances. "Miserable," the man said. Then Epictetus asked, "In what respect," men don't marry and have children in order to be miserable, usually quite the opposite. "But I," the man replied, "am so unhappy about my children that even lately, when my little daughter was sick and was supposed to be in danger, I couldn't endure to stay with her, so I left home until I heard that she had recovered." Well then, said Epictetus, do you think you acted correctly? "I acted naturally," the man replied. Please convince me that you acted naturally, and I will convince you, that everything which happens according to nature, happens correctly. "This is the case," said the man, "with all or at least most fathers." I don't deny that: but the matter which we are discussing is whether the behaviour was right; because, in respect to what you have said, we must also say that tumours come for the good of the body, because they do come; and so, we must say that to do wrong is natural, because nearly everyone or at least most of us do wrong. I can't show you how the behaviour was natural, but I ask if you can show me how it wasn't according to nature and why it was wrong.

Well, said Epictetus, if we were trying to distinguish white from black, what would we use for distinguishing? "The sight," he said. And the difference between hot and cold, and hard and soft, what do we use? "The touch." Well then, since we are distinguishing things which are done according to nature, and those which are done correctly or not, what do you think we use? "I don't know," he said. Well, not to know what distinguishes the colours or smells, also the taste, is perhaps no great harm; but if a man doesn't know the way to distinguish good from bad, and things done according to nature or not, can you see the harm in this? "The greatest harm." Is it the case that what seems to most people to be good and correct always appear to be; and at present there are Jews and Syrians, Egyptians and Romans, is it possible that the opinions of all of them in respect to what is good is right? "How could it be possible?" he said. Well, I suppose it would mean that, if the opinions of the Egyptians are right, the opinions of the rest must be wrong: if the opinions of the Jews are right, those of the rest can't be right. "Certainly." But where there is ignorance, there also there is also a need for teaching. Does affection to your family appear to you to be according to nature and to be good? "Certainly." Well, is affection natural and good, and is something which is consistent with reason not good? "Not at all. " So, is that which is consistent with reason in contradiction with affection? "I don't think so." You're right, because if it wasn't, wouldn't it create a contradiction with nature? "That's true," he said. So then, we have discovered to be affectionate is also consistent with reason, and reason we confidently declare to be right and good. "Agreed." Well then to leave your sick child isn't reasonable, I assume you won't disagree with that; but we have to determine if it is consistent with affection. "OK." If you had an affectionate disposition to your child, would it be right to run off and leave her; and has the mother no affection for the child? "Of course, she has." Should then, should the mother have left her as well? "Of course not." And the nurse, does she love her? "She does." So then, should she have also left her? "Not at all." So, should the child have been left alone without help, or should she have died in the hands of those who neither loved her or cared for her? "Certainly not." So, this is unfair and unreasonable, to allow those who have equal affection with her to do what you think to be ok for yourself to do. It is absurd. If you were sick, wouldn't you want your relatives to be affectionate, or everyone, including wife and child to leave you alone? "Not at all." And would you wish to be loved so much by people that they left you alone in sickness? Of course not, if that were so maybe you would rather pray, if it were possible, to be loved by your enemies? Of course not. The result we have is that your behaviour wasn't an affectionate act.

Was there something which induced you to desert your child? And how is that possible? What then caused the movement? The exact discussion of this does not belong to the present occasion perhaps; but it is enough to be convinced of this, if what the philosophers say is true, that we must not look for it anywhere externally, but in all cases it is one and the same thing which is the cause of our doing or not doing something, of saying or not saying something, of being excited or depressed, of avoiding something or pursuing: the very thing which is now the cause to me and to you, to you of coming to me and sitting and hearing, and to me of saying what I say. And what is this? Is it any other than our will to do so? "No other." But if we had willed otherwise, what else should we have been doing than that which we willed to do? This, then, was the cause of Achilles' sadness, not the death of Patroclus; because another man doesn't behave like that on the death of his companion; it is only because he chose to do so. So, do you think this was the cause of your running away, that you chose to do so; and on the other side, if you stayed with her, the reason will be the same. And now you are going to Rome because you choose; and if you change your mind, you won't not go. So, neither death or pain, or anything else is the cause of our doing, or not doing; but our own opinions and our will.

Are you convinced? "You have convinced me." So, then, as the causes are in each case, so are the effects. When, then, we are doing anything which isn't right, from this day we will understand it as nothing else than to the will from which we have done it: and it is that which we should endeavour to take away, more than the tumours and abscesses of the body. And we should take account of the cause of the things which we do correctly; and we shouldn't blame others as causes of evil to us, friend, neighbour, wife or child, being persuaded that, if we don't think these things we won't perform the acts which follow from those opinions; and as to thinking or not thinking, that is in our power and not in the external. "That's true," he said. From this day then we should examine all thoughts as opinions. "I hope so." If you really intend to examine your own opinions and know yourself: that isn't the work of one hour or a day.

CHAPTER 12 - ON CONTENTMENT

With respect to god, there are some who say that a divine being doesn't exist: others say that it exists, but is inactive and careless, and has no thought about anything; a third type say that such a being exists and exercises thought, but only about great and heavenly things, and about nothing on the earth; a fourth type say that a divine being exercises thought about things on earth and in heaven, but in a general way only. There is a fifth type which Ulysses and Socrates belong to, who say: "I don't move with without my knowledge."

Before it's necessary to discuss these opinions, what is important to confirm as true or false, is if a god exists or not, otherwise is there a point to discuss the opinions? And if god exists, but doesn't take care of anything, what would be the purpose to move on to the next opinion? And if god exists and looks after things, again there is no point to move on. The wise man, then, after considering everything chronologically, hands over his mind to the one who administers the whole, like good citizens do to the law of the state. He who is being taught should go to the teacher with this intention: How can I follow god in everything, and how can I be content with the divine administration, and how can I become free?" Because a man is free when everything happens according, to his will, and who no man can hinder. "But," you say, "I would then have everything just as I like, and in whatever way I like." Are you mad? Don't you know that freedom is a noble and valuable thing? But for me to inconsiderately wish for things to happen as I inconsiderately as I like, this appears not to be noble, but even worse: completely wrong. So, how would we proceed in the matter of writing? Would I wish to rewrite a name for example like Dion however I like? No, because I am taught to write it as it should be written. And how should I proceed in respect to music? In the same manner. And how universally in every art or science? The same. If it wasn't so, it wouldn't be of value to know anything, if knowledge were adapted to every man's idea. Is it, then, in this alone, in this which is the greatest and the main thing, I mean freedom, that I am permitted to will inconsiderately? Not at all; but to be thought this, to wish that everything happen as it should. And how do things happen? As the creator has created them? Like he has made summer and winter, abundance and scarcity, virtue and vice, and all the opposites for the harmony of the whole; and to each of us he has given a body, and parts of the body, possessions, and companions.

Remembering, this then, not that we can change the constitution of things- because we don't have the power to do that, and to know that it's not better that we should have the power - but in order that, as the things around us are what they are and by nature exist, we may maintain our minds in harmony with the anything that happens. We escape from men, but how is it possible? If we associate with them, can we change them? Who gives us the power? If you are alone, you call it solitude; and of you are with men, you call them thieves, and you find fault with your own parents and children, brothers and neighbours. When you are alone you should call this tranquillity and freedom, and think of yourself like god; and when you are with people, you shouldn't call it crowd, or trouble, or uneasiness, but a festival, and accept contentedly.

What is the punishment of those who don't accept? It is simply to be what they are. If a man is dissatisfied with being alone, let him be alone. If a man is dissatisfied with his parents? let him be a bad son, and be upset. If he is dissatisfied with his children? let him be a bad father. "Put him in prison." What prison? He will find himself there against his will; but that isn't necessary because any man who acts against his will, is already in prison. So, Socrates was not in prison, because he was there willingly. "Must my leg be injured?" Fool, do you then because of one bad leg find fault with the world? Wouldn't you willingly surrender it for the whole? Wouldn't you gladly part with it to him who gave it? And are you going to be angry and discontented with the things established by God, which he while spinning the thread of your generation, defined and put in order? Don't you know how small a part you are compared with the whole. I mean with respect to the body, because as to intelligence you are not inferior to god; because the magnitude of intelligence is not measured by length or height, but by thoughts which are endless.

So then, wouldn't you choose to place your good in that which you are equal to god? "How poor am I to have such a father and mother." Was it possible for you to exist, and to select, and to say: "Let this man at this moment unite with this woman so I can be produced?" It wasn't possible, it was a necessity that your parents existed first, and then for you to be born. What kind of parents are they? It doesn't matter, since they are such as they are, isn't a remedy offered to you? Now if you didn't know what purpose of vision is, you would be unfortunate, but if you could possess greatness of soul and nobility of spirit for every event that may happen in life, and you didn't know that you possess them, wouldn't you be even more unfortunate? Things appear to you which are proportionate to the power which you possess, but you turn away this power most particularly at the very time when you should maintain it. Wouldn't you rather thank god that he has allowed you to be above these things which haven't been placed in your power; and have made you accountable only for those things which are in your power? As to your parents, the gods have left you free from responsibility; and also with respect to your brothers, your body, possessions, death and life. For what, then, has god made you responsible? For that which alone is in your power, the proper use of appearance. Why then do you then feel upset about the things which you are not responsible for? This is only bringing trouble to yourself.

CHAPTER 13 – HOW EVERTHING MAY BE DONE ACCEPTABLY TO GOD

When someone asked, how may men eat acceptably to god, he answered: If he can eat contentedly, with equanimity, temperance and order, would that be acceptable to god? And when you have asked for warm water and the servant didn't hear, or he heard but only brought Luke warm water, and you are not angry, would that be acceptable to god? "But how can a man endure a servant like this?" Fool, can't you bear your own brother, who has god as his father, and is like a son from the same seed and of the same descent as you? You find yourself in a higher place in life, and now you make yourself a tyrant? Don't you remember who you are, and who you rule? Yourself only. These are your brothers by nature, they are the offspring of god "But I pay them, they don't pay me." Don't you see what direction you're looking? Toward the earth and laws established by men. But you don't look toward the laws of god.

CHAPTER 14 – THAT GOD OVERSEES ALL

When a person asked him how a man can be sure that all his actions are being watched by God, he answered, don't you think that all things are united in one? "I do," the person replied. Well then, would you agree that earth has a natural agreement and union with heaven "I do." And do you see regularly as if by God's command, when he asks the plants to flower, do they flower? When he asks them to produce fruit, do they produce fruit? When he asks the fruit to ripen, does it ripen? When he asks the fruits to fall, do they fall? What about the movement of the moon, and recession of the sun? Are plants and our bodies are united with the whole, but aren't are our souls much more? Aren't our souls united with God as parts of him and portions of him; doesn't God perceive every motion of these parts as being? If not his own motion? Now are you able to think of the divine administration, and about all things divine, and at the same time about human affairs, and not be moved by ten thousand things at the same time in your senses and in your understanding, and to rise to some, and to fall from others, and to the rest suspend your judgment; and don't you retain in your soul many impressions from so many and various things, and being moved by them, don't you conjure notions similar to those first impressed, and don't you retain numerous arts and the memories of thousands of things; and isn't God able to oversee this, and to be present with all, and to receive from everyone this communication? And isn't the sun able to illuminate a large part of the earth, and leave very little unilluminated, that part which is occupied by the earth's shadow; and he who made the sun, being a small part of himself compared to the whole, do you really think he can't perceive everything?

"I can't," the man might reply, "comprehend all these things at once." But who tells you that you have equal power with God? Nevertheless, he has placed by every man's side a guardian, a Demon, given the task of protecting the man, a guardian who never sleeps, and is never deceived. Because what better and more careful guardian could he have entrusted with each of us? When, you have shut the doors and your home is dark inside, remember never to say you are alone, because you're not; God is within, and your Demon is within, and what need do they have for light to see what you're doing? To God you should to swear an oath just as the soldiers do for Caesar. Those who are hired for a salary swear to protect Caesar; but you who have received so many great favours from God, won't swear, or when you have sworn, won't you honour your oath? What should you swear? Never to be disobedient, never to make any accusations, never to find fault with anything that he has given, and never unwillingly do or suffer anything, that is unnecessary. Is this oath like the soldier's oath? The soldiers swear not to prefer any man than Caesar: in this oath men swear to honour themselves before all else.

CHAPTER 15 – WHAT PHILOSOPHY PROMISES

When a man was asking him how he should persuade his brother to stop being angry with him, Epictetus replied: Philosophy does not propose to secure for a man any external thing. If it did philosophy would be allowing something which is not within its jurisdiction. Like the carpenter's material is wood, and the blacksmith's is metal, the art of living is each man's life. "What is my brother's?" That again belongs to his own art; but with respect to yours, it is one of the external things, like a piece of land, like health, like reputation. But Philosophy doesn't promise any of these.

"How then, will my brother stop being angry with me?" Bring him to me and I will tell him. But I have nothing to say to you about his anger.

When the man, who was asking him, said, "I want to know - how, even if my brother is not happy with me, I can maintain myself in a state conformable to nature?" Nothing great, said Epictetus, is produced suddenly; not even the grape or the fig is. If you tell me now that you want a fig, I will tell you that it requires time: let it flower first, then produce the fruit, and then ripen. Is, then, the fruit of a fig-tree perfected suddenly in one hour? Of course not. And you expect to possess the fruit of a man's mind in such a short space of time and so easily? Don't expect it, even if I tell you.

CHAPTER 16 – ON PROVIDENCE

There is no need to wonder if animals have everything they require for living, because food and shelter are provided by nature, they have no need for clothing or anything additional like us. Because animals were made to provide a service and not for themselves. It wasn't necessary for them to be made to need other things. Imagine what it would be like if we had not only to take care of ourselves but also the needs of animals: how they should be dressed and what they should eat and drink. Soldiers are ready for their commander, prepared with clothing and armed: but it would be a hard thing, for the leader to go around dressing his thousand men; and so, nature has formed the animals which are made for service, all ready, prepared, and requiring nothing else. Simple enough for one little boy with only a stick to move the cattle.

Now, instead of being thankful that we don't need to take the same care of animals as we do of ourselves, complain to God; and yet, in the name of God, any one of those things which exists should be enough for any man to perceive the existence of God, at least any man who is modest and grateful. Milk is produced from grass, and cheese from milk, and wool from skin. Who made these things or devised them? "No one," you say. Oh, how amazing shamelessness and stupid you are!

Well, let us put aside the great works of nature and contemplate its smaller acts. Is there anything less useful than hair on the chin? What subtle purpose has nature provided this hair for? Hasn't it been provided to distinguish the male from the female? Doesn't the nature of every man declare, "I am a man; approach me as such, speak to me as such; and this can be seen in the signs"? Again, in the case of women, a much softer in the voice, and no hair on the chin. You disagree and say: "the human should have been left without marks of distinction, and each of us should be obliged to declare, 'I am a man.' But how can you not see the beauty in the distinctions, what is more beautiful than the lion's mane? For this reason, we should preserve the signs which God has given us, we shouldn't throw them away, and we should hold on to as much as we can, the distinctions of the sexes.

Is this the only work of God in us? What words can we use to differentiate them according to their worth? If we had complete understanding, should we do anything else than sing hymns and worship God, and to tell each other of his benefits? Shouldn't we, when we are digging, ploughing and eating sing this hymn to God? "God is great, he has given us implements with which we will cultivate the earth: God is great, he has given us hands, the power of swallowing, a stomach, imperceptible growth and the power of breathing while we sleep." This is what we should be singing on every occasion, and to sing the greatest and most divine hymn for giving us the faculty of comprehending these things and using them in a proper way. Well then, since most of you have become blind, shouldn't there be some man to fill the job of reminding everyone, and on behalf of all to sing the hymn to God? What else can I do, as an old man than to sing hymns to God? If I was an eagle, I would act the part of an eagle: if I were a swan, I would act like a swan. But I'm a rational creature, and I should praise God: this is my work; I do it, I will not desert this post, as long as I'm allowed to keep it; and I encourage you to sign the same song.

CHPATER 17 – THAT THE ART OF LOGIC IS NECESSARY

As reason is the faculty which analyses and perfects the other faculties, it shouldn't be left unanalysed, but what could possibly analyse it? It is very simple, it should be done by either itself or by something else. But to analyse, this other thing, would have to be reason, or something superior to reason; which is impossible. And if we analyse reason with reason, again who will analyse that reason? And if that reason can do it for itself, that would mean our reason can also analyse itself. But if we did require something else to analyse our reason, that thing, will go on into infinity and have no end. Reason therefore is analysed by itself. "Yes: but it is more urgent to cure our false opinions." Well then, when we discuss those things and you say, "I don't know whether you true or false," and if I express myself in any way ambiguously, and you say to me, "Please distinguish," I will say to you "that what I am talking about now is more urgent." This is the reason, why they place the logical art first, just like when we are weighing our food, we first must examine the scales. And if we don't determine first what are scales, and what is a balance, how could we be able to measure or weigh anything?

Therefore, if we haven't fully learnt and accurately examined the analyser of all other things, by which those things are learnt, how can we examine accurately and learn fully anything else? "Yes; but logic is only wood, and produces no fruit." But it is a thing which can ascertain weight. "Logic produces no fruit you say?" We will see about that.

It is enough to know that logic has the power of distinguishing and examining other things, and, as we may say, of measuring and weighing them. Who says this? Is it only Chrysippus, Zeno, and Cleanthes? Don't the Antisthenes say this as well? Who was it that said the examination of names is the beginning of education? Wasn't it Socrates? And what did Xenophon write, that he began with the examination of names, what each name signified? Isn't this the great and wondrous thing to understand or interpret Chrysippus? What is the wondrous thing? To understand the will of nature. Well then are you yourself hindering your education by your own actions? Because it is true that all men do this occasionally involuntarily, but if you have learnt the truth, out of necessity you must act correctly. "But in truth I don't yet understand the will of nature." Who then can teach me what it is? Many say Chrysippus. I then inquire what this interpreter of nature says. If I don't understand what he says; I seek an interpreter of Chrysippus. "However, we shouldn't seek anyone who understands the will of nature but does not follow it himself.

So, I find an interpreter of the will of nature, and I say, "tell me what nature says." He replies, "you have a will, given to you by nature, free from hindrance and compulsion. Can any man stop you from becoming truthful? No man can. Can any man convince you to believe what you know is false? No man can. From this you can see you have the will, free from hindrance, free from compulsion, unimpeded." So, then, in the matter of desire and pursuit of an object, is it any different? And what can stop my pursuit except another pursuit? And what can stop desire except another desire? But, you object: "If you put me in a position to fear for my life, doesn't that mean you have altered my will." No, it's not what is in front of you that matters, but your opinion that it is better to live than die. In this matter, then, it is your opinion that gave you the fear not me. Because if God gave us will which could be hindered or altered by another, he wouldn't be God and he wouldn't be taking care of us as he should. If you choose, you are free; if you choose, you will blame no one. Everything will be according to your mind and the mind of God." For things like this I go to the philosopher, not admiring him for this interpretation, but admiring the things which he interprets.

CHAPTER 18 – WE SHOULDN'T BE ANGERED BY THE ERRORS OF OTHERS

If what philosophers say is true, that all men have these principles, that a thing is true, false or uncertain, and in the case of a movement toward anything the persuasion that this is for the man's advantage, and it is impossible to think that something is advantageous but to desire the opposite, and to judge one thing to be good and to move toward something else, why then are we angry with the most people? "They are thieves," you may say. What do you mean by thieves? "They are mistaken about good and evil." Should we really be angry with them, or pity them? We can show them their error, and you will see how they change. But if they can't see their errors, then they have nothing superior to their present opinion.

"Shouldn't that robber or adulterer be destroyed?" Not at all. We should be speaking in this way: "This man who has been mistaken and deceived about the most important things, and blinded, not in the faculty of vision which distinguishes white and black, but in the faculty which distinguishes good and bad, shouldn't we destroy him?" If you speak like that, you will see how inhuman what you said is, and that it is just as if you said, "should we destroy this blind and deaf man?" The greatest harm is blindness to the greatest things, and the greatest thing in every man is the will or choice such as it should be, and if a man is deprived of this will, why are you angry with him? You shouldn't be affected by the bad deeds of another. Pity him: drop your state of hate. Why are we angry with these people? Is it because we value so much the things which these men take from us? Don't admire your clothes, then you won't be angry with the thief. Do not admire the beauty of your wife, then you won't be angry with the adulterer. Learn that a thief and an adulterer have no place in the things which are yours, only in those which belong to others and which are not in your power. If you dismiss these things and consider them as nothing, who can you be angry with? As long as you value these things, you should be angry with yourself rather than the thief and the adulterer. Consider the matter as this: you have fine clothes; your neighbour hasn't: you have a window; you wish to air dry the clothes. The thief doesn't know what a man's true goodness consists of, and he thinks that it consists of having fine clothes, the very thing which you think as well. Shouldn't he come and take them away? When you show a cake to greedy people, and swallow it all yourself, do you expect them not to snatch it from you? Don't provoke them: don't have a window: don't air dry your clothes. Recently. I had an iron lamp placed by the side of my house: hearing a noise at the door, I ran down, and found that the lamp had been taken. I reflected that whoever had taken the lamp had done nothing strange. Tomorrow, I said, I will find another lamp: because a man only loses things that he has. "I have lost my garment." The reason is because you had a garment. "I have pain in my head." Why? Because, we only lose those things, and we only have pain over the things we possess.

"But the tyrant will take." What? the leg. "He will take away." What? the neck. What can't he take away? the will. This is why the ancient wise men taught the following, "Know yourself." Therefore, we should exercise ourselves in small things and, beginning with them, proceed to greater.

Who is invincible? He who allows nothing to disturb him which is independent from the will. Examining one circumstance after the next he observes and is not disturbed. For example, what if you throw money at a man, he will despise it. What if you put a young girl in his way? What about his reputation? What about if we praise him, and what about death? He overcomes all. What if there is heat, or rain, and what if he's in a bad mood, and what if he's sleeping? He will still conquer. This is an invincible man.

CHAPTER 19 – HOW WE SHOULD TREAT TYRANTS

If a man thinks he has a superior quality, when he doesn't, this man, if he is uninstructed, will be over inflated by it. For instance, the tyrant says, "I am the master of everything." What can you do for me? Can you give me desire which is unhindered? How could you? Do you have the power to avoid what you should avoid? Do you have the power of moving toward an object without error? And how do you possess this power? When you are on a ship, do you trust yourself or the captain? And when you are in a chariot, who else do you trust but the driver? And how is it in all of the other arts? Just the same. So? What is your power? "All men respect me." Well, I respect my plate, I wash it and wipe it. So? Is that really superior to me? No, but people supply some of my desire, and for that reason I take care of them. Don't I care about my cattle? Don't I wash their feet? Who would want to become like you? Who imitates you, in the same way as he imitates Socrates? "But I can cut off your head." Oh really. I forgot I must respect you.

What is it that scares most men? is it the tyrant and his guards? I hope not. It's shouldn't be possible that what is given by nature for free could be disturbed by anything else, or hindered by anything other than itself. It's a man's own opinions which disturb him: because when the tyrant says to a man, "I will chain your leg," the man who values his leg says, "Please don't": but the man who values his own will says, "If it appears more advantageous to you, chain it." "Don't you care?" I don't care. "I will show you that I am the master." You can't do that. God has set me free: do you think that he intended to allow his own son to be a slave? You can be the master of my dead body: take it. "S, when you approach me, you don't respect me?" No, but I respect myself; and if you want me to say that I have respect for you as well, I tell you that I have the same respect for you that I have for my plate.

This isn't a selfish self-respect; any animal has been created do look after itself. Even the sun does everything for itself; even God himself. But when he chooses to be the Giver of rain and the Giver of fruits, and the Father of gods and men, you can see we wouldn't even call him these names, if he was not useful to a man;

and, universally, he has made the nature of the rational animal in a way that it can't obtain one of its own proper interests, if it does not contribute something to the common interest. In this manner and sense, it is not unsociable for a man to do everything, for himself. What do you expect? That a man should neglect himself and his own interest?

When absurd notions about things independent of our will, as if they were good, lie at the bottom of our opinions, then of course people would pay respect to tyrants. How is it that a man becomes wise, when Caesar has made him superintendent? How is it that we say, "Feliciano spoke sensibly to me."? I wish he lost his position, so he could appear to be a fool again.

Epaphroditus had a shoemaker called Filicon, who he sold because he believed he was good for nothing. This man, by some good luck was bought by one of Caesar's men, and became Caesar's shoemaker. You should have seen the respect Epaphroditus paid him: How is Felicon doing? If any of us asked, "What is the master doing?" the answer would be "He is consulting with Caesar about Felicon." Didn't he sell this man as good for nothing? This is an instance of valuing something other than the things which depend on the will.

A man been given a position in the tribunal. Everyone meets him to offer their congratulations; one kisses his eyes, another the neck, and another the hands. He goes to his house, he finds torches lit. He goes to the capitol: he offers a sacrifice for the occasion. Whoever sacrificed something for having good desires? For acting conformable to nature? In fact, we thank the gods for those things in which we place our good.

A person was talking to me today about the priesthood of Augustus. I said to him: "Let's leave this topic as we will waste a lot of time." But he replied, "Those who draw up agreements can write any name." Do you stand next to the people who read them, and say to them, "that is my name written there;" And if you could be present on all occasions, what will happen when you die? "My name will remain." Write it on a stone, and it will remain. What else will there to be to remember about you "I wore a gold crown." If you desire a crown, take a crown of roses and put it on, because it would be more elegant in appearance.

CHAPTER 20 – ABOUT REASON, AND HOW IT CONTEMPLATES ITSELF

Every faculty contemplates certain things specifically. When it is alignment with these things, it must contemplate itself as well: but when it is out of alignment, it can't contemplate itself. For instance, the shoemaker's art is working with material, but the shoe is entirely distinct from the material itself: and because of that, it doesn't contemplate itself. Again, the grammarian's art is about articulate speech; but is the art itself articulate? Not at all. For this reason, it is not able to contemplate itself. What can contemplate itself? The right use of appearance. What is it then itself? A system of certain appearances. So, by its nature it has the faculty of contemplating itself. Again, this makes sense, because the contemplation of it belong to us. Good and evil, and things which are neither. What is it then itself? Good. And what about sense, what is it? Evil. Do you see then that good sense necessarily contemplates both itself and the opposite? For this reason, it is the primary and first work of a philosopher to examine appearances, and to distinguish them, and to admit none without examination. You see even in the matter of coins, in which our interest appears to be somewhat concerned, how we have invented an art, and how means there are which analysts use to value the coin, sight, touch, smell, and lastly hearing. He drops the coin on the table, and listens to the sound, and he's not content with doing this once, but through his great attention to detail he becomes a musician. In a similar manner, where we think that to be mistaken and not to be mistaken make a great difference, there we apply great attention to discovering the things which can deceive us. But in the matter of our miserable reasoning faculty, yawning and sleeping, we carelessly admit every appearance, because the harm is not noticed.

When you realise how careless you are with respect to good and evil, and how active with respect to things which are indifferent, observe how you feel with respect to being deprived of the sight of eyes, and how with respect to being deceived, and you will discover you are far from feeling as you should in relation to good and evil. "But this is a matter which requires much preparation, and much study." Do you really expect to acquire the greatest of the arts with little work? And yet the primary doctrine of philosophers is simple. If you want to know it, read Zeno's writings and you will see how few words it requires to say a man's life is to follow god, and that the nature of good is a proper use of appearances. But if you say "What is 'God,' what is 'appearance,' and what is 'particular' and what is 'universal nature'? then of course more words are necessary. If Epicurus came and said that the good must be in the body; in this case many words are also necessary, and we must be taught what is the leading principle in us, and the fundamental and the substantial; and as it is not probable that the good of a snail is in the shell, is it probable that the good of a man is in the body? But you yourself, Epicurus says, possess something better than this. What is in you that deliberates, what is in you which examines everything, what is in you which forms a judgement about the body itself, and the principle part? Why do you light your lamp and go to work, writing so many books for us? Is it so we won't be ignorant to the truth, who we are, and what we are in respect to you? This is a discussion which requires many words.

CHAPTER 21 – AGAINST THOSE WHO WISH TO BE ADMIRED

When a man holds his proper position in life, he doesn't strive for things beyond it. What do you want to happen to you? "I am satisfied if I desire and avoid what is conformable to nature, if I make movements toward and from an object as I am created by nature to do, my purpose and design emerge." My wish has always been that those who meet me, admire me, and those who follow me say, 'the great philosopher.'" Who do you wish to be admired by? Aren't they the people you used to say were mad? Do you really want to be admired by madmen?

CHAPTER 22 - ON PRECOGNITIONS

Precognitions are common to all men. Who among us doesn't believe that good is useful, and in all circumstances, we should follow and pursue it? And who doesn't assume that justice is beautiful? So, when does a contradiction arise? It arises in the adaptation of the precognitions to the particular cases. When one man says, "He has done well: he is a brave man," and another says, "Not really; he has acted foolishly"; then the disputes arise between men. This is the dispute among the Jews and the Syrians and the Egyptians and the Romans; not whether holiness should be preferred to all things and in all cases, it should be pursued, but whether it is holy to eat pig's flesh or not holy. You can find a similar dispute between Agamemnon and Achilles. Achilles said to Agememnon, don't you believe that what is good should be done? "I do." Adapt your precognitions to the present and here the dispute begins. Agamemnon says, "Should I return Chryseis to her father." Achilles says, "You should" Here people lose the difference between the precognition of should, or "duty." Then, Agamemnon says, "If I return Chryseis should I give up who I love" Achilles replies, "you should" So, I must be the only man without a prize? And so, the dispute begins.

What is education? Education is learning how to adapt natural precognitions to particular things conformably to nature; and then to distinguish which of these things are in our power, and which are not. In our power are our own will and all actions which depend on the will; things not in our power are the body, the parts of the body, possessions, parents, brothers, children, country, and, generally, who we live with in society. What should we say is good? And what things should we adapt it to? "To things which are in our power?" Isn't health a good thing, and soundness of mind? And aren't children, parents and country? Who would tolerate you if you deny this?

Let's then transfer the notion of good to these things. is it possible, then, when a man sustains damage and doesn't obtain life's good things, that he can be happy? "It's not possible." And can he maintain toward society appropriate behaviour? He can't.

Because I'm naturally formed to look after my own interest. If it's in my interest to have an estate of land, it's my interest also to take it from my neighbour. If it's my interest to have clothing, it's also my interest to steal it from the store. This is the origin of wars, civil commotions, tyrannies and conspiracies. And how could I still be able to maintain my duty toward God? Because if I sustain damage and am unlucky, he doesn't take care of me; and what is God to me if he allows me to be in that condition? I would begin to hate him. Why, then, do we build temples, why set up statues to God, and for evil demons? How is God the Saviour? And in truth if we place the nature of Good in these things, all this follows.

What should we do then? This is a question of a true philosopher who is working hard. "If I can't see what is good or bad, am I mad? Yes." But suppose that I place the good somewhere among the things which depend on the will: everyone will laugh at me. A grey-haired man will come wearing many gold rings on his fingers and he will shake his head and say, "Listen to me, my child. It's right that you should philosophize; but you should have some brains as well: all that you're doing is silly. You learn the syllogism from philosophers; but you know how to act better than the philosophers do." Why do you then blame me, if I know? What can I say to you? If I'm silent, you will burst. You have to speak in this way: "Excuse me, as you would excuse the ignorant: I am not my own master: I am mad."

CHAPTER 23 – AGAINST EPICURUS

Even Epicurus perceives that we are by nature social, but once we place our good in the outer layers of what is really meaningful, he's no longer able to say anything else. Because on the other hand he strongly maintains this, that we shouldn't admire or accept anything which is detached from the nature of good; and he is right in thinking this. How are we caring, if we have no natural affection for our children? Why do you advise the wise man not to have children? Why are you afraid that he will get into trouble? Does he get into trouble due to a mouse which has found it's was on to the house? What does he care if a little mouse in the house appears sad to him? But Epicurus knows that if a child is born, it is no longer in our power not to love it or care about it. For this reason, Epicurus says that a man who has any sense also does not engage in political matters; because he knows what a man must do who is engaged in such matters; because, if you intend to behave among men as you do among a swarm of flies, what hinders you? But Epicurus, who knows this, dares to say that we should not bring up children. A sheep doesn't desert its own offspring, or a wolf; and do you think a man will desert his child? What do you mean? That we should be as silly as sheep? They never desert their offspring: as savage as wolves can be, they never desert their young. Who would follow your advice, if he saw his child crying after falling on the ground? I think that, even if your mother and your father had been told by an oracle that you would say what you have said, they would never abandon you.

CHAPTER 24 – HOW WE SHOULDSTRUGGLE WITH CIRCUMSTANCES

It is circumstances that show what are true man is. Therefore, when a difficulty arises, remember that God, like a trainer of wrestlers, has paired you with a rough young man. "For what purpose?" you might ask, so you can become an Olympic conqueror; but that is not accomplished without sweat. In my opinion, no man has had a more profitable difficulty than you, if you choose to make use of it, as the wrestler would deal with the young man. If we needed to send a scout to Rome; no one would send a cowardly scout, who, if he hears the slightest noise and sees a shadow anywhere, comes running back in terror, reporting that the enemy is close by. So, if you came and told us, "I'm worried about the state of affairs at Rome, death is terrible, exile is scary; poverty is cruel; the enemy is near"; we would tell you to leave, you keep these imaginings to yourself, and that we have committed only one fault, that we sent such a scout."

Diogenes, who was sent as a scout before you, came back with a different report to us. He said that death isn't evil, neither is it bad: he said that fame is the noise of madmen. And what did this spy say about pain, pleasure, and about poverty? He said that to be naked is better than any luxury robe, and to sleep on the ground is the softest bed; and he gives us proof of each thing that he affirms, his own courage, his tranquillity, his freedom, and the healthy appearance and compactness of his body. "There is no enemy he said; "all is peace." How is that so, Diogenes? "See," he replied, "If I have been wounded, and ran away from a man." The duty of a scout is to go back, and see clearer when fear has been put to the side.

What should I do? What do you do when you leave a ship? Do you take away the helm? What do you take away then? You take what is your own, your bottle, your wallet; and if you think of what is your own, you will never claim what belongs to someone else. The emperor says, "remove your badge." I put on another one. "remove that as well." now, I have only my toga. "remove your toga." now, I am naked. "I still envy you." Take then my poor body;

when, at a man's command, I can throw away my poor body, would I still fear him?

"But what if no one is going to leave me as the heir to his estate." Have I forgotten that none of these things was mine? How could I then call them mine? You can't, they are just like the bed you sleep in at a hotel. If the hotelier died and left you the bed, but also left it to another, who would really own it? If he took it first, you won't find one, and you will sleep on the ground: which is better anyway, only sleep with good will, and remember that tragedies have their place among the rich, the kings and the tyrants, but no poor man takes part in a tragedy. Kings come into existence already with prosperity: You say a man like this is happy, because he knows many people, but they become bored very easy like little children, and when something no longer pleases them they say, "I won't play anymore," are you one of this kind? If so, please leave: but if you choose to stay, don't complain.

CHAPTER 25 – ON THE SAME

If these things are true, and if we are not silly, and are not acting hypocritically when we say that the good of a man is in his will, and the evil as well, and that everything else doesn't concern us, why are would we still be disturbed, why be afraid? The things we've been focusing on are in no man's power: and things which are in the power of others, we shouldn't care for. So, if we think like this, what kind of trouble would we have?

"You ask for directions." Why should I give you directions? Hasn't God given you directions? Hasn't he given what is yours, free from hindrance, and what isn't yours subject to hindrance? Keep by all means what is yours; and don't desire what belongs to others. Faithfulness is yours; virtuousness is yours; who can take these things away from you? Who else other than yourself can hinder you from using them? But how do you act? When you seek what isn't yours, you lose what is truly yours. Having what you need from God, what can you really ask me for? Am I more powerful than God, am I worthier of your trust? But he hasn't given these to me" you will say, I am unable to use them. Recall your precognitions, the proof of philosophers, produce what you have often heard, and produce what you have said yourself, produce what you have read, produce what you have meditated on (and you will then see that all these things are from God). How long, then, is it right to observe these precepts from God, and not to follow them? "Do you drink," "Do you mix wine," "Do you sing," "Do you go," "Do you come." Anything that is bad, who can compel me to think it's good?

Because as we behave in the matter of hypothetical arguments, we should also do in life. "Suppose it's night." I suppose it's night. "Well then; is it day?" No, because I added to the hypothesis that it was night. "Suppose that you think it's night?" OK. "But also think that it's day." That wouldn't be consistent with the hypothesis. And it is the same in this case also: "Suppose that you are unfortunate." I suppose so. "Are you then unhappy?" Yes. "And are you troubled by an unfavourable demon?" Yes. "and you think that you are also miserable." That isn't consistent with the hypothesis.

How long should we obey orders that make no sense? As long as it is profitable; and this means as long as I maintain that which is consistent. Also, some men have a bad temper, and they say, "I can't put up with this man, I have to hear him talking about how he fought in the war all day: But another man can say, "I prefer to get dinner and hear him talk as much as he likes." Can you see the difference? There is no need to do anything in a depressed mood, or as someone with an affliction, or thinking that you are in misery, because no man can compel you to that. Is there smoke in the chamber? If the smoke is moderate, I will stay; if it is excessive, I'll leave: because you must always remember this: the door is always open. But you say to me, "Don't live in Nicopolis." I won't live there. "or in Athens." I won't live in Athens. "or in Rome." I won't live in Rome. "Live in Gyarus." I'll live in Gyarus, but it seems like a great danger to live in Gyarus; so, I leave and go to the place where no man can hinder me from living, because that place is open for everyone; and as for the last garment, the body, no one has any power over me beyond this. This was the reason why Demetrius said to Nero, "You threaten me with death, but nature threatens you." If I place my admiration on the body, I make myself a slave: if on my possessions, I also make myself a slave: because I immediately make it clear that if I was captured; whichever part I choose to guard, this will be attacked. If you remember this and learn from it who could you possibly fear?

"But I like to sit where the Senators sit." Can't you see that you are squeezing yourself. "Well, there is no better view in the theatre?" Don't be a spectator at all; and you won't be squeezed. Why do you trouble yourself? Or wait a little, and when the spectacle is over, sit down in a place reserved for the Senators and enjoy. Remember this general truth, that it is us that squeeze ourselves, who put ourselves in narrow positions; that is, our opinions squeeze us and restrict our view. What is it to be admired? Stand by a stone and admire it; what will you gain? If, then, a man listens like a stone, what profit is there to the admirer? But if the admirer has as a man who listens, the weakness of the man who is

74

admired, allows the admirer to accomplish something. "Strip him." When the admiration stops, what good will it do for you?

This was the practice of Socrates: this was the reason why he always had one face. But we choose to practice and study anything rather than the method to be unhindered and free. You say, "Philosophers talk in paradoxes." But are there no paradoxes in the other arts? And what is more paradoxical than to remove a man's eye so he can see? Where is the wisdom, if in philosophy many things which are true appear to be paradoxical to the inexperienced philosopher?

CHAPTER 26 – MANY TYPES OF APPEARANCE AND WHAT WE CAN USE AGAINST THEM

Appearances come to us in four different ways: appearing as they are; or as they aren't and don't appear to be, or as they are and don't appear to be, or as they aren't but appear to be. In all of these cases to form the right judgement is an act of an educated man. So, whatever it is that we are judging, we should apply the right view. If the deception of Pyrrho and the academics are what we are judging, we have to apply the correct view. If it's the persuasion of appearances, by which some things appear to be good, when they are not good, we have to find the right view for this. If it's a habit which annoys us, we must find a resolution against the habit. What solution can we find for a bad habit: the opposite habit.

You hear the ignorant say: "That unfortunate person has died: his father and mother are struck with sorrow; his life was cut short by an untimely death and in a foreign land." Here is the contrary way of speaking: remove yourself from these expressions: oppose one habit with the opposite habit; to deception use reason, and the exercise and discipline of reason; against persuasive appearances we should have ready precognitions, clear from all impurity.

When death appears to be evil, we should have this rule ready, that it is normal to avoid evil things, but death is necessary. Because what can I do: how can I escape it? Suppose that I'm not the son of God, and unable to speak in this noble way: "I will live and I am determined to behave bravely or to give another the opportunity to do so; if I can't succeed in doing so myself, I won't grudge another for doing something noble." Suppose that it's above our power to act in a noble way; wouldn't it be in our power to reason in this way? Tell me how I can escape death: search the country, and show me the men who I have to go to, for who, death doesn't come. Find me a charm which works against death. If I have got one, what do you expect me to do? I can't escape death. So, shouldn't I escape from the fear of death, should I die in worry and fear? Because the origin of the disturbance is this, to wish for something not to happen. Therefore, if I am able to change the course of reality according to my wish, I would change them; but if I can't, should I tear a man's eyes out if he bothers me? Because the nature of a man isn't to endure being deprived of good, and not to endure falling into evil. So, as I am not able to change the circumstances or tear out the eyes of a man who bothers me, should I sit down and moan, and abuse whoever I can? Should I blame God, and say that he doesn't care for me, therefore who is he to me? You could say "Yes, but you will be a disrespectful man." And by doing all of this, in what respect will it be better for me than it is now? To sum this all up, remember that unless your interest and God be the same thing, respect can't be maintained by any man. Don't these things seem necessary?

Let the followers of Pyrrho and the Academics come and make their objections. Because on my part, I have no time for these disputes, and am not willing to waste my time preparing a defence against what commonly held as right. If I had a dispute about a bit of land, I would ask a lawyer to defend my interests. What am I satisfied with? With that which belongs to the matter in hand. How perception is effected, whether through the body or the mind, but perhaps I couldn't pinpoint: both opinions a potential truth. But you and I are not the same, I know that with perfect certainty. "How do you know?" When I swallow something, it doesn't go to your stomach.

Shouldn't we all, with all of our power, hold on to this: the maintenance of general opinion, and fortifying ourselves against the arguments which are directed against it? Who denies that we should do this? Well, anyone who is able to do it should, if he has the time for it; but for someone who has worry, fear and is inwardly broken in heart, he should use his time better on something else.

CHAPTER 27 – WE SHOULDN'T BE ANGRY TOWARD OTHER MEN, AND WHAT ARE THE SMALL AND GREAT THINGS THEY POSSESS

What is the cause of agreeing with anything? The fact that it appears to be true. It's not possible then to agree with something that doesn't appear to be true. Why? Because this is the nature of understanding, to accept the truth, and be dissatisfied with anything false, and in matters which are ambiguous to hold our judgement for now. What is the proof of this? "If you read this during the day, try to believe that it's night time." It's not possible. "Remove your reasoning that it's day time." It's not possible. "Persuade yourself." It's impossible. When any man agrees to something false, be assured that he didn't intend to agree, because every soul is unwillingly deprived of the truth, as Plato says; the false appeared to him to be true. So, we must be careful not to agree to that which is false, and for that we have the likely, unlikely, profitable, unprofitable, that which is suitable to a person and that which isn't. Would a man think that something is useful to him, but not choose it? He wouldn't? Medea says: "it's true, I know what evil I do, but passion overpowers my better judgement.'" She thought that to indulge her passion and take vengeance on her husband was more profitable than to spare her children. "It appeared to be so; but she was deceived." Show her that she has been deceived, and she wouldn't do it; but as long as you don't show her, what can she follow except that which appears to be true? Nothing else. Why, then, are you angry with the unhappy woman that has been deceived about the most important things? And why not, if it is possible, feel sorry for her instead, like we would the blind?

Whoever, then, can clearly remember, that a man the measure of every act is the appearance - whether it appears to be good or bad: if good, he is free from blame; if bad, he suffers the penalty, because it's impossible that someone who is deceived can be one person, and the one who suffers from it another person - whoever remembers this will not be angry with any man, or blame any man, or hate, or argue with any man.

"So, do all bad deeds have their origin in the appearance?" Yes, this origin and no other. The story of the woman names above, is nothing else than appearance and the use of appearances. It appeared to Paris to take the wife of Menelaus: and it appeared to Helen to follow him. If it appeared Menelaus that it would be better not to have a wife such a Helen, what would have happened? Not only would the Iliad have been lost, but we also wouldn't have the Odyssey. "On such small decisions can great things depend?" But what do you mean by great things? Wars and civil commotions, and the destruction of many men and cities. So, what great matter is this? "Is it nothing?" What great matter is the death of many sheep, many nests of birds being burnt or destroyed? "Are these things, then, like those?" Very similar. Bodies of men are destroyed, and the bodies sheep; the homes of men are burnt, just like the nests of birds. So, what in this, is good or bad? Or tell me what is the difference between a man's house and a bird's nest, as far as I know, each is a home; except that a man builds his out of beams, tiles and bricks, and the bird builds them with sticks and mud. "Is a man and a bird similar then?" What do you think?

"Doesn't a man differ at all in respect to a bird?" I think so, but there is no difference in these matters. "So, in what then, is there a difference?" Seek and you will find that there is a difference in another matter. You will find that in man he has the understanding of what he does, and you will see a difference in social community, in honesty, modesty, definiteness of purpose, and intelligence. Where is good and evil in men? It's found in the differences. If the difference is preserved and remains strong, modesty hasn't been destroyed, or honesty, or intelligence, then the man is also preserved; but if any of these traits have been destroyed and taken over like a city, then the man also perishes. Paris, you say, sustained great damage, when the Hellenes invaded and when they ravaged Troy, and when his brothers died. Not at all; because no man is damaged by an action which is not his own; what happened that time was only the destruction of bird's nests: the true ruin of Paris was when he lost his character of modesty, honesty, and his regard toward hospitality, and decency. When was Achilles ruined? Was it when Patroclus died? No. It happened when he became angry, when he cried over a girl, when he forgot that he was at Troy not find women, but to fight. These things are the ruin of men, being besieged by these things, this brings the destruction of cities, when the right opinions are destroyed, and have become corrupted.

"When women are taken, and children captured, and when the men are killed, isn't this the evil?" How can we add facts to these opinions? Explain this to me. "I won't do that; I could only say how you call this evil an opinion?" Let's find the rules: produce the precognitions: because if this is neglected we can't sufficiently determine good from bad, in the action that men do. When we intend to judge the weight, we can't judge by a guess: when we want to judge what is straight and crooked, we don't judge by guess. In all cases where it is our interest to know what is true or false, no man will do this with a guess. But in things which depend on doing right or wrong, of happiness or unhappiness, of being unfortunate or fortunate, there we find many inconsiderate and impatient men. There is nothing like scales, nothing like a rule: because with it an appearance can be presented, and straightway I can act accordingly. So, can I say that I'm superior to Achilles or Agamemnon, because they by following appearances suffer through much evil: shouldn't appearance be sufficient for me? What tragedy has any other beginning than appearance? What kind of a man would someone be, if he pays no regard to this then? And what do we name those who follow every appearance? "We call them madmen." Do we act differently?

CHAPTER 28 – ON CONSTANCY

A man of Good has a certain kind of Will; and a man of Bad has a certain kind of Will. What are external materials for the Will, which the will being familiar with can obtain its own good or evil. How can it obtain the good? If it does not admire the materials; because the opinions about the materials, if the opinions are right, make the will good: but perverse and distorted opinions make the will bad. God has fixed this law, and says, "If you want to have anything good, receive it from yourself." You say, "No, I have received it from another." This is not so: you receive it from yourself. Therefore, when the tyrant threatens and calls me, I say, "Who do you threaten If he says, "I will put you in chains," I say, "you threaten my hands and feet." If he says, "I will cut off your head," I reply, "you threaten my head." If he says, "I will throw you into prison," I say, "you threaten my body." If he threatens to banish me, I say the same. "Does he threaten me then?" If I feel that all these things don't concern me, he doesn't threaten me at all; but if I fear any of them, then he threatens me. Who do I fear then? The master of what? The master of things which are in my own power? If there were no such master, would I fear the master of things which are not in my power? And what are those things?

"Do philosophers then teach us to despise kings?" I hope not. Who would then teach us to claim the power over things which we really possess? Take my body, take my property, take my reputation. If I advised any people to claim these things, then they can truly accuse me. Someone says "I intend to be in control of your opinions." Who would give you this power? How can you conquer the opinion of another man? "By applying terror to it," he replies, "I will conquer it." Don't you know that opinion conquers itself, and is not conquered by another? Nothing can conquer the Will except the Will itself. For this reason, as well, the law of God is the most powerful. A man says "Let the stronger always be superior to the weaker." "Ten are stronger than one." For what? For putting men in chains, and for killing. The ten therefore conquer one in this way which they are stronger. "But in what then are the ten weaker," The one possesses the right opinions and the ten don't. "Well then, can the ten conquer in this matter?" How is it possible? If this was placed on the scales, wouldn't the heavier pull down that side of the scale?

"How strange, then, that Socrates was treated so badly by the Athenians." Why do you mention Socrates? Speak of it as it is: how strange the body of Socrates was taken and put in prison by stronger men. Do these things seem strange? Do they seem unfair, do you blame God? Didn't Socrates have an equivalent for these things? Where for him was the nature of good? Who should we listen to, you or him? And what does Socrates say? "Anytus and Meletus can kill me, but they cannot hurt me": and also, he says, "If it pleases God, let it be."

Show me how someone with inferior principles can overpower him. You could never show me this, or even come near to showing it; because this is the law of nature and of God that the superior will always overpower the inferior. In what? In that in which it is superior. One body is stronger than another: many are stronger than one: the thief can be stronger than the man who isn't. This is the reason why I lost my lamp, because I woke up and the thief was stronger than me. But the man pays for the lamp at a price: because for a lamp he became a thief, a dishonest man, and like a wild animal. This seemed to be a good bargain to him. Let it be. But what if a man threatens to behead me, "What is the use of these opinions?" What system of philosophy could make it so, if ten men try to put me in prison, I can avoid it? Have I learned nothing? I learned to see that everything which happens, if it's independent of my will, is nothing to me. Have you not gained any knowledge in this? Why would you then seek an advantage in anything other than in that which you can have full advantage?

Then sitting in prison, I say: "A man who cries about this doesn't hear what words mean, doesn't understand what is said, and doesn't care at all to know what philosophers say or what they do. Leave him alone."

But now someone says to the prisoner, "leave your prison." If there is no further need for me to be in prison, I leave: if need me again, I will enter the prison. "How long will you act like this?" As long as my reason requires me to: but when reason doesn't require this, take my body, I will say farewell. We shouldn't do this inconsiderately, or weakly, or for any slight reason; if, on the other hand, God doesn't want it to be done, and he has need of such a man in this world. But if he sounds the signal to leave, as he did for Socrates, we have to obey him, as if he were a general.

"Should we say this to everyone?" Why should we? Isn't it enough for a man to persuade himself? When you aren't able to make a man change his mind in regard to this, you can be assured that he's a child, you can either clap your hands with him, or if you not to, keep silent.

A man must keep this in mind; and when he finds himself in such difficulty, he should know that the time has come for showing what he has learnt, if he has been taught well. Because a man who has come into difficulty is like a young man from a school who has practiced reasoning; and if any person gives him an easy problem to solve, he says, "I would rather you propose something which is skilfully complicated so I can exercise my mind with it." Even wrestlers aren't satisfied with small young men, and say "he can't lift me." "This is a wise disposition." Because when the time comes, someone will say, "I wish I had learned more." A little more of what? If you didn't learn things in order to show them in practice, why did you learn them? I think that there is someone out there, who is suffering like a woman in labour, saying, "difficulties don't present themselves to me in the same manner as that which comes to a man. When would I face such a situation?" The disposition of preparation should be the same for all. Even among the gladiators of Caesar there are some who complain that they aren't challenged enough, so they pray to God for the next fight. You may say this is not the subject in which I wish to educate myself. Well, is it always in your power to choose the subject you want? You have been given a particular body, parents, siblings, and country, then you say, "change my subject." Don't you have the ability to manage the environment which has been given to you? I say, that man, are your material and subject.

Another example. "assume an attitude of ownership." I assume it, and now show how an educated man behaves. "Put aside the robe, and dress yourself in rags, and assume this character." What next, should I remove my powerful voice? How, would I appear? As a witness summoned by God. God can say "give a testimony for me, because you are worthy witness: is anything external to the will good or bad? Didn't I make every man's interest dependent on anyone else except himself?" What testimony do you have for me? "I am in a bad condition, master, I am unfortunate; no one cares for me, no one gives me anything; everyone blames me, and speaks in a bad way about me." Is this the evidence that you are going to give, and disgrace God, after he has placed so much honour on you, and thought you were worthy of being called to give a testimony?

Suppose someone says, "I judge you to be irreverent." What happened to you? "I have been judged to be irreverent?" Is that it? "Nothing else." But if the same person had given a judgment on a hypothetical argument, and declared, "the conclusion that, if it is day, it is light, I say is false," what happened to the hypothetical argument? Who is judged in this case? Who loses in this case, the hypothetical argument, or the man who has been deceived by it? Who has the power to declare about you if you respect or disrespect God? A man who has studied it, and has he learned it? Where? From who? If we accept this truth, then is it the fact that a musician pays no regard to a man who declares that the lowest chord is the highest; or a geometrician, if he declares that the lines from the centre of a circle to the circumference are not equal; should an educated man pay any regard to the uneducated man when he gives a judgment on what is respectful to God or disrespectful, or what is fair and unfair?

You should leave these small arguments to others, to lazy people, who sit in a corner and receive little pay, or main that no one gives them anything. Won't you rise above this and make use of what you've learned? Because it's not these small arguments that are needed now: the writings of the Stoics are full of them. What is needed now? A man who applies them, and by his acts proves his words. Assume, that there are no more examples of this character in schools so we must create our own.

Who should contemplate these matters? Any man that has time, because men are creatures that love to contemplate. But we shouldn't contemplate these things in a rushed manner; we should sit, as in a theatre, free from distraction, focused, and listen to the tragic actor, at another time to the piano player. The fool sits down and praises the actor and at the same time looks around. It is shameful for philosophers to contemplate the works of nature. What is a master? Man is not the master of other men; death is, life, pleasure and pain are; because he is born without them. When thundering and lightning come, and when I'm afraid of them, all I can do then is to recognise my true master.

CHAPTER 29 - HOW WE SHOULD BE PREPARED FOR DIFFICULT TIMES

When you find yourself in a position of power, remember that someone above can also see what's going on, and that you should please him rather those below. If he asked you: "In school what did you used to say about death and disgrace?" I used to say these things are indifferent. "What do you say about them now? Has that changed at all?" No. "Have you changed?" No. "What things are indifferent?" The things which are independent of the will. "Explain what you mean by that." The things which are independent of the will are nothing to me. "Tell me about Good, what was your opinion?" We should have a will to do what's good, and make the right use of appearances.

Go into the position of power boldly and remember these things; and you will see what it's like to be a man who has studied these things, and be among those who haven't. I already know you will have thoughts such as these: "why do we make so many preparations for nothing? Is this what it means to possess power? Is this the path to power? Is this what I listen to your lectures for? All of this is nothing: but I have been preparing you for something great."

CHAPTER 30 – CONFIDENCE IS NOT CONSISTANCE WITH CAUTION

The opinion of the philosophers appears to be a paradox to some people, so we should examine if it's true, that we are able to do everything with caution and confidence at the same time. Because caution seems the opposite confidence. The para contradiction seems to be a paradox to many. In my opinion: if we say that we should be cautious, in some things men will say that caution doesn't mix with this pursuit. So where is the difficulty in what I said? If this is true, which has often been said and proven, that the nature of good and evil is in the use of appearances, and that things independent of our will fall outside of our control. If philosophers say, where things are not dependent on the will, there you should have confidence, but where they are dependent on the will, there you should have caution, to me this is not a paradox. Because if bad consists in a bad exercise of will, caution should be applied towards things that are dependent on the will. But if things independent of the will and not in our power are nothing to us, with respect to these we must have confidence; and so, we exercise both cautiousness and confidence at the same time. We become confident because of our caution. because by having caution toward things which are really bad, it will result that we have confidence in respect to that which is good.

With respect to the condition of fear; there are deer that run from the huntsmen in fright, but where do they run in order to be safe? Right into the nets, and so, they are caught and killed by running from objects which they fear and towards that which they don't. It is the same case with humans: what things do we fear? Things which are not in our control. In what cases do we behave with confidence, and as if there were no danger? Things which depend on our control. So, to be deceived, or to act impatiently, or shamelessly or with evil desires doesn't concern us at all. But when death approaches, or pain or imprisonment, there we attempt to run away, or there we are struck with terror. Therefore, as we may expect it to happen with those who disregard the most important matters, we convert natural confidence into audacity, desperation, shamelessness; and we convert natural caution and modesty into cowardice and meanness, which are full of fear and confusion. But if a man transfers caution to the things which the will can be exercised, he will immediately, by willing to be cautious, also have the power to avoid anything he chooses: but if he transfers it to things which are not in his power and will, and attempt to avoid the things which are in the power of others, he will create fear, he will be unstable, and he will be disturbed. Because death and pain are not to be feared, but opinion of death and pain can create it.

We should have confidence against death, and caution against the fear of death. But people do the opposite, and have the intention to try and escape death; and to their opinion they apply carelessness and indifference. These things Socrates used to call "tragic masks"; because to children, masks can inspire fear as they are inexperienced, we are also scared in the same way, by events, for no reason, in the same way children are scared by masks. Because what is a child? Ignorance. What is a child? A lack of knowledge. Because when a child knows these things, he or she is no longer inferior to us. What is death? A "tragic mask." Examine it and you can see, it doesn't bite. The body must be separated from the spirit either now or later, as it was separated from it before. Why, then, are you worries, if you were separated from it now? Because if it's not separated now, it will be separated later. Why? So that period of the universe can be completed, because it always requires the present, future, and of course the past. What is pain? A mask. Examine it, the flesh can be damaged, but then, on the contrary, repaired. If that doesn't satisfy you, the door is open: if it does, just bear it. What comes from these opinions? That which comes only to the most noble and the really educated, the release from disturbance and fear: freedom. Because in these matters we shouldn't follow the crowd, who say that free people need to be educated; we should believe the philosophers, who say the educated are free. "How is this?". Is freedom anything other than the power to live as we choose? "Nothing else." Tell me then, do you wish to live doing bad things? "Not at all." No one then who lives like that is free. Do you want to live in fear? Do you want to live in sorrow? Do you want to live with disturbance? "Not at all."

No one, then, who is in a state of fear or sorrow or disturbance is free; but whoever has no sorrow, fear or disturbance, at the same time is also freed from mental slavery. How could we believe the legislators, when they say, "we only allow free people to be educated?" When philosophers say we allow no one to be free except the educated; God does not allow it. Is money your master, or a girl or a boy, or some tyrant, or some friend of a tyrant? Why do you tremble when you are called to a trial? I believe it's for this reason, so, study and keep in mind these principles with which you can determine what the things are, with which you should have confidence, and those which you should be cautious: courageous in thing which don't depend on your will; cautious in that which does.

"Do you know what I was doing?" In what? "In my little dissertations." Tell me how you now stand in respect to desire and avoidance; and tell me if you don't get what you want, and if you can't avoid what you don't: unfortunately, most won't be able to answer, most people will have read these sentences and ignored them.

"What did Socrates not write about?" Although he wrote so much. As he didn't always have someone to argue against his principles or to argue against someone else's, he used to argue with and examine himself, and he was always focusing one particular subject in a practical way. These are the things which philosophers write. But little dissertations, which I speak of, he left to others, to the stupid, or to those men who are free from disturbance and have time, or to those who are too foolish to understand the consequences.

So, now will you, when the opportunity presents itself, go forward and display the things which you possess, and announce them, saying, "See how I create dialogue?" Don't do that: you should say: "See how I haven't been disappointed by my desires. See how I haven't been trapped by that which I wish to avoid. Send death for me, and you will see. Send pain for me, prison, disgrace and condemnation." This is a true display of a young man who has been educated. But leave the rest to others, and let no one ever hear you say a word about these things; and if any man commends you for them, don't allow it; but think that you are nobody and know nothing. Only show that you know this: how not to be disappointed in your desires and how not to be trapped by that which you wish to avoid. Let others work at forensically toward other causes and problems: do you work at thinking about death, chains and pain, and do all this with confidence and reliance on him who has called you to do this, who has judged you worthy of the place in which, being stationed, you will show what things the rational governing power can do when it takes its stand against the forces which are not within the power of our will. And so, this paradox will no longer appear either impossible or a paradox, that a man should be cautious and courageous: courageous at the same time, toward the things which do not depend on the will, and cautious toward the things which are within the power of the will.

CHAPTER 31 - TRANQUILLITY

Consider, you have been called to court, for what you wish to maintain and what you wish to succeed in. If you wish to maintain a will conformable to nature, you have every security, every facility, and you have no troubles. If you wish to maintain what is in your own power and is naturally free, and if you are content with these, what else do you care about? Because who is the master of these things? Who can take them away? If you choose to be modest and faithful, who can stop you from being so? If you choose not to be restrained or pushed into wrong doing, who could make you do that which you don't desire to do? And who could make you avoid anything you think should be confronted? But, if you think the judge will find something against you to inspire fear, and you will also suffer in trying to avoid it, how can he do that? When then the pursuit of objects and the avoiding of them are in your power, what else do you desire? Let this be your introduction, this your narrative, this your confirmation, this your victory, this your conclusion, this your applause.

Therefore, Socrates said to someone who was reminding him to prepare for his trial, "Don't you think I have been preparing for it my whole life?" What kind of preparation? "I have maintained that which was in my own power." How then? "I have never done anything unfair either in my private or public life." But if you want to maintain external factors as well, your body and your property, I advise you from this moment to make the necessary preparation, and then consider the nature of your judge and your adversary. Because when you have proven to anyone in regards to the external possessions, what is your own, then you may need to beg to keep them, you can endure being beaten until you die or yield at once – but in regards to what is truly yours this can never be taken from you.

What do you think? Do you think, if Socrates wanted to keep any external belongings, he would have said: "Anytus and Meletus can kill me, but they are unable to harm me?" Do you think he was foolish knowing that this route wouldn't lead to the preservation of his life and fortune, but to another end? What is the reason then that he takes no account of his adversaries, and even irritates them? Just in the same way my friend Heraclitus, who had to attend court in Rhodes over a bit of land, and had proved to the judges that his case was true, said, when he had come to the conclusion of his speech, "I won't encourage you to do the right thing and I don't care what your judgment is, because it is you that is on trial, not me." And so, his business ended. What was the point of this? Was there a reason to irritate the judges on purpose, just like the case with Socrates. And to you, if you are preparing a similar conclusion, why do you wait, why do you obey the order summoning you to trial? Because if you wish to be crucified, wait and the cross will come: but if you choose to submit and to plead your cause as well as you can, you must do what is consistent with this objective, provided you want to maintain what is yours externally.

For this reason, it's also ridiculous to say, "Suggest something to me." What should I suggest? "Well, reshape my mind so it can accommodate itself to any event." That is like a man who hasn't read the letter, and says, "Tell me what name to write in response to this letter that has been presented to me." If I told him to write Dion, and then another letter came from Theon, what will he do? What will he write? But if you practiced writing, you are also prepared to write anything that is required. If haven't, what can suggest? Because if the circumstances require something else, what will you say or what will you do? Remember, this general rule and you won't need a suggestion. If you desire the externals, you will be obedient to the will of your master. And who is the master? Anyone, who has the power over the things which you seek to gain, or wish to avoid.

CHAPTER 32 – FOR THOSE WHO RECOMMEND OTHER PEOPLE OVER PHILOSOPHERS

Diogenes said to someone who asked from him for a letter of recommendation, "That you are a man, "he will know as soon as he sees you; and he will know whether you are good or bad, if he is experienced and skilful enough to distinguish the good from bad; but if he is inexperienced, he won't know, even if write him ten thousand letters." Because it's the same as if a piece of silver asked to be recommended to a person. If he's skilful in testing silver, he will know if it's authentic, and the quality will speak for itself. So, in life we should also have some skill, so that it can it can bring us anything and we will test it ourselves. But in the case of complex problems I would say, "bring any man you want, and I will distinguish for you the man who knows how to resolve problems and the man who doesn't." Why? Because I know how to resolve complex problems. I have the power, which a man must have who is able to discover those who have the same power. But in life how do I act? At one time, I call a something good, and at another time bad. What is the reason? The opposite of that which is needed to resolve complex problems, ignorance and inexperience.

CHAPTER 33 – AGAINST ADULTERERS

As Epictetus was saying that man is formed for fidelity, and that he who subverts fidelity subverts the peculiar characteristic of men, and at the moment entered a man, who had once been detected committing adultery. Then Epictetus continued: If we put aside fidelity, which we are formed for, and make plans to take a neighbour's wife, what are we doing? What other than destroying and overthrowing? Who? The man of fidelity, the man of modesty, the man of faithfulness. Is that all? Aren't we not also overthrowing the neighbourhood, friendship, and the community; and in where are we placing ourselves? What should I consider you as? As a neighbour, as a friend? What kind? As a citizen? How could I trust you? So, if you are a utensil, with such little worth, that no man could use you, you would be taken and thrown on the pile of animal shit, and no man would take you from there. And so, being a man, you are unable to fill any place in society, which befits you, or anyone else, what should we do with you? Would you be content to be thrown on the pile of animal shit, as a useless utensil, and a bit of shit? Then you'll say, "No-one cares about me"? They don't, because you are bad and useless. It's just as if the wasps complained that no man cares for them, because if a man can, he strikes them and knocks them down. You have such a poisonous sting that you create trouble and pain for any man that you wound with it. What would you expect us to do with you? There is no place in society where you can be put.

"Isn't it nature to take any woman we choose?" Just as common as pork being served to guests, when the portions have been served, if you think it's right, snatch the plate of the man who relaxes next to you, or slyly steal it, or take what you like off the plate with your hand, and if you can't break the meat, lick your fingers and try again. You would be a fine guest, wouldn't you? Much better than the cups! "Isn't the theatre a communal location to the citizens?" When they've sat down, come along if you like, and remove someone from their seat. Women are also common by nature, however, when the legislator, like a master of the feast, has distributed them, why don't you look for your own portion and not try to steal what belongs to another. "But I am an educated man, I understand Archedemus." Understand Archedemus then, and be an adulterer, and faithless, and instead of a man, be a wolf or an ape: because what's the difference?

CHAPTER 34 – HOW GENEROUSITY IS CONSISTANT WITH CARE

Situations themselves we should be indifferent to; but not to the use of them. How can a man preserve his firmness and tranquillity, and at the same time be careful and neither impatient or negligent? If he imitates people who play with dice. The dice are indifferent. How do I know what the numbers will be? I don't know, but to choose the numbers I want, is in my control. So, in life the main priority is this: distinguish and separate things, and say, "the external is not in my power: will is in my power. Where can I find the good and the bad? Within, in the things which are my own." But in that which doesn't belong to you, you can determine that nothing is either good or bad, profitable, or damaging.

"So, should we use our will power carelessly?" Not at all: because this is bad for the faculty of the will, and consequently against nature; so, we should act carefully because the use of the will is not something to be indifferent to. We should act with firmness and freedom from disturbance because the material world is something to be indifferent toward. If I am indifferent to the external, no man can hinder me. Where I can be hindered or compelled to try and obtain things not in my power, is an incorrect use of will, which can produce good or bad, and the use is in my power. But it is difficult to merge these two things, the carefulness of a man who is affected by the matter and the firmness of a man who has no regard for it; but it's not impossible; and if it was, happiness would be impossible. We should act as we would on a voyage. What can I do? I can choose the captain of the ship, the sailors, the day, the opportunity. Then a storm comes. What else do I need to do? My part is done. The situation now belongs to someone else - the captain. But the ship is sinking - what can I do? You do the only things you can do, not to be drowned full of fear, screaming, or blaming God, but knowing that what has been born must also die: because you aren't an immortal being, but a man, a part of the whole, as an hour is a part of the day: I must be present like the hour, and pass like the hour. What difference, then, does it make to me how I pass, whether by suffocation or a fever, because I must pass some way?

This is what you will see in young children playing football, they do not care if the ball is high quality or not, they have more interest in the actual game. This therefore is the skill, the art, the judgement, if I run in a certain direction I will be able to get the ball, and if I pass it, someone else can. But if with fear we receive or pass the ball, what kind of game would this be? Someone will say "pass"; or, "don't pass"; and will induce hesitation, this is more like arguing, not playing.

Socrates knew how to play the game of life. How?" By using pleasant phrases in the court where he was on trial. "Tell me," he said, "Anytus, how can you say I don't believe in God. These demons you speak of, who are they? Aren't they the sons of Gods, or a compound of god and man?" When Anytus admitted this, Socrates said, "Who then, can believe that there are mules, but no donkeys"; and this he said as if he were playing a game of football. And what was the ball in that case? Life, chains, banishment, separation from his wife and leaving his children as orphans. These were the things with which he was playing; so, he played well and passed the ball skilfully. We must use the same care that the players do, but show the same indifference about the ball. Because we by all means need to apply our art to some external material, not valuing the material, but, whatever it may be, showing our internal art through this external means. For example, the weaver doesn't make wool, but exercises his art with the material he receives. When you have received your material, work with it. If you come through without suffering anything, everyone who meets you will congratulate you on your escape; but someone who knows how to carefully look at these things, if he saw that you behaved properly, will commend you and be pleased with your behaviour; and if he discovered that you escaped due to inappropriate behaviour, he will do the opposite.

How can it be said that some external things are according to nature and others not? It is said as it might be said if we were separated from union: for example, the foot, if I believe according to nature it should be clean; it could be a benefit to walk through the mud, and sometimes to be cut off for the benefit of the whole body; otherwise it is no longer a foot. We should think in some way about ourselves also. What are you? A man. If you consider yourself detached from other men, it is according to nature to live to old age, to be rich, to be healthy. But if you consider yourself as a man and a part of the whole, it could be for the sake of the whole, that one day you become sick, and at another time take a voyage and run into danger, and at another time be in need, and, in some cases, die prematurely. Why are you disturbed? Don't you know, that a foot is no longer a foot if it's detached from the body, so you are no longer a man, if you are separated from other men. Because what is a man? To be part of a state, which consists of God and men. "So, do I need to go on trial; do others have to have fevers, sail the seas, and die?" Of course, because it's impossible in such a union, in this universe of things, among so many living together, that these things can't happen, some to one and some to another. It's your duty then, since you're here, to say what you should, to arrange these things in the right way. Then someone says, "I'll sue you for going against me." What good does that do for you: I've done my part; but whether you have done yours, you must look into that; because there is some danger here: that it might escape your notice.

CHAPTER 35 – INDIFFERENCE

A hypothetical proposition is indifferent: the judgment about it however is not, because it is either knowledge, opinion or error. Life is indifferent: the use is not. When any man then tells you that these things also are indifferent, don't become negligent; and when a man tells you to be careful, don't become struck with admiration of material things. It's good for you to know your own power, so that in matters which you haven't prepared for you can keep quiet, and not be angry, if others have any advantage over you. But you, in the resolution of complex arguments will claim to have the advantage over them; and if others are angered by this, you will pacify them by saying, "I have educated in this, and you haven't." So, where there is a need to practice, don't seek what is required from the need, but yield to those who have had the practice, and be content with firmness of your mind.

Find a teacher. "How?" Not without care. "But I've been locked out, I couldn't find the way to make it through the window; and when I finally did, I found the door shut, I have or come back or enter through the window again." Still try to find the teacher. "In what way?" Not without care. Imagine you found what you were seeking. Wasn't that what you wanted? Why don't you claim it, and not what belongs to others? Always remember what is your own, and what belongs to another; and you will not be disturbed. Chrysippus therefore said, "So long as the future is uncertain, I always stick with those who are more adapted to that which is according to nature; because God himself has given me the faculty to choose this path. "So, If I knew that it I would become sick, I would move toward it; because we must know in the case of men, it's a curse not to die. Since we must die, we also know that death approaches, and are angered by it; because we don't know what we, or what we have studied, and what belongs to man, in the same was as those who have studied horses know what belongs to horses. But Chrysantas, when he was going to strike the enemy, stopped himself when he heard the trumpet sounding to retreat: it seemed better to him to obey the general's command than to follow his own inclination. But none of us are ready to leave, even when it is necessary, to obey, instead we cry and moan that we are suffering. What do we suffer from? We call them "circumstances." What kind of circumstances? If you give a name to the circumstances around you, all things are circumstances; but if you call these things hardships, what hardship is there in the death of that which has been born?

That which destroys can be a sword, a wheel, the sea, or a tyrant. Why do you care which way you die? All ways are equal. If you listen to the truth, the way which the tyrant ends your life might be shorter. A tyrant never killed a man in six months: but a fever could last a year. All these things are only sound, and fuzzy noise.

"My life is in danger by Caesar." And isn't it dangerous to live in Nicopolis, where there are so many earthquakes: and when you are crossing the sea, what risks are there? Isn't that a hazard to your life? "But to be in danger is an opinion." Do you mean your own? Because who could inspire you to have an opinion which you don't choose? Is it another man's opinion? Then, what kind of danger would be yours, if others have false opinions? "But I am in danger of being banished." What is it to be banished? To be somewhere else than in Rome? "Yes: what if I'm sent to Gyara?" If that suits you, you'll go there; but if it doesn't, you can go to another place instead of Gyara, where the man who sends you to Gyara will also go, whether he choose to or not. If this is what happens, why do you want to live in Rome as if it were something great? It's not worth all this disturbance. An ingenuous youth would say, "It's not worthwhile to have heard so much, written so much, and to have been by the side of an old man who is not worth much." Only remember, that division of that which is your own and not your own are distinguished: never claim anything which belongs to others. A tribunal, and a prison are each a place, one high and the other low; but the will can be maintained in equilibrium, if you choose to maintain it in that way.

CHAPTER 36 – HOW WE SHOULD USE KNOWLEDGE

Due to an unreasonable disregard for knowledge many of us fail in many of our duties. Because what does God usually see other than death, danger or disease, generally things of that type? But if I have to expose myself to danger for a friend, and if it is my duty to die for him, what do I need to gain knowledge for? Don't I have inside me, God who has told me the nature of good and evil, and has explained to me the signs of both? What need do I then have to consult the various religious texts, or watch the flight of birds, and why do I give in, when someone says, "It's in your best interest"? Because does he know what is in my interest, does he know what is good; and as he has read these texts, has he really learnt the signs of good and evil? Because if he knows the sign of these, he knows the sign of both beauty and ugliness, and of the fair and unfair. Can you really tell me, what is in my interest: is it life or death, poverty or wealth? But whether these things are in my interest or not, I don't intend to ask your opinion. Why don't you give me your opinion on matters of grammar, instead of giving it for things which we are all in error and currently disputing with one another?

What leads us so frequently to seek knowledge? Cowardice, the fear of what will happen. This is the reason why we seek those who have knowledge. "Pray, God, will I be the heir to my father's property?" "Let's see: on this occasion." "Yes, as fortune chooses." "You will gain the inheritance," we thank God as if we received the inheritance from him.

What should we do then? We should have no desire to gain or avoid, as the man asks another man who he meets which of the two roads will he take, without any desire for either the right or left, because he has no wish to pick any road except the road which leads to his end. In the same way, we should seek God only as a guide; as we use our eyes, not asking them to show us what we want, but receiving the appearance of things as the eyes present them to us. But now we tremble to take any path, and, while we call on God, we avoid the path, and say, "God help me; allow me to come out of this difficulty safely." Fool, you should only seek what is best? Is there anything better than what pleases God? Why do you, so far as what is in your power, try to corrupt your judge and lead astray your adviser?

CHAPTER 37 – WHAT IS THE NATURE OF GOOD

God is beneficial. But the Good is also beneficial. It is consistent then that where the nature of God is, there we also find the nature of good. What then is the nature of God? The body? No. An estate of land? No. Fame? No. Is it intelligence, knowledge, and the right reason? Yes. So, simply seek the nature of good; because I suppose that you don't look for it in the nature of plants. No. Do you seek it in an irrational animal? No. So, if you seek it in a rational animal, why would you still seek it anywhere except in the superiority of rational over irrational animals?

Good requires the use of appearances. Therefore, we don't apply the term good to animals, because they don't possess the faculty of understanding the use of appearances; and there is good reason for this, because they exist for the purpose of serving others, and they exercise no superiority. The donkey, doesn't exist for the superiority over others. We needed a back which was able to carry something; and in truth we had needed the donkeys to walk carrying heavy loads. And that's where the matter stops. Because if donkeys had received the faculty of comprehending the use of appearances, it is plain that consistently with reason he would not have been subjected to us, and would not have done us these services, but he would have been equal to us and like us.

Will you now look for the nature of good in the rational animal? Because if it's not there, and you choose to say it exists in any something else. "Tell me where? Aren't plants and animals also the work of God?" They are; but they are not superior, and are not part of God. You are a superior being; you are a portion separated from God; you have in yourself a certain portion of him. Why are you so ignorant of your own noble descent? Why do you not know where you came from? Don't you think, when you are eating, who you are, who eat and who you feed? When you are with a woman, don't you remember who you are, and who does this? When you are in social intercourse, when you are exercising yourself, when you are engaged in discussion, don't you know that you are nourishing a god, that you are exercising a god? Fool, you are carrying god with you, whether you know it not. Do you think I mean some God of silver or of gold, and the external? No, you carry him within yourself, and you don't perceive that you are polluting him with impure thoughts and dirty deeds. And if an image of God were present, you wouldn't dare to do any of the things which you are doing: but when God himself is present within and sees all and hears all, you are not ashamed of thinking such things and doing such things, ignorant as you are of your own nature and subject to the anger of God. Then why do we fear when we are sending a young man from the school into active life, he shouldn't do anything inappropriately, eat inappropriately, have improper intercourse with women; and the clothes in which he dresses himself should protect him from the elements, there is no need for fine garments which make him proud. This youth does not know his own God: he doesn't know who he leaves his home with. How absurd is it when he says, "God, I wish I had you with me?" Don't you see you have God in you? Why do you seek for another when you have him? If you were a statue of Phidias, Athena or Zeus you would think both of yourself, and of the artist, and if you had any understanding you would try to do nothing unworthy of the artist who made you or of yourself, and try not to appear in shameful attire for those who look at you. But because God has made you, for this reason don't you care how you will appear? Being the work of such an artist, would you dishonour him? Not only has he made you, but also trusted you to govern yourself? You don't think of this, but if God had trusted you to look after an orphan, would you neglect him? He has trusted yourself to your care, and says, "I had no one fitter to look after you than yourself: keep yourself for me, as according to your nature, modest, faithful, upright, unafraid, free from passion and disturbance." But you chose to disregard this and keep yourself in a bad state.

People should say, let me get the confidence and the facial expression I should have, the right attitude, then I will show to you the statue, when it is perfected, when it is polished. My word is irrevocable, I will not fail. I will show myself to you, faithful, modest, noble, free from disturbance. This power I possess; and this I can do. I will show the nerves of a philosopher. "What nerves are those?" A desire never disappointed, an aversion which never hangs on that which I should avoid, a proper pursuit, a diligent purpose, a rise which isn't reckless. These things you will see.

CHAPTER 38 – WHEN WE CAN'T FULFIL THE CHARACTER OF A MAN, WE ASSUME THE CHARACTER OF A PHILOSPHER

It is not common, to fulfil the promise of a man's nature. Because what is a man? The answer is: "A rational and mortal being." Then, by the rational faculty, from what are we distinct? From wild animals. Take care then to do anything like a wild animal; because if you do, you have lost the character of a man; you have not fulfilled your promise. See that you do nothing like a sheep; but if you do, in this case the man is lost. What do we do as sheep? When we act gluttonously, when we act in a vulgar manner, when we act filthily, inconsiderately, what level have we declined to? To sheep. What have we lost? The rational faculty. When we act harmfully and violently, what level have we declined to? To wild animals. Consequently, some of us are great beasts, and others little beasts, of a bad disposition, which may say, "Let me be eaten by a lion." But in all these ways the promise of a man acting as a man is destroyed. When is a conjunctive proposition maintained? When it fulfils what its nature promises. That being the preservation of a complex proposition, a conjunction of truths. When is a disjunctive maintained? When it fulfils what it promises. Is it any wonder then, if man, is preserved or lost, in the same way? Each man is improved and preserved by corresponding acts, the carpenter by acts of carpentry, the grammarian by acts of grammar. But if a man accustoms himself to write ungrammatically, his art will be corrupted and destroyed. Therefore, modest actions preserve the modest man, and immodest actions destroy him: and actions of fidelity preserve the faithful man, and the contrary actions destroy him. And actions also intensify the current character: shamelessness strengthens the shameless man, faithlessness the faithless man, abusive words the abusive man, anger the man of an angry temper, and unequal receiving verses giving, make the greedy man greedier.

For this reason, philosophers urge us not to be satisfied with learning only, but also to add study, and then practice. Because we have been accustomed to do the opposite things, and we put into practice opinions which are contrary to true opinions. If then we don't put into practice the right opinions, we would be nothing more than people who explain the opinions of others.

Who among us isn't able to discuss according to the rules of art, about good and evil things? "Some are good, some are bad, and some are indifferent: the good then are virtues, and the things which participate in virtues; and the bad, is the contrary actions; and the indifferent are wealth, health, reputation." Then, if during our talk there's some greater noise than usual, or some of those who are present laugh at us, we are disturbed. Philosopher, where are the things from, which you were talking about? How did you find these things and speak about them? From my lips, and from there only. Why are you corrupting the advice provided by others? Why do you treat the biggest matters as if you were playing a game of dice? Because it's one thing to keep bread and wine in a storehouse, and another thing to eat. That which has been eaten, is digested, distributed, and becomes ligaments, flesh, bones, blood, healthy colour and healthy breath. Whatever is stored up, when you choose you can take and show it; but you have no other advantage, it except if you appear to possess it. Because what's the difference between explaining these doctrines to those men who have different opinions? If you explain, according to the rules, the art and opinions of Epicurus, perhaps you will explain his opinions in a more useful manner than Epicurus himself. Why do you call yourself a Stoic? Why do you deceive the masses? Why do you act the part of a Jew, when you are a Greek? Don't you see how each is called a Jew, a Syrian or an Egyptian? And when we see a man acting in two manners, we are accustomed to say, "This man isn't a Jew, but he acts like one." But when he has assumed the effects of one who has learnt the Jewish doctrine, and has adopted that sect, then he is in fact and he is named a Jew. So, we having similar knowledge of the Jews, are named Jews, but in fact we are something else. Our actions are inconsistent with our words; we are far from practicing what we say, and that of which we are proud, as if we knew it. Therefore, being unable to fulfil what the character of a man promises, we even add to it the profession of a philosopher, which is as heavy a burden, as if a man who is unable to lift ten pounds should attempt to raise a giant stone.

CHAPTER 39 – HOW WE CAN DISCOVER LIFE'S DUTIES FROM NAMES

Consider who you are. In the first place, you are a man; and man possesses nothing superior than the faculty of the will, of which all other things are subjected to; and the faculty itself he possesses is free from being controlled. Consider what things you have been separated from by reason. You have been separated from wild beasts: you have been separated from domestic animals. Further, you are a citizen of the world, and a part of it, not a lower class of animal, but one of the principal parts, because you are capable of comprehending the divine administration and of considering the connection of things. What does the character of a citizen promise? To hold nothing external as profitable to himself; to deliberate about nothing as if he were detached from the community, but to act as his hands and feet would, if they had reason and understood the constitution of nature, because they would never put themselves in motion or desire anything, without reference to the whole. Therefore, the philosophers say, if a good man had foresight of what would happen, he would cooperate toward his own sickness and death, since he knows that these things are assigned to him in accordance to the universal arrangement, and that the whole is superior to the parts: the citizens and state. But, because we don't know the future, it's our duty to stick to the things which are in our nature and are more suitable choices for us, because we were made for this.

After this, remember that you're a son. What is the character of a son? To consider that anything that the son possesses belongs to the father, to obey him, never to blame him, or to say or do anything which causes him harm, to yield to him in all things and give way, cooperating with him as much as you can. After this know that you are also a brother, and that this character it is able to make concessions; to be easily persuaded, to speak in a good way about your brother, never be in opposition to him in any of the things which are independent of the will, and read to give them up, so you can have a larger share in what is dependent on the will. See what a thing is and be prepared to give it up, for example, a lettuce, or a seat, to gain yourself a disposition of goodness. What a great advantage this is.

Next, if you are the senator of any state, remember that you are the senator: if you're young, that you are young: if an old man, that you're an old man; because each of these names, if it's examined, marks out its appropriate duties. But if you go and blame your brother, I'm telling you, "You've forgotten who you are and what your name is."

Next, if you were a carpenter, and used the hammer in the wrong way, you would have forgotten the carpenter; and if you've forgotten the brother and instead of a brother have become an enemy, wouldn't you appear to have changed one thing for another in that case? And if instead of a man, who is self-contained and social, you become a mischievous wild beast who uses deception, what have you lost? But, to lose money may make a man suffer and cause damage? Doesn't the loss of anything else do damage to the man? If you had lost the art of grammar, wouldn't you think the loss was damaging? And if you lost modesty, moderation and gentleness, do you think the loss is nothing? And yet the things I mentioned first are lost by some external cause, and are independent of the will, and the second by our own fault; and as to the first neither to have them nor to lose them is shameful; but as to the second, not to have them and to lose them is shameful and a serious matter which brings misfortune. What does the pathetic man lose? He loses the man. What does a man lose who makes the pathetic man what he is? Many things; and he also loses the man. What does the unfaithful man lose? He loses the modest, the temperate, the decent, the citizen, the neighbour. What does the angry man lose? Something else. What does the coward lose? Something else. No man is bad without suffering some loss and damage. If then you look for damage in the loss of money only, all these men receive no harm or damage; it may even seem, they've profited, when they acquire a bit of money by any of these bad deeds. But if you consider all damage to be caused by a small coin, not even the man who loses his nose is damaged in your opinion. "Yes," you say, "because his body has been mutilated." Isn't losing the sense of smell damaging too? Don't you see the energy of the soul an advantage to the man who possesses it, and damaging to the man who has lost it? "Tell me what you mean." Don't we have natural modesty? "We have." Does the man who loses this sustain no damage? Is he deprived of nothing, does he lose nothing that naturally belongs to him? Aren't we naturally faithful? And have a natural affection, a natural disposition to help others, a natural disposition for tolerance? The man then who allows himself to be damaged in these matters, can he really be free from harm and injury? "What are you saying? Shouldn't I hurt a man who has hurt me?" Firstly, consider what hurt is, and remember what you've heard from the philosophers. Because if the good consists in the will, and the evil can also dwell there, wouldn't you say this: "The man has hurt himself by doing an unfair act to me, wouldn't I hurt myself by doing some unfair act to him?" Why don't we take this view? But whenever there is some detriment our body or to our possessions, we see the harm there; and when the same thing happens to our faculty of the will, we don't sense the harm; because a man who has been deceived or has done an unfair act doesn't suffer from pain in the legs or hips, he doesn't lose his estate; and we wish for nothing else than to protect these things. But whether we have the will of modesty and faithfulness, we don't care at all.

CHAPTER 40 – WHAT THE BEGINNING OF PHILOSOPHY IS

The beginning of philosophy to a man who enters it the right way and by the door, is conscious of his own weakness in relation to necessary things. Because we come into the world with no natural notion of a right-angled triangle, or instrument notation; but we learn these things by transmission, according to art; and for this reason, those who don't know them, don't think that they know them. But in regards to good and evil, beautiful and ugly, happiness and misfortune, right and wrong, and what we should and shouldn't do, who came into the world without having an intuitive idea of them? We all use these names, and we endeavour to fit the preconceptions to the various cases, and so: "He has done well, he hasn't done well; he has done what he should, or not as he should; he's been unfortunate, he's been fortunate; he's unfair, he's fair": who doesn't use these names? Who among us defers the use of them these names until he's learned what they are? And the cause of this is that we come into the world already taught, as it were, by nature, some things on this matter, and proceeding from that we have added to them, self-conceit. "Why," a man says, "don't I know the beautiful and the ugly? Don't I have a notion of it?" You so. "Don't I adapt it to various things?" You do. "Don't I adapt it properly?" That is the basis of the whole question; this is where conceit is added.

Beginning from these things which are added, men proceed to that which is a matter of dispute: unsuitable adaptation; because if they possessed this power of adaptation from the beginning, what would cause them to be wrong? And now, since you think that you properly adapt the preconceptions to things, tell me how you gained this ability? Because you think so? But it doesn't appear so to another, and he thinks that he also makes a proper adaptation; doesn't he? He does. Is it possible then that both of you can properly apply the preconceptions to things when you have opposing opinions? It's not possible. Can you then show us anything better toward adapting the preconceptions beyond your thinking that you do? Does the madman do anything else other than the things which seem right to him? Is this then the criterion for him as well? It's not sufficient. Then tell me something which is superior. What is this?

This is the beginning of philosophy, a perception of the disagreement of men with one another, and an inquiry into the cause of the disagreement, and a condemnation and distrust of that which only "seems," and a certain investigation of that which "seems" whether it "seems" right, and the discovery of an indicator, like we have discovered the balance in the determination of weight, and a carpenter's rule in the case of straight and crooked. This is the beginning of philosophy. "Should we say that all things are right because they seem so to everyone?" How is it possible that contradictions can be right? " Not all can, but people believe all that seem to be right." Why do some things seem more right to you than those which seems right to the Syrians? Why do some things seem more right to you than what seems right to the Egyptians? So, "seems" to every man is not sufficient for determining what "is". In the case of weights or measures are we satisfied with the appearance? No, in each case we have discovered a certain tool to measure. In this matter then, is there a rule for that which "seems?" And how could it be possible that the most necessary things to men would have no sign, and be incapable of being discovered? There is a rule then. So why don't we seek the rule and discover it, and afterward use it without deviating from it?

This I think, is that which when it's discovered cures the madness of those who use mere "seeming" as a measure, and misuse it; so that in the future proceeding from knowing the rule, we can make clear and use in the case of things, the preconceptions which are distinctly fixed.

Take whatever you're inquiring about. For example, "Pleasure." Subject it to the rule, put it on the scales. Shouldn't there be something that could do this, so we can have confidence in it? "Yes.

"What should we confide in? Should we trust anything which is insecure? "No." So, is pleasure something which is secure? "No." Take it off the scale and throw it away, and drive it far away from the place of good things. So, things are tested and weighed when the rules are ready. And to philosophize is this, to examine and confirm the rules; and then to use them when they are known is the act of a wise and good man.

CHAPTER 41 – ON DISPUTE OR DISCUSSION

The things that a man must learn in order to be able to apply the art of disputation, has been accurately shown by our philosophers, but with respect to the proper use of these things, we are entirely without practice. Give any of us, whoever you want, an illiterate man to have a discussion with, and he won't know how to deal with the man. But when he has spoken to the man a little, if he replies off subject, he doesn't know how to treat him, so he either abuses or ridicules him, and says, "He's an illiterate man; it's not possible to do anything with him." However, a guide, when he finds a man on the wrong road, leads him right way: he does not ridicule or abuse him and then leave him. Show this illiterate man the truth, and you will see that he follows. But as long as you don't show him the truth, don't ridicule him - see your own incompetence.

How did Socrates act? He used to encourage his adversary in disputes to give evidence to him, and he wanted no other witness. Therefore, he could say, "I don't care about other witnesses, because I am satisfied with the evidence of my adversary, and I don't want the opinion of others, only the opinion of the man who is in dispute with me." Because he used to make conclusions drawn from natural notions so clear that every man could see the contradiction and cease arguing: "Does an envious man have joy?" "Not at all, he suffers pain." Well, "Do you think that envy over evil causes pain? Who can have envy toward evil?" Therefore, he made his adversary say that envy is pain over good things. "So, would any man envy people who are nothing to him?" "Not at all." So, having completed the notion and distinctly fixed it he would go away without saying to his adversary, "Define for me what envy is"; and if the adversary had defined envy, he didn't say, "You've defined it badly, because the terms of the definition don't correspond to what we've defined." These are technical terms, and for this reason disagreeable and hardly intelligible to illiterate men, however, these are terms that we can't put to one side.

The illiterate man himself, who follows the appearances presented to him, should be able to concede anything or reject it, and we can't by the use of these terms encourage him to do otherwise. Accordingly, being conscious of our own inability, we don't attempt it; well, at least those of us that exercise caution wouldn't. But most people have little patience, and when they have a dispute, they confuse themselves and others; and finally abusing their adversaries and abused by them, they walk away.

Now this was one of the primary objectives of Socrates, never to be irritated in an argument, never to say anything abusive, anything insulting, but to have patience for abusive people and put an end to the argument. If you want to know the great power he had by doing this, read Symposium of Xenophon, and you will see how many arguments he put an end to.

Now; the matter isn't very safe, and particularly in Rome; because a man who attempts to do it, mustn't do it in a corner, you must be sure, if you go to a man of higher ranking, or to a rich man, and ask him, "Can you tell me, Sir, who do you trust to look after your horses?" "I can tell you." You have entrusted them to a person without care, to someone who has no experience with horses? "Not at all." Well then; can you tell me who you trust with your gold or silver? "I don't entrust these to anyone indifferently." Well; what about your own body, have you considered entrusting the care of it to anyone? "Certainly." To a man of experience, I suppose, and one acquainted with remedies, or with the healing art? "Without a doubt." Are these the best things that you have, or do you also possess something else which is better than all of these? "What kind of things do you mean?" Something that makes use of these things, and tests each one, and deliberates. "Do you mean the soul?" You have thought correctly. "In truth, I do believe that the soul is a much better thing than anything else I possess." Can you then show me, in what way you've taken care of your soul? Because it's not likely that you, who are such a wise a man, and have a reputation in the city, inconsiderately and carelessly allow the most valuable thing that you possess to be neglected and to perish? "Certainly not." But have you taken care of the soul yourself; and have you learned from another person how to do this, or have you discovered how to yourself? Here comes the danger, that he might say, "What is this to you, my good man, who are you?" Next, if you persist in troubling him, there is a danger that he may raise his hands and give you blows. I use to admire this type of inquisition, until I experienced these dangers.

CHAPTER 42 – ON ANXIETY

When I see an anxious man, I say, "what does that man want? If he didn't want something which is not in his power, would he be anxious?" For this reason, a musician when singing by himself has no anxiety, but when he enters the theatre, he is anxious even if he has a good voice and plays his instrument well; because not only does he wish to sing well, but also to be liked by the crown: but this isn't in his power. Accordingly, where he has skill, there he has confidence. Bring anyone who knows nothing about music, and the musician wouldn't care. Why does this matter? Well, because he doesn't know what will please the crowd. He has learned to strike the lowest chord and the highest; but what will bring praise from the crowd, and what power it has in life, he doesn't know, neither has he thought about it. Therefore, he trembles and becomes pale. I can't say that the man isn't a musician if I see him afraid, but I can say something else, and not one thing, but many. First of all, I'll call him a stranger and say, "This man doesn't know which part of the world he is in, although he's been here so long, he is ignorant of the laws of the State and the customs, and what is permitted and what is not; and he has never employed any lawyer to explain the laws." A man doesn't write a will, if he doesn't know how it should be written, neither does he rush to seal a bond or write a security. But he uses his desire without a lawyer's advice. "What do you mean without a lawyer?" He doesn't know that he wills what is not allowed, and does not will that which is necessary; and he doesn't know what is his own or what is another man's; but if he did know, he would never be obstructed, he would never be hindered, he wouldn't be anxious. "How's that? " Is any man afraid of things which aren't evil? "No." Is he afraid about things which are evil, but as long as they are within his power they may not happen? "Certainly not." If, then, the things which are independent of the will are neither good or bad, and all things which do depend on the will are within our power, and no man can either take them from us or give them to us, if we choose, where there any room left for anxiety? But we are anxious about our body, our property, about the will of Caesar; but not anxious about the internal things. Are we anxious not to form false opinions? No, because this is in my power. About not exerting our movement contrary to nature? No, not even about this. So, when you see a man who is pale, as the physician says, judging from the complexion, this man's spleen is damaged, or it's the man's liver; so, I also say, this man's desire and aversion are disordered, he's not in the right state, he has a fever. Because nothing else changes the colour, or causes trembling or chattering of the teeth, or causes a man to sink to his knees: than anxiety.

Because of this, when Zeno was going to meet Antigonus, he wasn't anxious, because Antigonus had no power over any of the things which Zeno admired; and Zeno didn't care for the things which Antigonus had power over. But Antigonus was anxious when he was going to meet Zeno, because he wanted to please Zeno; this was an external thing. But Zeno didn't want to please Antigonus; because no man who is skilled in any art wishes to please someone who has no such skill.

Should I try to please you? Why? I suppose, you know the measure by which one man is estimated by another. Have you been through the pain of education to learn what's a good man and what's a bad man, and how a man becomes one or the other? Why, then, are you not good yourself? "How," he replies, "am I not good?" Because no good man moans and cries, no good man is pale and trembles, or says, "How will someone else view me, will he listen to me?" Fool, just as it pleases him. Why do you care about things that belong to others? Is it his fault if he receives badly what comes from you? "Certainly." And is it possible that the fault can be one man's, and the evil in another? "No." Why are you anxious about that then, when it belongs to others? "Your question is reasonable; but I'm anxious how I'll speak to him." Can't you speak to him as you choose? "But I'm worried I might not be composed." If you were going to write the name Dion, would you be afraid that you wouldn't be composed? "Not at all." Why? Isn't it because you've practiced writing? "Certainly." Well, if you were going to read the name, wouldn't you feel the same? Yes. And Why? Because every art has a certain strength and confidence in the things which belong to it. Haven't you practiced speaking? What else did you learn in school? Sophisticated propositions? For what purpose? Wasn't it for the purpose of speaking skilfully? and isn't speaking skilfully the same as speaking seasonably, cautiously and with intelligence, and also without making mistakes and without hindrance, and besides all that, with confidence? "Yes." When, then, you are on a horse and find flat land, are you anxious at being matched against a man who's on foot, and anxious in a matter in which you have practiced, and he hasn't? "Yes, because that person has power to kill me." Fool, speak the truth, unhappy man, do not brag, or claim to be a philosopher, or refuse to acknowledge your masters, as long as you present this nonsense, you will follow every man who is stronger than you. Socrates used to practice speaking, and he talked as he wanted to tyrants, to the judges, and to whoever talked in his prison. Diogenes had practiced speaking, he spoke as he liked to Alexander, to the pirates, and to the person who bought him. These men were confident in the things which they practiced. But you want to walk off to your own affairs and cling to them: go and sit in a corner, and weave hypothetical arguments, and oppose them to one another. I can't see in you a man who can rule a state.

CHAPTER 43 – TO NASO

When a man entered with his son and listened to the man reading, Epictetus said, "This is the method of instruction"; and stopped. When the man asked him to continue, Epictetus said: Every art, when it is taught, creates hard work for the person who is unacquainted with it and is unskilled in it, and indeed the things which proceed from the arts immediately show their use in the purpose for which they were made; and most of them contain something attractive and pleasing. Because, to be present and to witness how a shoemaker learns is not pleasant; but the shoe is useful and also not bad to look at. You will see this much more in music; because if you were present while a person is learning, the discipline will appear so challenging; and yet the results of music are pleasing and delightful to those who know nothing about music. And here we believe the work of a philosopher to be something of this kind: he must adapt his wishes to what's going on, so that none of the things which are taking place, take place contrary to our wishes, and any of the things which don't take place, take place when because we wish they should. From this, the result is, to those who have arranged the work of philosophy, not to desire, or to peruse that which we should avoid; to be without nervousness, without fear, without worry to pass through life, together with their associates maintaining the relations, naturally acquired, such as the relationship of son, father, brother, citizen, man, woman, husband, wife, neighbour, ruler, or ruled. The work of a philosopher we conceive to be something like this. It remains next to inquire, how this is accomplished.

We see that the carpenter when he has encountered certain things becomes a carpenter. Wouldn't it be in philosophy, not sufficient enough to wish to be wise and good, without the necessity to learn certain things? We inquire then what these things are. The philosophers say that we should first to learn that there is a God and that he provides for all; also, that it is not possible to conceal from him our acts, or even our intentions and thoughts. The next thing, is to learn what is the nature God is; and any man who would please and obey God, must try with all his power to be like him. If the divine is faithful, man must be faithful; if it is free, man must also be free; if generous, man must also be generous; if forgiving, man must also be forgiving; as a being, an imitator of God, he must do and say everything consistently with this fact.

"What do we begin with?" If you enter this path, I tell you that you first must understand names. Because, If I don't understand them, how can you use them? You would use them how the illiterate uses written language: because use is one thing, understanding is another. But if you think you understand them, say any name you like, and let's see whether we understand it.

What do you lack? If, I show you that you lack the most necessary things and the primary of things for happiness, and that up until now you have looked after everything other than that which you should, and, to crown all, that you don't know what God is, or what a man is, or what is good, or what is bad; and what I've said about your ignorance toward other matters, that may perhaps be endured, but if I say that you know nothing about yourself, how is it possible that you could endure me if I produce the proof and stay here? It's not possible; you would immediately run away in anger. And yet what harm have I caused you? Unless the mirror also causes injury to the ugly man because it shows him to himself as he is. If the doctor said to a man "You have a fever: no food or drink for a day." No one says, "What an insult!" But if you say to a man, "Your desires are inflamed, your aversions are low, your intentions are inconsistent, your pursuits are not comfortable to nature, your opinions are false," the man immediately goes away and says, "he's insulted me."

Our way of dealing with this, is like a crowded market. Animals are brought to be sold; and the greater part of men come to buy and sell, but there are a few who come to look at the market and inquire how it's conducted, and why, and who determines the opening times, and for what purpose. And it's the same here in this assembly: some trouble themselves with nothing except the unimportant. To everyone who is busy with possessions, land, and magisterial offices, these are all unimportant. But there are a few who attend the assembly, men who love to look and consider what is the world, and who rules it. Does it have a ruler? And how is it possible that a city or a family could continue to exist, not even for the shortest time without an administrator and guardian, and that such a great and beautiful system could be administered with such order and yet without a purpose and by chance? There is then an administrator. What kind of administrator and how does he rule? Who are we? Were we produced by him? If so, for what purpose? Are we connected to him, have some relation to him, or none? This is the way in which these few people are curious, and then they apply themselves to this. But, they are ridiculed by many, as the spectators at the market are by the traders; and if the animals had any understanding, they would also ridicule those who admired anything other than the unimportant.

CHAPTER 44 - TO OR AGAINST, THOSE WHO STUBBORNLY PERSIST IN WHAT THEY HAVE DETERMINED

When some people have heard these words, that a man should be constant, and that the will is naturally free and not subject to compulsion, but that all other things are subject to hindrance, and are in the power of others, they suppose that they should without deviation abide by everything which they have been determined. But in a different way, something similar is felt by those who listen to these discourses in the wrong manner; which was the case with one of my companions who for no reason decided to starve himself to death. I heard of it during the third day of his abstinence from food and I went to ask what had happened. "I have decided," he said. Tell me what has induced you to decide this; because if you've decided correctly, I will sit with you and assist you to die; but if you've made an unreasonable decision, change your mind. "We should stick to our decisions." What are you doing? We shouldn't keep to all our decisions, only to those which are right. Have you first laid the foundation and inquired whether the decision is right or wrong, and then build on it firmness and security? But if you've laid no foundation, wouldn't a miserable little building fall down, sooner than if you laid more and stronger materials? So, without any reason you are going to withdraw from life, a man who is a friend, a companion, and a citizen of the same city? Then, while you are committing murder and destroying a man who has done no wrong, you say that we should abide by our decisions? And if it ever in any way came into your head to kill me, should you to abide by your decision?

Now this man, with difficulty, was persuaded to change his mind. But it's impossible to convince some people at present; so now I seem to know, what I didn't know before, the meaning of the common saying, "That you can't persuade or break a fool." If it weren't that I had such a wise fool for a friend: nothing could be more unmanageable. "I am determined," the man says. Madmen are also determined; and the more firmly they form a judgment on things which don't exist, the more elaborate you must be. Wouldn't you act like a sick man and call the doctor? "I'm sick, doctor, help me; what should I do: it's my duty to listen to you." So, should be like this as well: "I don't know what I should do, but I have come here to learn." No; it should be: "Speak to me about things: on which I have based my decisions." What things? Greater and more useful things for you to be persuaded by, so you see it's not sufficient to make your decision and not be open to change it – if it is wrong. That is the tone of madness, not health.

CHAPTER 45 – THAT WE DON'T STRIVE TO USE OUR OPINIONS ABOUT GOOD OR EVIL

Where can the good be found? In the will. Where can the evil be found? In the will. Where is neither of them? In the things which are independent of the will. Well then? Does anyone among us contemplate these lessons on leaving the schools? Does anyone meditate by himself to find an answer to important questions? Is it day? "Yes." Is it night? "No." Is the number of stars even? "I can't say." Why do you wonder then, in the cases which you have studied, in those you have improved; but in those which you have not studied, in those you remain the same? When the author knows he has written well, that he has committed to memory what he has written, why is he still anxious? Because he isn't satisfied with having to study. What does he want then? To be praised by the audience? For the purpose, then, of being able to practice speech, he's been disciplined: but with respect to praise he's not been disciplined. Because, when have we heard from anyone what praise is, and what kind of praise should be strived for? When has he practice this discipline? Why do you still wonder if, in the matters which a man has educated, there he surpasses others, and in those which he hasn't been disciplined, there he shows no improvement. So, the musician knows how to play, sings well, and has a fine dress, and yet he worries when he steps on the stage; because music he understands, but he doesn't know what a crowd is, or what a crowd may shout, or what ridicule is. Neither does he know what anxiety is, whether it is a result of ourselves or of others, and whether it is possible to stop it or not. Because of this, if he's been praised, he leaves the theatre inflated with pride, but if he's been ridiculed, his ego is punctured.

This is exactly the case with ourselves also. What do we admire? External things. And what things are we busy with? External things. And then can we have any doubt why we fear or why we're anxious? What happens when we think about things which are coming to us as evil? It's not in our power not to be afraid, it's not in our power not to be anxious. Then we say, "God, how can I stop being anxious?" Fool, don't you have hands? Didn't

God make them for you, sit down and pray that your nose doesn't run. Wipe tears instead and don't blame him. Hasn't he given you nothing to deal with the present case? Hasn't he given you endurance? Hasn't he given you nobility of character? Hasn't he given you manliness? When you have hands, do you really look for someone else to wipe your nose? But we don't bother to study these things and we don't care for them. Give me a man who cares how he does anything, not for obtaining things, but someone who cares about his own energy. What man, do you see walking about, who cares for his own energy? Who, when he is calculating, cares about his own calculations, and not about obtaining the things over which he calculates? And if he succeeds, he is ecstatic and says, "How well we have calculated; didn't I tell you, brother, that it is impossible, when we have thoroughly thought about anything, that it would not turn out to be?" But if it turned out otherwise, the bad man is humbled; he doesn't even know what to say about what's taken place. Who here has consulted a prophet? Who here in regards to his actions haven't slept in indifference? Who? Name someone, so I can see the man who I've long been looking for, who is truly noble and ingenuous, whether young or old; name him.

Why then, are we still surprised, if we have practiced well in thinking about matters, but in our actions, we move without decency, worthless, cowardly, impatient of work, and in a work: bad? Because, we don't care about things, and we don't bother to study them. But if we fear, not death or punishments, but fear itself, we would have studied how to avoid those things which appear to be evil to us. Now in school we are prepared; for any little question, because when it arises about any of this subject, we can examine fully. But ask us to practice, and you will find us shipwrecked. Let some disturbing experience come to us, and you'll know what we've been studying and in what we've been exercising. Consequently, through our desire for discipline, we are always adding something to the experience and representing things to be greater than what they are. For instance, in regards to myself, when I'm on a voyage and look down at the deep sea, or look around and see no land, I'm out of my mind and imagine that I have to drink all of this water if were to be shipwrecked, and it doesn't occur to me that three pints would be enough. What is it that disturbs me? The sea? No, it's my opinion. Again, if an earthquake where to happen, I imagine that the city is going to fall on me; but isn't one little stone enough to knock my brain out?

So, what are the things which weigh heavy on us, and disturb us? None other than our opinions? What else, other than an opinion weighs heavy on a man, who goes away and leaves his companions, friends, familiar places and habits of life?

In regards to young children, for instance, when they cry about the nurse leaving them for a short time, they forget their sorrow as soon as they receive a small cake. Would you like us to compare you to a young child? No, because I don't wish to be pacified by a small cake, but rather, the right opinions. And what are those opinions? Those which a man should study all day, and not to be affected by anything that's not in his own power, neither by a friend or by his own body, but to remember the law and to have it in front of him at all times. And what is this divine law? To keep a man's will, not to claim anything which belongs to others, but to use what is given, and anything that's not given, not to desire it; and when a thing is taken away, to be ready to let it go immediately, and to be thankful for the time that God gave you use it.

"When will I see Athens again?" Fool, aren't you content with what you see daily? Don't you have anything better or greater to see than the sun, the moon, the stars, the whole earth, and sea? If you comprehend he who administers the whole, and carry him in yourself, would you still desire small stones, when you have a beautiful rock? When it's your time to leave all of these beautiful things behind, what will you do? Will you sit and cry like children? What have you been doing in school? What have you heard? What did you learn? Why would you call yourself a philosopher, you should have said the truth; that, "I had an introduction, and I read Chrysippus, but I didn't even approach the door of a philosopher." Because how could I possess anything of the kind which Socrates possessed, who died as he did, who lived as he did, or anything such as Diogenes possessed? Do you think that any of these men cried or grieved, because he wasn't going to see a certain man, or woman, or to be in Athens again? Because if a man can leave dinner whenever he chooses, would he still stay and complain? But if I leave, I'll cause others sorrow." You cause them sorrow? Not at all; only that will cause them sorrow which also causes you sorrow, opinion. What do you need to do then? Take away your own opinion, and if others are wise, they'll take away their own: if they don't, they will grieve through their own fault.

My man, as the proverb says, make a desperate effort on behalf of tranquillity of mind, freedom and kind-heartedness. Lift your head up as if at last you were released from slavery. Look up to God and say, "Hand me anything in the future that you like; I have the same mind as you; I'm yours: I will refuse nothing that pleases you: lead me wherever you want: dress me in any clothes that you choose: is it was your will that I hold the office of a magistrate, that I should be in the condition of a private man, that I faced exile, or were to be rich, or poor? I will prepare a defence for men on behalf of all these conditions. I will show the nature of each thing and what it is." Other men won't do this, they sit and wait until their mother's feed them. Who would Hercules have been, if he had sat at home? He would have been Eurystheus and not Hercules. And in his travels through the world how many people did he meet, and how many friends did he have? But no one dearer to him than God. For this reason, it was believed that he was the son of God, and he was. In obedience to God, then, he went away cleansing injustice. But you aren't Hercules and you aren't able to cleanse the wickedness of others; and neither are you Theseus, who was able to cleanse the evil things in Attica. Cleanse whatever is bad inside yourself. Cleanse your thoughts, be clear, instead of having, sadness, fear, desire, envy, malevolence, greed, effeminacy and intemperance. But it it's not possible to eject these things without looking toward God, by fixing your sight on him, by being willing to follow his commands. If you choose anything else, you will find yourself being compelled to follow what's stronger than yourself, always seeking tranquillity and never able to find it; because if you seek tranquillity, where it doesn't exist, and you neglect to seek it where it is lives.

CHAPTER 46 – HOW WE MUST ADAPT PRECONCEPTIONS TO PARTICULAR CASES

What is the first objective of a man who philosophizes? To remove vanity. Because it's impossible for a man to begin to learn anything which he thinks he knows already. In regards to things which should and shouldn't be done, the good and bad, beautiful and ugly, all of us who talk about them go to the philosophers; and on these matters, we praise, we condemn, we accuse, we blame, we judge and determine which principles are honourable and dishonourable. But why do we go to the philosophers in the first place? Because we want to learn what we think we don't know. And what is that? Rules. Because we want to learn what philosophers say, because it is seen as something elegant; and some want to learn because they think they might gain profit from it. It's ridiculous to think that a person wants to learn one thing, but will seek to learn another; or further, that a man will make a start in that which he doesn't want to learn. But many are deceived by things which also deceived the writer Theopompus, of which he blamed many, including Plato for wishing everything were defined. Because, what does he say? "Didn't any of us use the words 'good' or 'fair' before, or do we simply make the sounds in an unmeaning and empty way without understanding what they each signify?" Who told, Theopompus, that we didn't have a natural notion of each of these words and preconceptions? You may say, it's not possible to adapt preconceptions to their correspondent objects if we haven't distinguished them, and understood what object must be assigned to each preconception. You may make the same claim against doctors as well. Because who among us hasn't uses the words "healthy" and "unhealthy" before Hippocrates lived, or did we just say these words as empty sounds? Because we have a certain preconception of health, and we aren't able to adapt it. For this reason, someone can say, "Abstain from food"; another says, "Give food"; another says, "Bleed." What's the reason? Could it be any other reason than a man properly adapting to the preconception of health?

So, it's in this matter also, the things which concern life. Who doesn't speak about good and bad, useful or un-useful; because who doesn't possess a preconception of these things? Is it a distinct and perfect preconception? Show me it. How can I show you? Adapt the preconception properly to these things. Plato, for instance, gave definitions to the preconception of what's useful, and you gave to the preconception of what's useless. Is it possible that both of you are right? How's that possible? Doesn't one man adapt the preconception of good to wealth, and another to the opposite, to the matter of pleasure and health? Generally, if all of us who use those words know sufficiently their meanings, and need no assistance in resolving, the notions of the preconceptions, why do we differ, why do we argue, and why do we blame each another?

If you yourself properly adapt your preconceptions, why are you unhappy, why are you worried? Let us forget for the moment the second topic about the pursuits and the study of duties which relate to them. Let us forget the third topic, which relates to the validation: I will put aside these two topics. Let us concentrate on the first, which presents an almost obvious demonstration that we don't properly adapt the preconceptions. Do you desire that which is possible to you, over merely that which is possible? Why are you worried then? Why are you unhappy? Are you trying to avoid the unavoidable? Why do you fall toward anything that you want to avoid? Why are you unfortunate? Why, when you desire something, doesn't it happen, and, when you don't desire it, it happens? Because this is the greatest proof of misery and unhappiness: "I wish for something, and it doesn't happen." And who is more of a fool than I?

It was because she couldn't endure this that Medea murdered her children: because she had opinion over what it means for someone not to succeed in securing their wishes. She says, "I am seeking vengeance against him who done me wrong and insulted me; what have I gained by being punished like this? How should I seek my vengeance? I'll kill my children, but that will punish myself as well: but what do I care?" This is a deviation of the soul which possesses great energy. Because she didn't know where the power lies in gaining that which we wish; you can't get this from the outside, or by the alteration and new adaptation of things. Don't desire any external thing and there can be no sorrow. Only desire what God wills. And then who could obstruct you? Who could alter your path? No man could more than he could persuade God.

When you have a guide like this, and your wishes and desires are the same as his, why do would you fear disappointment? Give up your desire for wealth and your aversion to poverty, and you will be disappointed by one, you move toward the other. But, if you give up a desire for wealth in exchange for health, you will be fortunate: so, give up any external desire, the court, country, friends, children, in summary, any of the things which are not in a man's power. Give them up to God, let him steer the way, let your desire and aversion be on the side of god, and then will you be unhappy any longer? But if, you're a fool, and you envy, and complain, and are jealous, and fear, and never cease for a single day complaining both to yourself and to God, why do you say you are educated? What kind of an education do you have? Do you mean that you have been busy theorising? Won't you, if it's possible, unlearn all the things you have acquired on this subject, and start again from the beginning, and see at the same time that up until now, you haven't even touched the matter; and then, commencing from this foundation, you will build all that comes after, so that nothing will happen that you don't choose, and nothing will fail to happen that you do choose?

Show me one young man who has come to the school with this intention, who has become a champion for this matter and says, "I give up everything, and this is enough for me if it will be in my power to live my life free from obstruction, and free from trouble, and to experience life like a free man, and to look up to heaven as a friend of God, and fear nothing that can happen." If any of you can point out a man like that, I would say "Young man, you have come into the possession of that which is your own, it is your destiny to live philosophy: these are your possessions, these are your books, and these are your discourses." Then when he has worked hard and exercised himself on this matter, let him come back and to again and say, "I also desire to be free from passion and free from disturbance; and I wish as a religious man and a philosopher and a diligent person to know what is my duty to God, what it is to my parents, what it is to my brothers, what it is to my country, and what it is to strangers." On this second matter: this also is yours. "I have now sufficiently studied the second part as well, and I would like to be secure and unshaken, and not only when I'm awake, but also when I'm asleep." You are a god, you have great design.

"No: but I want to understand what Chrysippus says in his writings." Do you want be a fool, with such an intention? What good will it do you? You will read the whole writings with sorrow, and you'll speak to others with fear. Then, having told your dreams to one another, you will return to the same things: your desires are the same, your aversions the same, your pursuits are the same, and your design and purpose: the same, because you wish for the same things and work for the same things. And you will no longer seek for someone to give you advice. You might be annoyed to hear this but if I didn't, one day you will say "That old man, when I was going away, he didn't cry, and he didn't say, 'be careful of what danger you are getting into: if you return safe, my child, I will celebrate for you.' This is what a good-natured man should do." It would be a great thing for you if you could return safe, and it will be worthwhile to celebrate for such a person: because you would have to be immortal and exempt from disease.

Putting aside that for now, as I say, this vanity of thinking we know something useful, when we don't will not allow us to ever approach to proficiency of the subject, even if we read all the collections and commentaries of Chrysippus, Antipater and Archedemus.

CHAPTER 47 – HOW WE SHOULD STRUGGLE AGAINST APPEARANCES

Every habit and faculty is maintained and increased by the action itself: the habit of walking by walking, the habit of running by running. If you want to be a good reader, read; if a writer, write. But when you haven't read for thirty days in succession, and have been doing something else, you'll know the consequence. In the same way, if you lay down for ten days, get up and attempt to take a long walk, and you'll see how your legs are weakened. Generally, then, if you want to make anything a habit, do it; if you don't want to make it a habit, don't do it, but accustom yourself to do something else instead.

And it's the same in respect to the soul: when you've been angry, you know that this isn't the only evil thing which has happened, you have also increased the habit, and literally thrown fuel on fire. When you have experienced sexual intercourse with a person, don't think this is the only defeat you suffer, know that you've also nurtured, and increased your incontinence. Because it's impossible for habits and faculties to emerge if they haven't been used before, and those that exist to be increased and strengthened by opposing acts.

So, in this manner, as the philosophers say, diseases of the mind also grow. Because when you start to desire money, if reason can be applied and leads to a perception of evil, the desire is stopped, and the ruling faculty of our mind is restored to its original authority. But if you don't apply a cure, it doesn't return to the same state, but, being again excited by the appearance of money, it is inflamed to desire more than before: and when this takes place continually, it is hardened, and the disease of the mind confirms the love of money. Because any man who has had a fever, and has been relieved from it, is not in the same state that he was before, unless he has been completely cured. That same happens also in diseases of the soul. Certain traces and blisters are left behind, and unless a man can completely remove them, when he's poked in the same places, this time it will produce not blisters but sores. If you then wish not to be angry, don't feed the habit; add nothing to it which will increase it: at first keep quiet, and count the days which you haven't been angry. I used to be in passion every day; now every second day; then every third, then every fourth. But if you have abstained thirty days, thank God. Because the habit is beginning to be weakened, and then subsequently will be completely destroyed. "I haven't been angry today, or the day after, or on any succeeding day during two or three months; but I took care when some exciting things happened." Today when I saw an attractive woman, I didn't say to myself, "I wish I could lie with her," Neither do I imagine the woman present, stripping herself and lying down by my side. I rub my head and say, "well done, Epictetus, you have solved a fine riddle, much finer than that which is called the master riddle." And if even the woman is willing, and gives signs, and sends messages, and if she touches me and comes close to me, and I will abstain and be victorious, that would be a riddle which is named "The Liar," and "The Inactive." A victory like this a man can be proud of; not for proposing, the master riddle.

How can this be done? Be willing to approve of yourself, be willing to appear beautiful to God, desire to be combined, your own pure self with God. Then when any appearance visits you, Plato says, "Be willing to repent, go a on protest against evil." It's sufficient if "you return to the society of noble and fair men," and compare yourself with them, whether you its someone who's living or dead. Go to see Socrates, see him lying down with Alcibiades, and view his beauty: consider what a victory he gained over himself; what an Olympian victory; we should salute him, "Socrates, the wondrous man, who has conquered these sorry men."

Don't be drawn in by appearance, but say, "appearances, wait for me: let me see who you are, and what you're about: let me put you to the test." And then don't allow the appearance to lead you and draw pictures of things which may cause you to follow; because if you do, these appearances can take you wherever they please. So instead, you should display an opposing appearance, something beautiful which repels these bad appearances. And if you are accustomed to act in this way, you will see what shoulders, what ligaments, what strength you have. But now it's only words, and nothing more.

The true athlete, is the man who exercises himself against appearances. Don't stop, fool, don't be taken away. Combat is great, it is divine work; for freedom, for happiness, for to remove disturbance. Remember God: call to him as your helper and protector, like men at sea call to him during a storm. Because is there a greater storm than that which comes from appearances which are violent and drive away our reason? Because the storm itself, what else is that but an appearance? Take away the fear of death, and face as much thunder and lightning as you please, and you will see what calm and serenity there is in the ruling faculty. But if you've been defeated and you say that you'll conquer afterwards, be careful, you should be assured that you don't find yourself in this condition and so weak that you won't even know what afterward is.

CHAPTER 48 - AGAINST THOSE WHO EMBRACE PHILOSOPHY ONLY IN WORDS

The argument called the "ruling argument" appears to have been created from these principles: there is a contradiction between each of these three positions, two of them are in contradiction with the third. The propositions are, that everything that has past must be true; that an impossibility can't occur if something is possible; and that something is possible which neither is true or will be true. Diodorus observing this contradiction said the following: "That nothing is possible which isn't true and never will be." Against this: "That something is possible, even if currently it's not true and never will be": and "That an impossibility doesn't occur if something is possible," And he wouldn't allow that everything which has past is necessarily true, as the followers of Cleanthes seem to think, and we know Antipater furiously defended this. Others still hold the other two propositions, "That a something is possible which isn't currently true and may not become true": and "That everything which has past is true"; but then they will believe that an impossibility can occur although something is possible. We can see which ever view is taken it's impossible to hold all three beliefs, because of their common contradiction. If anyone asked me which I believe, I would say that I don't know; but I do have a story tell, that Diodorus believed one opinion, the followers of Panthoides, I think, and Cleanthes believed another opinion, and the followers of Chrysippus believed another also. "What's your opinion?" I wasn't made for this purpose, to examine and compare what others say and to form an opinion on this one thing. But what else can I say about the ruling argument? Nothing. But, if I was a vain man, especially at a dinner party, I might surprise the guests by detailing those who have written on this matter. Chrysippus has written wonderfully in his first book about "Possibilities," and Cleanthes has written especially on this subject, and so has Archedemus. Antipater has written not only in his work about "Possibilities," but also separately in his work on the ruling argument. Haven't you read the work? "I haven't." Read. And what will a man gain from it? He will be even more uncivil than he is now;

because what else will you gain by reading it? What opinion have you formed on this subject? None; but you'll gladly tell us about Helen and Priam, and the island of Calypso which never was and never will be. And this also is of no great importance if you retain the story or not, and have formed no opinion of your own. But In matters of morality this happens to us much more than the things we are currently speaking about.

"Speak to me about good and evil." Listen: The wind comes from the shore and brought me. "Some good things, some bad, and others I view indifferently. The good are the virtues and things which work toward creating the virtues; bad are the vices, and things which lead to their creation; and the things which lie between the virtues and the vices are those that are indifferent, for example, wealth, health, life, death, pleasure and pain." How do you know this? "Hellanicus said it in his Egyptian history"; and was there any difference when "Diogenes said it in his work on Ethics?" Have you read any of these and formed an opinion of your own? Can you tell me how to behave on a boat during a storm? Do you remember this division, when the sail rattles and a man, who knows nothing about the times and seasons, stands by you while you're screaming and says, "Tell me, please, what were you saying just now? Is it a vice to suffer shipwreck: is it the creation of vice?" Wouldn't you pick up a stick and hit him on his head with it? What should I do with you? Here we are about to die, and you come to say this? But if Caesar asked you to answer a question, wouldn't you remember this distinction? If, when you are going to see him, pale and trembling, a person came up to you and said, "Why are you trembling? What's the matter? Does Caesar who awaits you give virtue and vice to those who go to see him?" You reply, "Why are you mocking me to add to my current sorrow?" Tell me, philosopher, why are you trembling? Are you afraid of death, a prison, pain inflicted on the body, banishment, or disgrace? What else is there? Is there any vice or anything which creates vice? What did you use to say about these things? "What can be done to you? Your own evil is enough for you." That was right. Your own evil is enough for you, your cowardice, the boasting which you showed

146

when you were in the school. Why did you claim for yourself that which belonged to others? Why did you call yourself a Stoic?

Therefore, observe yourself in your actions, and you will find what group you really belong to. You will find that most are Epicureans, a few Peripatetics, and many the feeble kind. Because where can you see those that really consider virtue equal to everything else or even superior? Show me a true Stoic, if you can. Where you say. But you can easily show me an endless number who discuss arguments created by the Stoics. Don't the same people also repeat the Epicurean opinions? Don't they recall them with equal accuracy? Who is a Stoic then? Show me a man whose actions are in alignment with the doctrines which he speaks of. Show me a man who is sick and happy, in danger and happy, dying and happy, in exile and happy, in disgrace and happy. Show me: I desire, to see a Stoic. You can't show me one; so, show me then, at least one who is forming, who has shown a tendency to be a Stoic. Do this favour for me: don't grudge me for wanting to see something which I haven't seen yet. Do you think that you have to show me God, or a work of ivory and gold? Can anyone simply show me a human soul ready to think as God does, who doesn't blame God or another man, who's not disappointed about anything, doesn't consider himself damaged by anything, not angry, envious, or jealous? Show me this man. You can't. So, why does everyone delude themselves and cheat others? Why do they put on a disguise of an appearance which doesn't belong to them, and walk about being thieves of that which doesn't belong to them?

Now I am your teacher, and you are instructed in my school. And I have the responsibility, to make you free from restraint, compulsion, hindrance, to make you free, prosperous, happy, looking toward God in everything small and large. And you are here to learn and practice these things. Why, don't you finish the work, if you have this purpose? What is lacking here? When I see a student and the material next to him, I expect the work. Isn't it in our power then? The only thing that's in our power: it's not wealth, health, reputation, or anything other than the right use of appearances. This is by nature free from restraint, this alone is free from impediment. Why don't you finish the work? Tell me the reason. Because it's either my fault that you don't finish it, or your own fault, or through the nature of it. It's possible, and in our power. Therefore, the fault is either in me or in you, or, what's could be closer to the truth, in both. So, from today, are you willing to begin to bring this purpose into the school, and take no notice of the past? Let's make a start. Trust me, and you will see.

Propositions which are true and evident, are out of necessity used even by those who contradict them: and a man perhaps would consider it to be the greatest form of proof, of a thing being evident, even for him who denies it, when they make use of it. For instance, if a man denies that there's anything universally true, he must make the contradictory negation, that nothing is universally true. What a fool, who would make such a statement? Because what is this, other than to assert that whatever is universally affirmed: to be false? Again, if a man came forward and said: "Know that there is nothing that can be known, as all things are incapable of perfect evidence"; or if another said, "Believe me and it will be better for you, that a man shouldn't believe anything"; or again, if another man said, "Learn from me, that it's not possible to learn anything; I say this but will teach you, if you choose." In what respect does this differ from those? Who should I name? Those who call themselves Academics? "Men, agree that no man agrees: and believe that no man believes anything."

Epicurus also, when he designs to destroy the natural fellowship of mankind, at the same time makes use of that which he destroys. Because what does he say? "Men, don't be deceived, led astray, or mistaken: there is no natural fellowship among rational animals; believe me. Those who say otherwise, are deceiving you and trying to seduce you by false reason." What is this to you? Allow us to be deceived. Would it be worse, if all of us are persuaded that there can be a natural fellowship among us, and that it should be preserved? Not at all, it will be much better and safer for us. Why do you trouble about us? Why do you stay awake for us? Why are your lights on at night? Why do wake up early? Why do you write so many books, so that none of us will be deceived about God and believe that he takes care of men; or so people will believe the nature of good is pleasure? If this is so, lie down and sleep, and lead the life of a worm, which you judge yourself to be worthy of: eat and drink, enjoy women, relax yourself, and snore. What is it to you, how the rest of us should think about these things, whether they're right or wrong? What should we do with you? You take care of sheep because they supply us with wool, and milk, and, last of all, with their flesh. Wouldn't it be desirable if men could be enchanted by the Stoics, be put to sleep and presented to you, and those like you, to be slaughtered and milked? You should say this to your fellow Epicureans: and conceal it from the rest of us, but really you should be persuading them that we are by nature adapted for fellowship, and that temperance is a good thing. We should maintain fellowship with some and not with others. Who should we maintain it with? With those who also maintain it, or those who violate it? And who violates it more than you who establish this type of doctrine?

What awoke Epicurus from his sleepiness, and compelled him to write what he wrote? Anything other than that which is the strongest thing in men, nature, which draws a man to his own will although he could be unwilling and complaining? A man's nature is so strong and invincible. How can a vine become an olive tree? Or an olive tree become a vine? It's impossible: it can't be conceived. Therefore, it's not possible for a man to completely lose the movements of a man; and even those who have had their genitals removed are not able to deprive themselves of a man's desires. Epicurus mutilated a man, a father of a family, a citizen, a friend, but he didn't mutilate human desires, because he couldn't; not more than the lazy Academics have tried to remove their own senses, although they have tried with all their might to do it. What a shame is this? When a man has received from nature, rules for the knowing of truth, and doesn't strive to add to those rules and to improve them, but, just the opposite, endeavours to take away and destroy whatever enables us to discern the truth?

What do you say philosopher? Spirituality and holiness, what do you think they are? "If you like, I will demonstrate that they are good things." Well, demonstrate it, so that our citizens can turn and honour God and may no longer be ignorant about the things of the highest value. "Have you heard the demonstrations?" I have, and I'm thankful for them. "But since, you pleased with them, hear the opposite: 'That there are no Gods, and, if there are, they don't care about men; there is no fellowship between us and them;

and that this spirituality and holiness which is spoken about among most men, is the lies of tricksters, for the purpose of terrifying the wrong-doers.'" Well done, philosopher, you have done something for our citizens, you have made all the young men despise the divine things. "Does this satisfy you?" If not, teach us, that justice is nothing, that modesty is foolishness, that a father is nothing, a son nothing." Well done, philosopher, continue, persuade the young men. Because, from your principles Sparta was founded: Lycurgus taught these opinions to the Spartans through his laws and education, and their condition was horrible not honourable, consider those who died at Thermopylae died due to those opinions. Then those who hold those beliefs, marry and have children, and take up public affairs and make themselves priests and interpreters. Of who? Of God who doesn't exist to them?

Modest men are grateful, if they do nothing else, other than eat their daily bread, yet are shameless enough to say, we don't know if there's a Pluto; not to mention that they are enjoying the night and the day, the seasons of the year, the stars, the sea, and the land, and the co-operation of mankind, and yet they are not moved in any degree by these things to turn their attention to them; but they only seek to moan out their little problems, and when they have exercised their stomach, they go and relax in the bath. Why should a man say any more in reply to people such as this, give them any reason, listen to any reason from them, or try to convince them of anything? We might as well try to make a certainty change than try to change those who have become so deaf and blind to their own evil.

CHAPTER 50 – ON INCONSISTENCY

There are some things that men will easily confess, and others they don't. No man will confess that he's a fool or lacks understanding; but, quite the opposite, you will hear all men saying, "I wish that I was as rich as my understanding." However, they will confess that they're timid, they say: "I'm quite timid, I confess; but I'm not foolish." A man won't confess that he's self-indulgent; and unreasonable? No, he would never confess that. He would never admit to being envious or a nuisance. However, most men will confess that they're compassionate. What's the reason for this? The main thing is inconsistency and confusion in the things which relate to good and evil. But different men have different reasons; and generally, what they imagine to be bad, they won't confess. Yet they believe timidity to be a good characteristic, along with compassion; but silliness to be the characteristic of a fool. They won't admit things which are offensive in society. But when it comes to most errors, they are induced to confess them, because there is something involuntary in them, as in timidity and compassion; and if a man confesses that he's in any respect self-indulgent, he declares love as an excuse for what is involuntary. But men don't imagine injustice to exist in this.

Living among such men, who are so confused and so ignorant of what they say, and of the evil which they possess, and why they have it, or how they can be relieved of it, I think it's worth the trouble for a man to be on guard constantly "Whether I'm also one of them, what I imagine about myself, how I conduct myself, whether I conduct myself as a prudent man, whether I conduct myself as a self-controlled man, whether I ever say this, that I have been taught to be prepared for everything that might happen. Do I have the consciousness, which a man who knows nothing should have? Do I visit my teachers as a man goes to oracles, prepared to obey? Or like a whining boy who goes to school to learn history and understand the books which I didn't understand before, and then, to explain them others?"

You've had a fight at home, you've turned the family upside down, you've frightened the neighbours, and you come to me as if you were a wise man, and you take a seat and judge how I've explained some word, and how I have spoken whatever came into my head. You come full of envy, and humbled, because you bring nothing from home; and you sit during the discussion thinking of nothing else than how your father and brother are at home hoping you learn. "What are they saying about you there? Now they think that you're improving, and are saying, 'He will return with a lot of knowledge.' You wish you could learn everything before you return: but a lot of work is required.

People like you don't value the education, then those you return to say, "No one gains anything from the school." Why? Who comes to this school, who comes for the purpose of being improved? Who comes to present his opinions and to be purified? Who comes to learn what he really needs to? Why do you wonder then if you return from the school with the same things which you brought to it? Because you don't come to put aside or to correct them or to receive other principles in place of them. Not at all, nothing like it. You rather look at this, whether you already possess that which you come for. You wish to discuss theories? Why? Do you want to become a better theorist? Do your little theories give you the opportunity to display something? You solve arguments. But do you examine the assumptions of the argument named "The Liar"? Don't you examine hypothetical arguments? Why, then, are you angry if you leave with that which you come to the school for?

"If my child died or my brother, or if it's my time to die, what good will these things do for me?" Did you come for this? Is this why you sit by my side? Did you ever stay up at night contemplating this? Or, when you went out for a walk, did you ever analyse an appearance that had been presented to you instead of a hypothetical argument, and did you and your friends discuss it together? Where and when? Did I say, "Theories are useless." To who? Only to those who make bad use of them. Prompting is not useless. Dumbbells are not useless; these things are useless to some, and useful to others. If you asked me now if hypothetical arguments are useful, I will tell you that they are, and if you choose, I will prove it. "How are they useful?" Are you asking if they're useful to you, or in general? If a man who was in pain asked me if pain killers are useful, I would say yes, but if he asked is it useful to me, I would say no.

Be tranquil in your mind, bring it free from distraction to the school, and you will discover what power reason has.

CHAPTER 51 – ON FRIENDSHIP

A man apply himself sincerely, to that which he naturally loves. Do men naturally apply themselves sincerely to things which are bad? Not at all. Do they apply themselves to things which don't concern them? No. Therefore, we understand that they apply themselves sincerely to things which are good; and if they sincerely apply themselves to these things, they also love these things. Whoever understands what is good, can also know how to love. Can a man who can't distinguish good from bad, and things which are neither good or bad, possess the power to love? No. To love, then, is a power only found in the wise.

"How is this?" A man might say; I'm foolish, but I love my child." I firstly would be surprised, that you he would begin by making the admission that he's foolish. What are you deficient in? Can't you make use of your senses? Don't you distinguish appearances? Don't you use food which is suitable for your body, and clothing and habitation? Why would you admit that you're foolish? Is it because you are often disturbed by appearances and perplexed, and their power of persuasion often conquers you; and sometimes you think these things to are good, and sometimes believe the same things to be bad, and lastly neither good or bad; and in short you fear, envy, and are disturbed. This is the reason why you confess that you're foolish. Aren't you changeable in love? Do you think wealth and pleasure are sometimes good and sometimes bad? Don't you think a man can be at one time good, and at another time bad? Don't you sometimes have a friendly feeling toward them and at another time they feel like an enemy? Don't you praise them sometimes and at other times blame them? "Yes; I have these feelings." Well then, do you think that a man who's been deceived by a man can be his friend? "Certainly not." And when a man has selected a man as his friend, but has a changeable disposition toward him, does he have good-will toward him? "He doesn't." What if he abuses the man, and afterward admires him? "This man also has no good-will toward the other." Well, have you ever seen little dogs caressing and playing with each other, you might say there's nothing friendlier? But, so you can understand what friendship is, throw a bit of meat between them, and you will soon learn. Show your son the total value of your estate, and will see how soon he wishes to bury you. Then you will change your tone and say, "What a son I've brought up! He's been wishing to bury me." Throw a beautiful and intelligent girl between you; and you the old man, will love her, and your son will love her too, and if it were fame, or danger, the outcome will be the same.

Do you think that Admetus didn't love his own son when he was little? That he wasn't in agony when the child had a fever? That he didn't always say, "I wish I had the fever instead of my son?" But when the test came, these words changed. Weren't Eteocles and Polynices from the same mother and father? Weren't they brought up together, hadn't they lived together, drunk together, and slept together? If any man had seen them, he would have ridiculed the philosophers for the paradoxes they create when they talk about friendship. But when an argument started between them about the royal power, as between dogs over a bit of meat, they placed themselves against each other like men in opposing towers with intent to kill. So, universally, don't be deceived, every animal is attached to nothing as to its own interest. Whatever appears to be an impediment toward this interest, whether a brother, a father, a child, or a lover, it hates, and curses: because its nature is to love nothing as much as its own interest; which paradoxically should be his father, brother, friends, country, and God. So then, when even God appears to be an impediment to our interest, we abuse him, destroy statues and burn temples, just like Alexander ordered the temples of Aesculapius to be burned when his dear friend died.

For this reason, if a man actually made his interests, holiness, goodness, country, parents and friends, all of these things will be secured: but if he places his interest in other things, in direct opposition to his friends, country and justice itself, all of these things will be destroyed by the weight of his interest. Wherever the "I" and "Mine" are placed, that's the place out of necessity the animal inclines.

If were to place them where my will is, then I would be a friend, son, and father as I should be; because this would be my interest, to maintain the character of faithfulness, modesty, patience, abstinence, active cooperation, and observing my relations. But if I put my interest in something else other than honesty, then the doctrine of Epicurus becomes strong, which declares that either there is no honesty, or there's an opinion which believes it's honest.

It was due to this ignorance that the Athenians and the Lacedaemonians argued, and the Romans argued with the Getae. Even earlier that this the Trojan war happened for the same reasons. Alexander was a guest of Menelaus; and if any man had seen their friendliness toward each other, he wouldn't have believed anyone who said that they weren't friends. But there was something which came between them, a beautiful woman, and because of her a war arose. So now, when you see brothers appearing to be friends, don't conclude from this anything about their friendship, not even if they say it and swear that it's impossible for them to be separated from one another. Because the ruling principle of a bad man can't be trusted, it has no certain rule by which it is directed, and is overpowered at different times by different appearances. So, examine, not what other men examine, that they came from the same parents and were brought up together; but examine this only, where do they place their interest, whether in the external reality or in the will. If in the external, don't call them friends, no more than you could call them trustworthy or constant, brave or free: don't even call them men, if you have any judgment. Because placing interest in the will is not a principle of human nature which makes them bite one another, abuse one another, act with intemperance, become adulterers and corrupters, nor doing anything which makes them do whatever else men do against one another through placing their interests in the things which are not within the power of their will. But if you find that in truth these men think the good resides where the will is, where there is a right use of appearances, don't trouble yourself whether they are your father, son, brother, or have associated with you from a long time and are companions, but when you have ascertained this, you can confidently declare that they are friends. Where else do we find friendship than where there is loyalty and modesty, where there is a communion of honesty and nothing else?

"But," you might say, "someone treated me in a nice way for a long time; doesn't she love me?" How do you know, fool, she might regard you in the same way she wipes her shoes with a sponge, when you are no longer useful as a vessel, she might throw you away like a broken plate? "But this woman is my wife, and we've lived together a long time." And how long did Eriphyle live with Amphiaraus, and was the mother of his children? But a necklace came between them. "And what importance does a necklace have?" It's the opinions about things such as this. This was the thing tore apart the friendship between a husband and wife, that no longer allowed this woman to be a wife or to be a mother. Every man who has seriously resolved either to be a friend himself or to have someone as his friend, should cut out these opinions, hate them, drive them out of his soul. Therefore, he will not accuse himself if there is a failure in the friendship. And in addition, when he finds someone who is like himself, there he will find a real friend. But he will have to put up with a man who isn't like himself, he can be kind to him, gentle, ready to excuse him for his ignorance, or being mistaken about things great importance; he will be harsh to no man, being well convinced of Plato's doctrine that every mind is deprived of truth unwillingly. If you can't do this, but you can do everything else friends do: drink together, sail together, and you may have even come from the same parents; these will not be real friends, and you can't call yourself one either, as long as you maintain these cursed opinions.

CHAPTER 52 – ON THE POWER OF SPEAKING

Every man will read a book with even more pleasure, if it's written in finer characters. Therefore, every man will also listen more willingly to what is spoken, if it's conveyed using charming words. We mustn't say, that there is no faculty of expression: because this affirmation is the characteristic of a timid man. Of an irreverent man, because he undervalues the gifts which come from God, just as if he would remove the power of vision, hearing, or seeing. Didn't God give you your eyes for a purpose? And there's no purpose for them to be infused into the spirit, so strongly and with such skill, that they can see into a long distance and outline to us the form of these things which are seen? What messenger is so swift and vigilant? And of course, no purpose for the intervening atmosphere so valuable and elastic that the vision penetrates through the atmosphere which is in constant movement? And no purpose for light, without the presence of which there would be no use for anything else?

Man, shouldn't be ungrateful for these gifts or forget the things which are superior to them. But indeed, for the power of seeing and hearing, and indeed for life itself, and for the things which contribute to support it, for the fruits, and for wine and oil everyone should thank God: but remember that God has given you something better than all of these things, I mean the power of using them and estimating the value of each. Because what is it that gives us information about each of these powers, and what each of them is worth? Is it each faculty itself? Did you ever hear the faculty of vision saying anything about itself? Or the faculty of hearing? Or wheat, barley, a dog or a horse? No, because but they're appointed to serve the faculty which has the power of making use of the appearance of things. And so, if you inquire what the value of each thing is, who do you inquire with? Who answers you? How can any other faculty be more powerful than this, which uses the rest as servants and articulates them? Which of the faculties knows what itself is, and what its value is? Which of them knows when it should use itself or not? What faculty is it, that opens and closes the eyes, and turns them away from objects to which it shouldn't view and places their gaze on other objects? Is it the faculty of vision? No; it's the faculty of the will. What is that faculty which opens and closes the ears? What makes them curious and inquisitive, or, on the contrary, unaffected by what is said? Is it the faculty of hearing? It's no other than the faculty of the will. This faculty then, knows that it's above the other faculties which are blind, dumb and unable to see anything else except the acts which they are appointed to do in order to serve. This faculty sees sharp and understands the value of the rest; will this faculty say to us that anything else is better, or that it is? What else does the eye do when it's opened than see? But whether we should look at a woman, or a certain person, and in what manner, what tells us this? The faculty of the will. And whether we should believe what's said to us, and if we believe, whether we are moved by it or not, what tells us? Isn't it the faculty of the will? But this faculty of speaking and remodelling words, if there is such a faculty, what else does it do, when there happens to be discourse about something than beautify words and arrange them like hairdressers do to the hair? But whether it's better to speak or be silent, and better to speak in this way or that way, what else tells us this, other than the faculty of the will?

"So," it says, "if this fact is acknowledged, can that which serves be superior to that which it serves, can the horse be superior to the rider, or the instrument to the musician, or the servants to the king?" What is it that uses the rest? The will. What takes care of all faculties? The will. What creates or destroys a man? The will. So, is anything stronger in men than this? And how is it possible that the things which are subject to serve, become stronger than that which isn't. What things are naturally formed to obstruct the faculty of vision? Both the will and things which don't depend on the will. It's the same with the faculty of hearing, and with the faculty of speaking. But what has a natural power of deterring the will? Nothing which is independent of the will; but only the will itself, when it has become corrupted.

Being such a great faculty and situated above the rest, would it tell us that the most excellent of all is the body. Not even if the body if it could say this itself, would be believed by anyone.

None other than Epicurus, who wrote about "The End of our Being," and "The Nature of Things," was dying, however, he said on the last day that he was happy. Was this, his body or will? Can you admit that you possess nothing superior to the will?

Would any man despise the other faculties? I hope not. Would any man say that there's no use or excellence in the speaking faculty? I hope not. That would be foolish, irreverent, and ungrateful toward God. But a man gives to each thing its appropriate value. Because there's even some use in the donkey. But just because somethings are superior, should we undervalue the use which other things have. There is a certain value in the power of speaking, but it's not as great as the power of the will. Therefore, when I speak, I don't was you to neglect the power of speaking, or to neglect the eyes, ears, hands, feet, clothing or shoes. But if you asked me, "What's the most excellent out of all things?" What should I say? I can't say the power of speaking, because it's certainty the power of the will. Because it's this which uses the others, all of them, no matter how small or great.

When this faculty of the will is set straight, a man who isn't good becomes good: but when it's corrupted, a man becomes bad. It's through the will that we are either fortunate, or unfortunate, that we blame one another, or are pleased with one another. In simple terms, it's this which if neglected causes unhappiness, but if we look after carefully it creates happiness.

However, not to undervalue the other faculties either, if a man would see no value in speaking, this would not only be an act of ungrateful man, but also the act of a cowardly man: because men like this to me seem to be in fear, and if there is such faculty known as fear shouldn't we despise it? This is a great matter; to acknowledge the power of each thing, but to learn what's the most excellent of all, and to pursue it always, to be diligent about it, considering all other things of secondary value compared to it, but yet, as far as we can, not to neglect all those other things. We must take care of the eyes, not as if they were the most excellent thing, but we must take care of them to be readily called upon by the most excellent thing, the will.

How should the will be used? Men generally act as a traveller would on his way to his own country, when he enters a good hotel, and being pleased with it wants to remain there. Have forgotten your purpose? You weren't traveling to this hotel, it was meant to be a brief stay on your way to your chosen destination. "But this is a nice hotel." And how many other hotels are nice? Your purpose is to return to your country, to relieve your friends of anxiety, to marry and have children. You are not here to select more pleasant places, but to live in where you were born, of which you were made a citizen. Since, by the aid of speech and communication you receive here, you must advance to perfection, and clean your will, and correct the faculty which makes use of the appearances of things; and since it's possible due to the teaching of theory to be effected by expression, some people captivated by this and accept it, one captivated by the expression, another by false assumptions, another by deception, and another by some kind of hotel; and there they stay and waste away.

Your purpose was to make yourself capable of using conformably to nature the appearances presented to you, not to be frustrated by your desires, not to move toward that which you wish to avoid, not to count on good or bad luck, to be free, not obstructed, or encouraged, conforming yourself to the administration of God, obeying it, satisfied with it, blaming no one, able from your whole soul to say this: "Lead me God, to my destiny."

Then claiming this purpose, if some form of expression pleases you, if some theory pleases you, do you dwell there, forgetting the original will, and say, "These things are fine"? No one said they weren't fine, but they are just things to be seen on the way home, as hotels are. Because what can stop you from being an unfortunate man? What prevents you, even if you can resolve arguments from sorrow, from being disturbed, from being unhappy? Only the will. You see then that these hotels are worth nothing; and that the original purpose was something else. When I speak about this to some people, they think that I'm rejecting the faculty of speaking, or care about more about theory. I'm not rejecting that at all, but I am rejecting those things which appear, like hotels on the way home, which people put their hope in. If a man does harm to those who listen to him, consider me to have done this harm as well: because I'm not able, when I see something as excellent and supreme, to say that something else is, in order to please you.

CHAPTER 53 – A PERSON NOT VALUED

A certain person said: "I want to hear you and came to you frequently, and you never gave me an answer: and now, if it's possible, I'm asking you to say something to me." Do you think, said Epictetus, that, as there's art in everything, there' also an art in speaking, and a man who has that art, will speak skilfully, and a man who doesn't, will speak in an unskilful manner? "I do." A man then, who by speaking receives benefit himself and is able to benefit others, will speak skilfully: but a man who is damaged by speaking and does damage to others, isn't he unskilled in the art of speaking? You may at times find people who are damaged and others benefited by the same speech. Are all those who hear, benefited by what they hear? Or will you find that among them some are benefited and some are damaged? "You will find both types among these too," he said. In this case, then, are those who hear skilfully are benefited, and those who hear unskilfully damaged? He admitted this. Is there then a skill in hearing also, as there is in speaking? "It seems so." Consider this then. The practice of music, who does it belong to? "To the musician." And the making of a statue, who does that belong to? "To the sculptor." And looking at a statue skilfully, doesn't this require the aid of art? "This also requires the aid of art." Then if speaking properly is the business of a skilful man, do you see also, that to hear with benefit is the business of a skilful man? Now in regards to speaking and hearing perfectly, and usefully, let us for the present, if you don't mind, say no more, because both of us are a long way away from anything of the kind.

I think that every man will agree, that a man goes to hear philosophers speak, requires some amount of practice in hearing.

Tell me then, what should I talk to you about: what are you able to listen to? "About good and evil." Good and evil in what? In a horse? "No." Well, in a donkey? "No." What then? In a man? "Yes." Do you know what a man is, and what the notion is that we have of him? Do you understand what nature is? Can you even in any degree understand me when I say, "I will use demonstration on you? " How? Do you understand what demonstration is, or how anything is demonstrated; or what things are like demonstration, but aren't demonstration? Do you know what's true or what's false? What is consistent or inconsistent? Could I show you the revulsion in the opinions of most men, through which they differ about what is good and evil, when you don't know revulsion is? Tell me then, what I will accomplish by discussing these with you; what would give me the inclination to do this. Like the grass when is suitable, is presented to a sheep, gives it the inclination to eat, but if you present it a stone, it doesn't eat; so, within us, are certain natural inclinations to speak. When the hearer appears to be worth it, he excites us: but when he sits next to us like a stone, how can he excite a man's desire to speak? Do the crops say to the farmer, "pick me?" No, but the crops by displaying themselves to be profitable to the farmer, encourages him to harvest.

"Why don't you say anything to me?" I can only say this to you, that a man who doesn't know who he is, what purpose he exists for, what the world is, who he's associated with, what things are the good and bad, beautiful and ugly, who doesn't understand speaking or demonstration, what's true or false, and isn't able to distinguish them, will not desire according to nature, to turn away, move upward, intend, ascend or descend, or hold his judgment: to this in a few words, he will drift, dumb and blind, thinking that he's somebody, while being a nobody. Is this a present fact? Isn't it a fact that, ever since the human race existed, all errors and misfortunes have developed due to this ignorance? Why did Agamemnon and Achilles argue with each another? Wasn't it because they didn't know what things are profitable and unprofitable? Didn't one say its profitable to return Chryseis to her father, and the other say that it wasn't? Didn't one think he should claim her as his prize and the other think he shouldn't? Didn't they both forget who they were and what purpose they were here for? What purpose they come for? To gain mistresses or to fight? "To fight." With who? The Trojans or the Hellenes? "The Trojans." So why did they leave Hector to fight against their king? They neglected the duties of the king, these men who were meant to be the people's guardians were arguing about a girl with the most warlike intentions. Do you see what kind of things ignorance over what is profitable can cause?

This is all I have to say to you; and I didn't even say this willingly. "Why?" Because you have not excited me to. Do you think you clothing excites me? Or your behaviour? Or your look? These things are the same as nothing. When you listen to a philosopher, don't say to him, "You've told me nothing"; just show yourself worthy of hearing; and you'll see how you awaken the speaker.

CHAPTER 54 – LOGIC IS ALWAYS NECESSARY

A man who was present said, "Can you prove to me that logic is necessary," he replied: Do you want me to prove this to you? The answer was, "Yes." Then I must use a demonstrative form of speech. This was agreed. How will you know if I'm cheating you during this argument? The man was silent. Can you see, said Epictetus, that you yourself are admitting that logic is necessary, because without it you won't even know, whether logic is necessary or not necessary.

CHAPTER 55 – WHAT IS ERROR

Every error has a contradiction: because those who make errors don't want to, they actually want to be right, therefore, it is plain to see that they don't do what they really want. What does the thief want to do? That which is for his own interest. If, then, the theft isn't for his interest, he's not doing what he wants. But every rational soul is by nature offended by contradiction, and so long as the soul doesn't understand this contradiction, it is not held back from doing contradictory things: but when it understands the contradiction, it must, out of necessity avoid the contradiction and avoid it as much as he would from the false when he realises it's not true. However, as long as he is unaware of what's false, he may believe it to be true.

A man is strong in argument, when he has the faculty of persuading and disproving, and can show a man the contradiction through which he makes an error, and clearly can prove how he doesn't do what he really wants, and actually does the opposite. Because if a man can show this, the other man will himself stop doing what he does; but as long as you don't show him, don't be surprised if the man persists in his practice; due to having the appearance of doing right, he does what he does. For this reason, Socrates, also trusting this power, used to say, "I am used to calling on no witness of what I say, but I am always satisfied with a man, who I am having a discussion with, when I ask him to give his opinion, and although he's only one person, he's sufficient to take the place of all." Because Socrates knew what the rational soul is moved by, just like a pair of scales, and that it must lean in favour, whether it chooses to or not. Show the rational governing faculty a contradiction, and it will cease to contradict; but if you don't show it, blame yourself rather, than the man who's not persuaded.

CHAPTER 56 – ON FINE CLOTHING

A young man came to see me, with his hair tidier than what was common at that time, and his clothing was very stylish; I asked him: do you think that some dogs and horses are beautiful, and some out of all the other animals. "I do," the young man replied. So, are some men beautiful and others ugly too? "Certainly." We see a dog is naturally formed for one thing, and a horse for another, yet we don't claim them to be beautiful according to their purpose, and since the nature of each is different, each of them seems to me to be beautiful in a different way. Isn't that true? He admitted that it was. That then which makes a dog beautiful, makes a horse ugly; and that which makes a horse beautiful, makes a dog ugly, if it is true that their natures are different. "It seems to be."

I think, what makes the high jump contestant beautiful, makes the wrestler ugly, and a runner to be ridiculous; and the man who is beautiful for the high jump, is very ugly for wrestling. "That's true," said he. What, then, makes a man beautiful? Is it the same as that which makes both a dog and a horse beautiful? "It is," he said. What makes a dog beautiful then? Being an excellent dog. And what makes a horse beautiful? Being an excellent horse. What makes a man beautiful? Isn't it being an excellent man? And so, if you wish to be beautiful, young man, work at this, the acquisition of human excellence. But what is this? Observe who you praise, when you praise many people without partiality: do you praise the fair or the unfair? "The fair." Do you praise the moderate or the immoderate? "The moderate." And the temperate or the intemperate? "The temperate." Therefore, you know if you make yourself a person like those who you praise, you will know that you will make yourself beautiful: but so long as you neglect these things, you must be ugly, even though you arrange all you can to appear beautiful.

I don't know what else to say to you: because if I say to you what I think, I'll offend you, and you will perhaps leave the school and not return to it: and if I don't say what I think, how would I be acting, if you've come to me to be improved, and I won't improve you at all, and if you've come to me, a philosopher, and I say nothing to you as a philosopher, how cruel would it be for me to leave you uncorrected. If in the future you acquire sense, you will with good reason blame me and say, "What did Epictetus see in me that, when he saw me in such a predicament coming to him in such a shameful condition, he neglected me and never said a word? Didn't he care? Wasn't I young and in need of help? Wasn't I able to listen to reason? And how many other young men at this age commit many errors like this? I heard that a very self-indulgent young man underwent a great change. Well, I suppose that he didn't think that I could. He could have fixed my hair, and removed my decorative clothing, he could have stopped me from plucking the hair off of my body; but when he saw me dressed like that - he was silent."

So, if you came to me in the future saying this, how could I defend myself? I don't know, whether you'll be persuaded by me or not. Was Socrates able to persuade all of his listeners to take care of themselves? Not all of them. Am I the man to change you? Maybe. And are you a man who can listen to the truth? I hope you are. Since I have been condemned to have a long white beard and a cloak, and you've come to see me, as a philosopher, I won't treat you in a cruel way, or as if I was disappointed in you, but I will say: young man, who do you wish to make beautiful? Firstly, know who you are and then enhance yourself appropriately. You are a human being; and this is a mortal animal which has the power of using appearances rationally. But what is meant by "rationally?" Conformably to nature and completely. What, then, do you possess which is unique? Is it the animal part? No. Is it the condition of mortality? No. Is it the power of using appearances? No. You possess the rational faculty as a unique thing: adorn and beautify this; leave your hair to God who made it as he chose. Come on, what other titles do you have? Are you a man or a woman? "Man." Adorn yourself as a man then, not as woman. Women are naturally smooth and delicate; and if she has a lot of hair on her body, she's a monster and is displayed in Rome among monsters. And on a man it's monstrous not to have hair; and if he has no hair, he's a monster. If he cuts off his hair and pulls them out, what should we do with him? Where should we put him on display? And as what gender? "I will show you a man who chooses to be a woman rather than a man." What a terrible sight! There is no man who wouldn't shake his head, disapprovingly at such a spectacle. However, I think that the men who pluck their hair, don't realise what they are doing. What fault are you trying to find with your nature? That it made you a man? What? Would it be better if nature made all humans women? What advantage would you gain by being beautiful? Who would you have beautified yourself for, if all humans were women? You act as if you aren't pleased with the matter: and start working on this business. Try to even remove the cause of the hairs. If this is the case make yourself a woman in all respects, so we're not mistaken: don't make one half man, and the other half woman. Who do you want to please? The women? Please them as a man then. "Well; I think they like smooth men." Will you please go and hang yourself? and if women were interested in homosexuals, would you become one? Were you born for this purpose, that degenerate women like you? Could we give you some importance in society? Put you in charge of the youth, or general or superintendent of the games? And if you have a wife, do you intend to have your hairs plucked out? To please who and for what purpose? And when you've had children, will you introduce them into this world with the habit of plucking their hairs out? A beautiful citizen, senator or leader. We should pray that such young men are born among us and brought up correctly.

Don't do this, I ask you young man: when you've heard these words, go away and say to yourself, "Epictetus didn't say this to me; how could he? Some good has flowed through him: because this would have never come into his thoughts, since he's not accustomed to talk like that with anyone. So I say to you, let us obey God, so we're not subject to his anger."

Do you realise the crow through his croaking can signify something to you? Is it the crow which signifies, or God through the crow? And if he signifies anything through a human voice, is it not so you can see the power of divinity? The chief signifies through the noblest of messengers. What do the poets say: we ourselves have warned him, and have sent a careful watcher. The husband not to kill or wed the wife.

And now God says this to you and sends a messenger, to warn you not to pervert that which is already well arranged, or busy yourself which such things, but to allow a man to be a man, and a woman to be a woman, a beautiful man to be a beautiful man, and an ugly man to be an ugly man, because you are not just flesh and hair, you are will; and if your will is beautiful, then you will be beautiful. But at the present time I'm sorry to say that you are ugly, because I think you are prepared to hear anything other than this. But remember what Socrates says to the most beautiful and prospering men: "Try to be beautiful." He didn't say: "Dress your hair and pluck the hairs from your legs." Nothing of the kind. But "Adorn your will, and take away bad opinions." "And with the body?" Leave it as it is by nature. Another looks after these things: trust in him. "Does that mean a man shouldn't be clean?" Of course not; but what you are and are made of by nature, cleanse this. A man should be clean as a man, a woman as a woman, a child as a child. You say no: let's also pluck out the lion's mane, so he won't be dirty.

CHAPTER 57 – WHAT SHOULD A MAN EXERCISE HIMSELF IN, AND WE SHOULDN'T NEGLECT THE PRIORITY

There are three things a man should exercise himself in, if he wishes to be wise and good. The first concerns the desires and the aversions, so a man won't fail to get what he desires, and so he can avoid that which he doesn't desire. The second concerns the movements toward, and the movements from an object, and generally in doing what a man should do, that he may act according to order, to reason, and not carelessly. The third thing concerns freedom from deception and impulsiveness in judgement. Out of these topics the main and the most urgent is that which relates to the affects; because an affect is produced in no other way than by a failing to obtain that which a man desires or a falling into that which a man wants to avoid. This then creates disturbance, disorders, bad fortune, misfortunes, sorrows and envy; that which makes men envious and jealous; and by these causes weren't able to listen to the instructions of reason. The second topic concerns the duties of a man; because I don't want to be still like a statue, but I should maintain the correct natural relations as a sincere man, a son, a father, andas a citizen.

The third topic is that which immediately concerns those who are making proficiency, that which concerns the security of the other two, so that not even in sleep any appearance unexamined may surprise us. "This," it must be said, "is above our power." But the present philosophers neglecting the first topic and the second, busy themselves on the third, using sophisticated arguments, making conclusions from questioning, creating theories, and lying. "A man must," as it is said, "when working on these matters, take care that he's not deceived." Who must do this? The wise and good man. This then is all that is required of you. Have you successfully worked out the rest? Are you free from deception in the matter of money? If you see a beautiful girl, do you resist the appearance? If your neighbor obtains an estate by will, are you not angry? Now, there should be nothing else you want except unchangeable firmness in the mind? You are a fool, if you hear these things with fear and anxiety and think that some people may despise you, and then wonder what people might say about you.

Let's look at your principles. Because it's plain to see that you don't value at all your own will, and you look externally to things which are independent of your will? For instance, what could a certain person say about you? And what will people think of you? Will you be considered an educated man? Want me to tell you what type of man you have shown us that you are? You have exhibited yourself to us as a mean fellow, argumentative, passionate, cowardly, finding fault with everything, blaming everybody, never quiet, vain.

Fool, you shouldn't dismiss these things that don't concern you? These things are suitable for people who are able to hear them without any internal disturbance, who can say: "I am not subject to anger, grief, or envy: I'm not hindered, I'm not restrained. What's left? I have leisure, I'm tranquil: let's see how we should deal with sophisticated arguments; let's see how when a man has accepted a hypothesis he's not led to anything absurd."

CHAPTER 58 – WHAT SHOULD A GOOD MAN FOCUS ON AND PRACTICE

The material for the good and wise man is his own ruling faculty: and the body is material for the doctor; the land is for farmer. The business of the wise and good man is to use appearances conformably to nature: and as it is the nature of every soul to agree with truth, to disagree with the false, and to remain uncertain in regards to that which is ambiguous, it is its nature to move toward good, and to avoid evil; and with respect to that which is neither good or bad it feels indifferent. When good appears, it is immediately attracted to it; and is repelled from evil. But the soul will not reject the appearance of good. This principle is the basis of every movement, both of man and God.

For this reason, good is preferred to every intimate relationship. There is no intimate relationship between me and my father, but there is between me and good. "Are you hard-hearted?" Yes, because that is my nature. For this reason, if good is something different from beautiful and fair, my father is gone, and my brother, my country, and everything else. Should I overlook my own good, so you can have it, and should I hand it over to you? Why? "I'm your father." But you are not my goodness. "I'm your brother." But you are not my goodness.

If we value good highly and place it in our will, the very observance of the relations of life is good, and accordingly he who gives up any external things obtains that which is good. Your father takes away your property. But he does not injure you. Your brother will have the larger part of the estate. Let him have as much as he chooses. Will he have a greater share of modesty, of fidelity, of brotherly affection? Who can take this possession from you? Not even God, because he hasn't chosen to do so; and has placed this in my own power, and he has given it to me just as he possesses it himself, free from obstruction, compulsion, and impediment.

As soon as you go out in the morning, examine every man you see, every man you hear; and then answer this question, "What have you seen?" A handsome man or woman? Apply the rule: Is this independent of the will, or dependent? Independent. Take it away. What have you seen? A man crying over the death of a child. Apply the rule. Death is a thing independent of the will. Take it away. Has the officer met you? Apply the rule. What is an officer? Independent of the will, or dependent on it? Independent. Take this away: it does not warrant examination, throw it away as if it is nothing to you.

If we practiced this and exercised ourselves daily in this, from morning to night, something would be done. But now we are caught half-asleep by every appearance, and it is only, if ever, that in the school when we see a little. Then when we go out, if we see a man crying, we say, "He's incomplete." If we see an officer, we say, "He's happy." If we see an exiled man, we say, "He's miserable." If we see a poor man, we say, "He's foolish: he has nothing to eat."

We should eradicate these bad opinions, and direct all our efforts toward this. Because what is crying? Opinion. What is bad fortune? Opinion. What is treason, what is divided opinion, what is blame, what is accusation, what is immorality? All these things are opinions, and nothing more, and opinions about things independent of the will, as if they were good and bad. Let a man transfer his opinions to things dependent on the will, and I appoint him to be firm and constant, whatever the state of things around him is.

External appearances are like a ray of light shining on the water. When the water moves, the ray also seems to move, but it hasn't. So, when a man is paralyzed with fear, it isn't the art of the virtues which is confused, but the spirit on which they are impressed; but if the spirit is restored to its natural state, those things will also be restored.

CHAPTER 59 – INAPPROPRIATE BEHAVIOUR

The governor of Epirus showed his favor to an actor in an inappropriate way and after he was publicly blamed for this, reported to Epictetus that he was blamed and was angry at those who blamed him, Epictetus said: What harm have they done? These men also were also acting, and so were you. The governor replied, "Do, people show their support in this way?" When they see you, said Epictetus, as their governor, a friend of Caesar and his deputy, not showing support, how can it be expected? Why are you angry if they followed your example? Who else do they have to imitate except you, who are their superiors, who's example should they look toward except yours? You should know when you enter the theatre that you enter as an example to the rest. Why did they blame you? Because every man hates that which is a interference to him. They wanted one person to be crowned; but you wanted it to be another. They were a hindrance to you, and you were a hindrance to them. You were found to be stronger; and they did what they could; they blamed the man who hindered them. What do you expect? That you do whatever you want, and they shouldn't say what they want? What is the surprise? Don't farmers abuse God when they are hindered? What about sailors? Do they ever stop abusing God? What doesn't God know? And isn't what's said reported to Caesar? What does he do? He knows that, if he punished all who abuse him, he would have nobody to rule over. So then? When you enter the theatre, you shouldn't say, "Let Sophron be crowned", you should say this, "Let me maintain my will in this matter so that it's conformable to nature: no man is dearer to me than myself. It would be ridiculous, then, for me to be hurt in order that another man who is an actor may be crowned." Who do I wish to gain this prize? Whoever I wish to gain it. "I wish Sophron to be crowned." Celebrate what you do in your own house. But in public don't claim more than your entitled, or attempt to assign to yourself that which belongs to everyone. If you don't consent to this, you have to bear being abused: because when you do the same as everyone else, you put yourself on the same level with them.

CHAPTER 60 – AGAINST THOSE WHO CLAIM SICKNESS AND LEAVE HOME

"I'm sick," said one of the pupils, "and I want to go home." At home, I suppose, you're free from sickness. Don't you consider whether you're doing anything here which may be useful to the exercise of your will, or that it might be corrected? Because if you're not moving toward this goal, there was no purpose for you to come. Go home then. Because if your ruling power can't be maintained in a state conformable to nature, maybe it's possible that you can maintain your land this way, or you'll be able to increase your money, perhaps take care of your father in his old age, attend public places, or even hold a position in the office: but being bad, you will always do badly in anything that you have to do. However, if you understand yourself, and know that you are removing bad opinions and adopting others in their place, and if you have changed your state of life from things which are not within your will to things which are within your will, and if you can ever say you're not speaking on behalf of your brother or father, but on behalf of yourself, would you still claim to be sick? Don't you realise, disease and death surprise us if we are busy doing something? The farmer while he's preparing the ground, the sailor while he's on a voyage? What will you be doing when death attempted to surprise you, because you have to be surprised if you are busy. If you can be doing something, when you are surprised, do it. Because I want to be surprised by disease or death when I am looking after nothing else than my will, that it can be free from distress, and free from hindrance, free from compulsion, and in a state of liberty. I want to be found practicing these things so I am able to say to God, "have I in any respect disobeyed your commands? Have I in any respect misused the powers which you gave me? Have I misused my perceptions or my preconceptions? Have I ever blamed you? Have I ever found fault with your administration? I have been sick, because it was your will, and so have others, but I was content to be sick. I have been poor because it was your will, but I was content with this as well. I haven't taken a place in the office, because it wasn't your will. I have never desired pleasure. And for that reason, have you ever seen me discontented? Haven't I always approached you with a cheerful expression, ready to do follow your commands and signals? If it were your will now, that I should leave from the gathering of men? I would leave. And I would give you thanks for that. You have allowed me to join in this gathering of men and to see my work, and have allowed me to comprehend your administration." May death surprise me while I am thinking of these things, while I am reading and writing.

"But my mother will look after me when I'm sick." Go to your mother then; because you're a person fit enough to have your head held when you're sick. "At home, I can lie down on a comfortable bed." Go to your bed then: because you're fit to lie on such a bed even when you are in good health: of course, you don't want to lose what you can do there.

What does Socrates say? "As one man," he says, "is pleased with improving his land, another with improving his horse, I am pleased each day, by observing that I'm growing better." "Better in what? In using nice words?" Don't say that. "In matters of speculation?" What are you saying? "I don't see anything else that philosophers use their time for." Does it appear to be nothing to you, to never find fault with another person, in regards to God or men? To have never blamed anybody? To have the same face when going out or returning home? This is what Socrates knew, and yet he never said that he knew anything or taught anything. But if any man asked him for nice words or speculations, he would refer him to Protagoras or Hippias; and if any man came to ask for herbs, he would refer him to the gardener. Who then among us has this purpose? Because if you had it, you would be content with sickness, hunger, and death. If any among us have been in love with a charming girl, he will know what I say is true.

CHAPTER 61 – MISCELLANEOUS

When some man asked him how it occurred that reason has been greatly cultivated by the men of the present time, but the progress made by the previous generations was greater. In what respect, he answered. In what respect was the progress greater then? Because if it has now been cultivated well, that cultivation of the past would be included in this. At present, it has been cultivated for the purpose of resolving hypothetical arguments and progress has been made. But in former times it was cultivated for the purpose of maintaining the governing faculty in a condition conformable to nature, and progress was made. Do not, then, mix things which are different and do not expect, when you are working toward one thing, to make progress in another. Take a look to see if any man among us when he is intent to keep himself in a state conformable to nature doesn't make progress. I assure you, you won't find such a man.

The good man is invincible, because he doesn't enter a contest where he's not stronger. If you want to have his land and all that is on it, take the land; take his servants, take office, and take his poor body. But you can't make his desire change, in that which it seeks, or his aversion move toward that which he wishes to avoid. The only contest he enters in to, is that about things which are within the power of his will; how then could he not be invincible?

Someone once asked, what is common sense, Epictetus replied: It may be called a common hearing which distinguishes vocal sounds, and that which distinguishes musical sounds isn't common, but artificial; so, there are certain things which men, who are not totally perverted, can see by the common notions which all possess. Such a constitution of the mind is named common sense.

It's not easy to encourage weak young men; and neither is it easy to hold cheese with a hook. But those who have a good natural disposition, even if you try to negatively influence them, hold on stronger to reason. Rufus generally attempted to discourage, and he used this method as a test for those with a good natural disposition and for those who without. "Because," it was his habit to say, "just like a stone, if you throw it into the air, it will be brought back down to the earth by its own nature, and so, the man whose mind is naturally good, the more you repel him, the more he returns toward that to which he is naturally inclined."

CHAPTER 62 – TO THE ADMINISTRATOR

When an administrator came to visit, and the man was an Epicurean, Epictetus said: It's important for us who aren't philosophers to inquire about those who are philosophers, in the same manner those who come to a strange city pose questions to citizens who are acquainted with it, what is the best thing in the world, in order that we after inquiring, can search for that which is best and view it, as strangers do with the things in cities. For this, there are three things which relate to a man: body, soul, and things which are external. Very rarely does any man deny this. It remains for you philosophers to answer what is the best. What should we tell all men? Is it the flesh? Was this the reason Maximus sailed as far as Cassiope during winter with his son, just so he could be gratified in the flesh? The man replied, "it wasn't for that, that is far from his style". It is highly important Epictetus said, to be actively seeking the best. What, then, do we possess which is better than the flesh? "The soul," he replied. And is this the best of the good, or the worst of the bad? "The best of the good." And are the best things of the good within the power of the will or not within the power of the will? "They are within the power of the will." Is, then, the pleasure of the soul a thing within the power of the will? "It is," he replied. And what does this pleasure depend on? On itself? That cannot be conceived: because there must first exist a certain substance or nature of good, and by obtaining this we will have pleasure in the soul. He agreed with this as well. On what, then, do we depend for this pleasure of the soul? Because if it depends on the soul only, then the substance of good can be discovered; but good can't be one thing, and the things we are delighted with another; and neither can something be bad, and that which comes after be good, because in order that things which come after to be good, that which precedes must also be good. But you wouldn't affirm this, if you're in your right mind, because then you would say it's inconsistent with Epicurus and the rest of your doctrines. It remains, then, that the pleasure of the soul is in the pleasure of the body.

For this reason, Maximus acted foolishly if he made the voyage for any other reason than the sake of the flesh, that is, for the sake of the best.

And also, a man acts foolishly if he abstains from that which belongs to others.

But, I wouldn't agree, let's consider this, how these things can be done secretly, and safely, and that no man will know. Because not even Epicurus declares stealing to be bad, but he admits that the detection is; and because it is impossible to have security against detection, for this reason he says, "don't steal." But I say, if stealing is done cleverly and cautiously, we won't be detected: some men are weak, and no man will follow the thieves because of this. But why would you refrain from your own good? This is senseless and foolish. And even if you tell me that you do refrain, I won't believe you. Because it's impossible to agree with which appears false, and to turn away from that which is true, so it's also impossible to abstain from that which appears good. But wealth is a good thing, and certainly most efficient in producing pleasure. Why won't you acquire wealth? And why shouldn't we corrupt our neighbor's wife, if we can do it without detection? and if the husband foolishly talks about the matter, why not throw him out the house? If you want to be a philosopher such as you should be, a perfect philosopher, consistent with your own doctrines. Then you won't differ at all from us who are called Stoics; because we also say one thing, but do another: we talk about things which are beautiful, but we do what is ugly. But you will be perverse in the opposing way, perhaps teaching what is bad, and practicing what is good. In the name of God, are you thinking of a city of Epicureans? "I wouldn't marry anyone." "Or have children, or engage in public matters." What will happen? Where will the citizens come from? Who will bring them up? Who will be governor of the youth? Who will teach them? And what will he teach them? Will he teach them what the Lacedaemonians were taught, or what the Athenians were taught? Take a young man, bring him up according to your doctrines. The doctrines are bad, perverse, malicious to families, and not appropriate to women. Dismiss them. You live in a great city: it's your duty to be a magistrate, to judge justly, to abstain from that which belongs to others; no woman should to seem beautiful to you except your own wife, and no youth, no silver, no gold. Seek for doctrines which are consistent with what I say, and, by making them your guide, you will with pleasure abstain from things which have such persuasive power to lead us and overpower us. But if to the persuasive power of these things, we also devise philosophy which helps to push us on toward them and strengthens their hold on us, what will be the consequence? In a piece of design, what is the best part? The silver or the workmanship? The substance of the hand is the flesh; but the work of the hand is the principal part. There are also three duties; those which are directed toward the existence of a thing; those which are directed toward its existence in a particular kind of way; and third, the principle leading things themselves. And also in a man we shouldn't value the material, the poor flesh, but the principal. What are these principles? Engaging in public business, marrying, having children, respecting God, taking care of parents, and, generally, having desires, pursuits of things and avoidances, in the way in which we should do, and according to our nature. And how are we constituted by nature? Free, noble, modest: because what other animal blushes? What other is capable of receiving the feeling of shame? And we are constituted by nature, to experience these things, so it can keep us constant in acts which are conformable to nature.

"But I am rich and I want nothing." Why, then, do you pretend to be a philosopher? Your gold and silver vessels are enough for you. What need do you have for principles? "But I am also a judge of the Greeks." Do you know how to judge? Who taught you to know? "Caesar gave me the position." Well, let him write and give you an order to judge music; how useful will you be? How did you become a judge? Whose hand did you kiss? The hand of Symphorus or Numenius? Whose bed did you sleep in? Who have you sent gifts to?

"But I can throw into prison any man I please." And you can also do that with a stone. "But I can beat with sticks anyone I please." And you can also do that to a donkey. This is not how to govern men. Govern us as rational animals: show us what is profitable to us, and we will follow: show us what is unprofitable, and we will turn away from it. Make us imitators of yourself, as Socrates made men imitators of himself. Because he was like a governor of men, who made them subject to him their desires, their aversion, their movements toward an object and their turning away from it. "Do that. Don't do this: if you don't obey, I will throw you in prison." This is not governing men like rational animals.

But I: As God has ordained, act like this: if you don't act as I say, you will feel the penalty, you will be punished. What will be the punishment? Nothing else than not having done what you ask: people are already losing the character of faithfulness, modesty, and righteousness. Don't look for greater penalties than these.

CHAPTER 63 – TO AN ORATOR GOING TO ROME

When a certain person came to him, who was going to Rome in regard to his rank, Epictetus asked what the reason was for him to go to Rome, and the man then asked what he thought. Epictetus replied: If you ask me what you'll do in Rome, whether you will succeed or not, I have no idea about this. But if you ask me how you will roughly do, I can tell you: if you have the right opinions, you will do well; if they are false, you won't do well. And for every man, the cause of his actions are his opinions. Because what is the reason you desire to be elected governor. Your opinion. What is the reason that you are now to Rome? Your opinion. And going in winter, during such a dangerous time on such an expensive trip. "I must go." What tells you this? Your opinion. Then if opinions are the causes of all actions, and a man has bad opinions, the cause is bad, and the effect is also. Do we all have sound opinions, both you and your adversary? And how do you differ? Do you have sounder opinions than your adversary? Why? You think so. And he does as well, he thinks that his opinions are better. And madmen do to. This is a bad benchmark. Show me that you've made some inquiry into your opinions and have taken some careful consideration about them. And as now you are sailing to Rome in order to become governor, and you're not content to stay at home with the honors which you had, but you desire something greater and grander, when did you ever make a voyage for the purpose of examining your opinions, and throwing them out, if you have any that are bad? Who have you approached for this purpose? What time have you assigned for it? At what age? Go over the times of your life by yourself, if you are ashamed to discuss them with me. When you were a boy, did you examine your own opinions? And when you were a little older, didn't you attend schools practice their teachings, what did you imagine that you were deficient in? And when you were a young man and engaged in public matters, and were gaining reputation, who then seemed equal to you? When would you have submitted to any man examining and showing you that your opinions are bad? What, then, do you wish me to say to you? "Help me in this matter." I have no rule for this. Neither have you, if you came to me for this purpose, come to me as a philosopher, but coming as a seller of vegetables or a shoemaker. "What purpose does a philosopher's rule serve?" For this purpose: that whatever may happen, our ruling faculty may be and continue to be conformable to nature. Does this seem to you a little thing? "No; it's the greatest." So, then? Doesn't it require only a short time? And is it possible to seize it? Therefore, if you can, seize it.

Then you will say, "I met with Epictetus and it was like meeting a stone or a statue": because you saw me, and nothing more. But he who meets with a man as a man, who learns his opinions, and shows his own. Can then say he visited. Let's examine one another: if I have any bad opinions, take them away; if you have any, show me. This is the meaning of meeting with a philosopher. "If you don't agree, then this is only a passing visit, and while you're hiring a boat, you say let's go to see Epictetus. Let's see what he says." Then you go away and say: "Epictetus was nothing: he made errors and spoke in a vicious way." As judges, what else do you come for? "Well, a man might say to me, "If I care about this kind of thing, I'll have no land, as you have none; I'll have no silver cups as you have none, I'll have no animals, as you have none." In answer to this it is perhaps sufficient to say: I have no need of these things: because if you possess many things, you then have a need from more: whether you choose or not, you are poorer than I. "What do I need of?" Of that which you lack: firmness of a mind which is conformable to nature, of being free from distress. Whether I have customers or not, what is that to me? But that means something to you. I'm richer than you: I'm not anxious what Caesar will think of me: and for that reason, I flatter no man. This is what I possess instead of boats of gold and silver. You have utensils of gold; but your discourse, your opinions, your agreements, your movements, your desires are poor. When I have these things conformable to nature, why shouldn't I dedicate my time to the study of reason? Because I have leisure: my mind is not distracted. What should I do, since I have no distraction? What more suitable for a man than this? When you have nothing to do, you are disturbed, you go to the theatre or you wander about without a purpose. Why shouldn't a philosopher work to improve his reason?

You work for crystal: I work for "The Living": you work for jewels; I work for "The Denying." To you, everything you possess appears small: to me all that I have appears great. Your desires are insatiable: mine are satisfied.

Children put their hand into a narrow jar and try to take figs and nuts; if they fill the hand, they can't take it out, and then they cry. When they drop a few of them, you'll be able to take some. Let go of your desires: don't desire many things and you'll have what you want.

CHAPTER 64 – HOW WE SHOULD TOLERATE SICKNESS

When we require opinions, we should have them ready: for example, breakfast, opinions relating to breakfast; in the gym, opinions concerning the gym; in bed, those concerning bed.

Don't allow yourself to sleep, before each daily action should be analysed: what's done, what's left undone; from the first to last action, examine all of them, and then blame yourself for what is wrong, and for what is right be happy.

And should retain these verses in such a way that we can use them, not just saying them, for example when we exclaim "Paean Apollo." Again, we need our opinions ready; when we have a fever, we should already have opinions relating to fever, and we shouldn't, as soon as the fever begins, lose them all and forget. A man who has a fever may "If I philosophize might die: wherever I go, I must take care the body, so a fever doesn't come." But what is philosophizing? Isn't it a preparation against events which may happen? Don't you understand that's what you're saying? "If I prepare myself to have patience what happens, should I die?" This is just as if a man after receiving blows should give up the boxing match. In the boxing ring it's in our power to avoid and not to receive blows. But in other matters, if we give up philosophy, what do we gain? When something painful happens what should a man say? "This is what I exercised for, for this I disciplined myself." God says to you, "Give me proof that you have really practiced athletics, that you have eaten what you should, that you have exercised, that you have obeyed the coaches." If you have, would you appear weak when the time comes for action? Now is the time for a fever. Let it be handled well. Now is the time for thirst, well; now is the time for hunger, you should be ready for it. Isn't this in your power? Who could hinder you? The physician could hinder you from drinking; but he can't prevent you from being able to handle thirst well: and he could hinder you from eating; but he can't prevent you from being able to handle hunger well.

"But I can't attend to my philosophical studies." For what purpose do you do them? Fool, isn't it so you can be happy, so you can be constant, isn't it so you can be in a state conformable to nature and live like that? What hinders you when you have a fever from having your ruling faculty conformable to nature? Here is the proof of this thing, here is the test of the philosopher. Because this is also a part of life, like walking, like sailing, like exploring the land, just as fever is. Do you read when you're walking? No. And neither when you have a fever. if you walk about when well, you have all that is required for a man who walks. If you handle fever well, you have all that belongs to a man suffering from fever. How do we handle a fever well? Not to blame God or any man; not to be afflicted by that which happens, to expect death, to do what must be done: when the physician comes, not to be frightened at what he says; or if he says, "you're doing well," to be satisfied by that. Because what good has he told you? Just as if he said that when you were in good health, what good is that to you? And even if he says, "You're not doing so well," don't despair. Because what is it to be ill? Isn't it that you are near the severance of the soul from the body? What harm is there in this? If you are not near now, wouldn't you be near afterward? Is the world going to be turned upside down after you die? Why then do you flatter the physician? Why do you give him an opportunity of raising his eyebrows? Don't you value a physician, as you do a shoemaker when he's measuring your foot, or a carpenter when he's building your house. He who has a fever has an opportunity of doing this: if he does these things, he has what belongs to him. Because it's not the business of a philosopher to look after these external things, neither his wine, his oil or his poor body, but his own ruling power. But in regard to the externals how should he act? As much as he can, not to be careless about them. Where then is there a reason for fear? Where is there, then, a reason for anger, and fear about what belongs to others, which are of no value? For should have these two rules ready: nothing except the will is good or bad; and that we shouldn't lead events, but follow them. "My brother shouldn't have behaved like this toward me." No; but he will realise that: and, however he may behave, I will conduct myself toward him as I should. Because this is my own business: his actions belong to him; no man can alter what I chose through my will, external things can be hindered.

CHAPTER 65 – CERTAIN MISCELLANEOUS MATTERS

There are certain penalties fixed by law for those who disobey the divine administration. Whoever thinks any other thing to be good except those things which depend on the will, let him envy, let him desire, let him flatter, and let him be disturbed: whoever considers anything else to be evil, let him grieve, let him feel sad, let him cry, and let him be unhappy.

CHAPTER 66 – ABOUT EXERCISE

We shouldn't exercise in a way which is opposing our nature and adapted purely to cause admiration, because, if we do, we, who call ourselves philosophers, would not differ at all from jugglers. Because it's difficult to walk on a rope; actually, not only is it difficult, but it is also dangerous. Should we practice walking on a rope for these reasons? Not at all. Everything, which is difficult and dangerous isn't suitable for us to practice; only that which is worth exercising should be practiced. Mainly to control our desires and avoid that which is bad for us. What does this mean? Not to be disappointed by that which you desire, or to move toward anything which you want to avoid. This is where our exercise should be. However, since it's very difficult to not have our desires disappointed and our aversions free from failure, a great and constant effort is required. You must know that if you allow your desire and aversion to turn to things which are not within the power of the will, you will not be capable of attaining this objective, or your aversion free from the power of avoiding that which you want to avoid. And since strong habits move us, and we are accustomed to desire and avoid things which are not within the power of our will, we should oppose this habit with a contrary habit.

I like pleasure: I will take the contrary route for the sake of exercise. Who is this type of practitioner in exercise? He who doesn't practice using his desire, and applies his aversion only to things which are within the power of his will, and practices most in the things which are difficult to conquer. For this reason, one man must practice more against one thing and another against another thing.

Practice, if you are irritable, to endure if you are abused, not to be angry if you're treated with dishonour. Also exercise yourself to drink moderately, in this there are men who don't know how to practice, well for a start, you should abstain from it.

Be obedient to reason, so you don't do anything out of season or place. Study things which are persuasive and attractive.

Because as Socrates said, "we shouldn't live a life without examination," so we shouldn't accept an appearance without examination, but we should say, "wait, let me see what you are and where you come from"; And finally whatever exercise is applied to the body, if they are conformable to nature, then they are a fit means of exercise; but if they are for display, that is an indication of someone who has turned himself toward something external, and who is hunting for something else, and who looks for spectators who will say, "oh what a great man." For this reason, Apollonius said, "when you intend to exercise yourself for your own advantage, and you are thirsty from heat, take a mouthful of cold water, and spit it out, and then tell nobody."

CHAPTER 67 – WHAT SOLITUDE IS, AND WHAT KIND OF PERSON A SOLITARY MAN IS

Solitude is the condition of a helpless man. But just because a man is alone, it doesn't necessarily mean he is solitary; and when a man is among many, it doesn't necessarily mean he's not solitary. When we've lost either a brother, or a son, or a friend who we were accustomed to having in our life, we say that we are alone, though we are often in Rome, and although such huge crowds are around us, and so many live in the same place.

The man who is solitary, as it is imagined, is considered to be a helpless person and exposed to those who wish to harm him. For this reason, when we travel, we say that we are lonely, because it's not the sight of a human that removes us from solitude, but the sight of one who is faithful and modest and helpful to us. Because if being alone is enough to create solitude, you could say that even God is solitary.

They do not understand how a man passes his life when he is alone, because they possess a certain principle: the natural desire of community and mutual love and from the pleasure of conversation among men. However, a man should be prepared to be sufficient for himself and to be his own companion. Just as God dwells with himself, and is tranquil by himself, and thinks of his own administration and of its nature, and is processing thoughts suitable for himself; we should also be able to talk with ourselves, not to feel in need of others, to be present with ourselves when passing our time; to observe the divine administration and the relation of ourselves to everything else; to consider how we formerly were affected by things that happen and how at present; we observe what things currently give us pain; how these can be cured and removed; and if any things require improvement, to improve them according to reason.

Can you see that Caesar appears to offer us peace, that there are no longer any enemies, or battles, or associations of robbers, or pirates, so we can travel at any time, and we can sail from east to west. But can Caesar give us security from fever as well, can he save us from shipwreck, from fire, from earthquake or from lightning? Can he give us security against love? He can't. From sorrow? He can't. From envy? He can't. He can't protect us from any of these things. But the doctrine of philosophers promises to give us security even against these things. And what does it say? "Men, if you will attend to me, wherever you are, whatever you are doing, you will not feel sorrow, anger, compulsion, or hindrance, but you will pass your time without disturbance and free from everything." When a man has this peace, not offered by Caesar, but by God through reason, isn't he content when he's alone? When he sees and reflects, "now no evil can happen to me; to me there is no robber, no earthquake, everything is full of peace, full of tranquility: every way, every city, every meeting, neighbor, and companion is harmless. One person whose business it is, supplies me with food; another with clothing; another with perceptions, and preconceptions.

What kind of solitude remains? What kind of wanting? Why do we make ourselves worse than children? And what do children do when they're left alone? They pick up stones and build something, then they pull it down, and build something else, and are happy passing time alone. Should I, if you sailed away, sit down and cry, because I've been left alone and solitary? Don't I have any stones? But children do what they to learn, and we through our own knowledge are unhappy.

Every great power is dangerous to beginners. You must then handle things as you are able to, but conformably to nature. However, you must abstain from food, drink water, and abstain sometimes altogether from desire, in order that you may at some point desire consistently with reason; and if consistently with reason, when you have anything good in you, you're desires will be well. "But some don't do this; they wish to live like wise men immediately and to be useful already." Useful how? What are you doing? Have you even been useful to yourself? "But, I suppose, you wish to encourage people." You encourage them because you wish to be useful to them. Show to them through your own example what kind of men philosophy makes, don't make false displays.

When you're eating, be good to those who eat with you; when you're drinking, to those who are drinking with you; bearing with them, do good to them, and don't spit on them.

CHAPTER 68 – CERTAIN MISCELLANEOUS MATTERS

Some people cannot walk alone. But if you are able, you should walk alone and talk to yourself. Don't hide yourself from yourself. Look around inside so you can know who you are.

When a man drinks water, or does anything for the sake of practice, whenever there's an opportunity he tells everyone: "I drink water." Does he drink water for the purpose of drinking water? If it's good for you to drink, drink; but if not, then you are just acting. Therefore, if it's good for you and you do drink, don't say anything about to others. Do you need to please others?

Out of the things which can be done some are done with a final purpose, some according to the occasion, and others with reference to circumstances, others for the purpose of complying with others, and some according to a fixed scheme of life.

You must root out of men these two things, arrogance and distrust. Arrogance, then, is the opinion that you want and need nothing: but distrust is the opinion that you can't be happy with the circumstances which surround you. Arrogance is removed by disproving it; and Socrates was the first who practiced this. It's impossible not to need or want anything. Inquire and seek, this search will do you no harm. This is philosophizing, to seek how it is possible to have desire and aversion without impediment.

"I am superior to you, because my father is a man of high ranking." Another says, "I have been a member of the court, but you haven't." If we were horses, would you say, "My father was faster?" If, then, while you were saying this, I said, "So be it: let's run then." But is there nothing more in a man which he can be known for, as superior or inferior? Isn't there modesty, fidelity and justice? Show yourself superior in these, so you can be a superior man. If you tell me that you can kick violently, I would say to you that you are proud of an act which belongs to a donkey.

CHAPTER 69 – PROCEED WITH CAUTION IN EVERYTHING

In every act consider what comes before and what follows after, and then execute the act. If you don't consider, you will first begin with spirit, since you haven't thought about the things which follow; but afterward, when some consequences have shown themselves, you will stop. "I wish to conquer at the Olympic games." "So do I: because that would be such a fine thing." But consider first, what comes before and what follows; and then, if it's for your good, undertake it. You must act according to rules, follow strict diet, abstain from delicacies, exercise yourself by compulsion at fixed times, in heat, in cold; drink no cold water or wine. In other words, you must surrender yourself to the trainer like you do to your doctor. In the contest, you must be covered with sand, sometimes dislocate a hand, sprain an ankle, swallow a quantity of dust, be tormented with the whip; and after undergoing all this, you must sometimes be conquered. After weighing up all of these things, if you still have an inclination, go to the athletic practice. If you don't consider all of these things, you will behave like a child who at one time acts as a wrestler, then a gladiator, then blows a trumpet just because they have seen and admired these things. So, you will also: at one time act the wrestler, then a gladiator, then a philosopher; but with your whole soul you are nothing: like the ape, you imitate all that you see; and always one thing after another pleases you, and anything that becomes familiar displeases you. Because you have never undertaken anything after careful consideration, neither have you explored the whole set of circumstances with strict examination; but you have undertaken things with a cold desire. Therefore, some people after seeing a philosopher and having heard one speak - wish to be philosophers themselves.

So first consider what the matter is, then what your own nature is, and what it is able to bear. If you are a wrestler, look at your shoulders, your thighs, your core: because different men are naturally formed for different things. Do you think that you can be a philosopher? Do you think that you can eat and drink as you do now, and in the same way be angry and out of humour? You must watch, work and conquer certain desires, you must leave some friends, be despised by others, laughed at by those who meet you, in external things, you must be inferior, in regards to the public office, In honours, and in the court. When you have considered these things completely, then, if you think correctly, approach philosophy, and you would gain in exchange for these things freedom from disturbance, liberty and tranquillity. If you haven't considered these things, don't approach philosophy: don't act like children, being at one time a philosopher, then a tax collector, then a teacher, then an agent of Caesar. These things are not consistent. You must be one man, either good or bad: you must either work on your own ruling faculty or at external things: you must either work at things within or external: that is, you must either occupy the place of a philosopher or that of the common people.

CHAPTER 70 – THAT WE SHOULD CAUTIOUSLY ENTER INTO CONVERSATION WITH MEN

If a man has frequent discussions with others, either for talk, or drinking together, or generally for social purposes, he must either become like them, or change them. Because if a man places a piece of burnt wood close to a piece that's burning, either the burnt wood will quench the other, or the burning wood will relight that which has been burnt. The danger is great, we must cautiously enter into conversation with common people, and remember it's impossible for a man to keep company with someone who's covered with dirt without covering himself as well. What would you do if a man speaks about gladiators, horses, athletes, or, what is worse, about men? "Such a person is bad," "Such a person is good."

Socrates had such a power in his social conversations, that he could lead his companions to his own purpose. Would you like to have this power? If so, think is it necessary to be carried about by the common kind of people.

Why are the common more powerful than you? Because they speak useless words from their real opinions: but you speak elegant words only from your lips; and for this reason they lack strength, feel dead, and it's sickening to listen to your speech. Because of this the common people have an advantage over you: because their opinions are strong and invincible. Until the good opinions are fixed in you, and you have acquired a certain power for your security, I advise that you're careful in your associations, because like wax in the sun anything you inscribe in your mind will be melted away. Withdraw yourself far from the sun as long as you have these wax opinions. For this reason, philosophers also advise men to leave their native country, because ancient habits distract them and don't allow a new beginning to be made of different habits; neither can we tolerate those who meet us and say: "See, so and so is now a philosopher, who was once a nobody." Even doctors send those who have lingering diseases to a different country with different air; and the rightly do so. Do you want to introduce new habits other than those which you already have? Fix your opinions and exercise yourself in them. But you don't do this, so: you go to a spectacle, to a show of gladiators, to a place of exercise, to a circus; then you come back, and again off to another place you go, and still you are the same person. And there is no new habit, attention, or care about the self and any observation of this kind, "How can I use the appearances presented to me? According to nature, or opposing nature? How do I answer people? As I should, or as I shouldn't? Do I say to the things which are independent of the will, that they don't concern me?" Because if you're not yet in this state, leave your former habits and leave the common people, if you ever intend to begin to be something.

CHAPTER 71 – ON PROVIDENCE

When you make accusations against God, you will learn that the thing has happened according to reason. "Yes, but the unfair man has the advantage." In what? "In money." Yes, because he's superior to you in this regard, he is free from shame, and is watchful. What's the wonder? But see if he has an advantage over you in being faithful, in being modest: because you won't find it to be so; but where you are superior, there you will find that you have the advantage. And I once said to a man who was angry because Philostorgus was fortunate: "Would you choose to sleep with Sura?" "I hope that never happens," he replied. "Why are you angry then, if he receives something in return for that which he sells; or how can you consider him to be happy if he acquires those things in ways which you disapprove of. What wrong does God do, if he gives better things to better men? Isn't it better to be modest than rich?" He admitted this. Why are you angry then, when you possess better things? Remember, then, always, and have in mind, the truth that this is a law of nature, that the superior has an advantage over the inferior in that in which he is superior; and you will never be angry.

"But my wife treats me badly." Well, if any man asks you, say, "My wife treats me badly." "Is there more?" Nothing. "My father gives me nothing." But to say that this is evil is something which must be added externally, and added falsely. For this reason, we must not get rid of poverty, but the opinion about poverty, and then we will be happy.

CHAPTER 72 – WE SHOULDN'T BE DISTURBED BY ANY NEWS

When you receive any news which by its nature can disturb, have this principle in mind, that the news is about nothing which is within the power of your will. Can any man tell you that you've formed a bad opinion, or had a bad desire? Not at all. But perhaps he will tell you that some person has died. What is that to you? He might tell you that some person speaks in a bad way about you. What is that to you? Or that your father is planning something or other. Against who? Against your will? How can he? Or is it against your body, or against your property? You're quite safe: as it's not against you. But the judge declares you have committed an act of irreverence to God. Didn't the judges make the same declaration against Socrates? Does it concern you that the judge has made this declaration? No. Why would you trouble yourself with it any longer then? Your father has a certain duty, and if he doesn't fulfill it, he loses the character of a father, of a man of natural affection, of gentleness. Don't wish that he loses anything else then. Because never does a man do wrong in one thing, and then suffer in another. On the other side it's your duty to make your defense firmly, modestly, without anger: but if you don't, you also lose the character of a son, of a man of modest behavior, of generous character.

Is the judge free from danger? No; he's in equal danger as well. Why then would you be afraid of his decision? What does another man's evil have to do with? It's your own evil to make a bad defense: be on your guard against this only. Because being condemned or not being condemned is the act of another person, so it's the evil of another person. "A certain person threatens me." Well if he's going to condemn you unfairly, then he's a fool.

CHAPTER 73 – THE CONDITION OF THE COMMON MAN VS THE PHILOSOPHER

The first difference between a common person and a philosopher is this: the common person says, "poor me, for their children, siblings or parents." The philosopher, if he ever says, "poor me," stops and says, "but this is for myself." Because nothing which is independent of the will can hinder or damage the will, and the will can only hinder or damage itself. If, then, we ourselves follow this direction, so as, when we are unlucky, to blame ourselves and to remember that nothing else is the cause of our disturbance or loss of tranquility except our own opinion, I swear to God that we have made progress. But in the present state of affairs we have gone another way from the beginning. For example, while we were children, the nurse, if we ever fell and hurt ourselves and required care, did not blame us, but blamed the stone. But what did the stone do? Should the stone be moved due to the child's lack of balance and coordination? Again, when we find nothing to eat, the lecturer doesn't blame our appetite, but he blames the cook. Did we make you the lecturer of the cook and not of the child? Correct the child, improve him. In this way, even when we are grown up we are still like children. Because one who is unmusical is a student of music; one without letters is a child still studying language: and he who is untaught, is a child in life.

CHAPTER 74 – HOW WE CAN DERIVE ADVANTAGE FROM ALL EXTERNAL THINGS

In the case of appearances, which are the objects of the vision, nearly all have allowed the good and the evil to be within, and not in the externals. No one calls the day good and the night bad. But what do men say? They say that knowledge is good, and that error is bad; but that would mean by accepting false knowledge this would still be a good result. And what about life. "Is health a good thing, and sickness a bad thing" No. "Then what is it?" To be healthy, and healthy in the right way, is good: to be healthy in a bad way is bad; that means it's possible to gain advantage even from sickness. Isn't it possible to gain advantage even from death, and isn't it possible to gain advantage from mutilation? Do you think that Menoeceus gained little by death? "Could a man who says so, gain so much as Menoeceus gained?" Didn't he maintain the character of being a lover of his country, a man of great mind, faithful and generous? And if he had continued to live, wouldn't he have eventually lost all of these things? Wouldn't he have gained the opposite? Wouldn't he have gained the name of coward, a hater of his country, a man who feared death? So, do you think that he gained little by dying? "I suppose not." But did the father of Admetus gain much by prolonging his life so miserably? Didn't he die afterward anyway?

"Can't advantage then be derived from all of these things?" From all; and even a man who abuses you. How does the man who coaches before combat profit the athlete? A great deal. The coach exercises me in endurance, in keeping my temper, in mildness. You say no: but he, who disciplines my legs and shoulders, does good to me; and the coach is right when he says: "Lift him up with both hands, and the heavier he is, the more advantage he has." But if a coach exercises me in controlling my temper, doesn't he also do good? "Is my neighbour bad?" Bad to himself, but good to me: because he exercises my good disposition, my moderation.

This is Hermes rod: "Touch it with whatever you want," as the saying goes. "and it will turn to gold." I don't say this, but: bring whatever you want, and I will make it good. Bring disease, bring death, bring poverty, bring abuse, bring trial on capital charges: all these things through Hermes rod will be made profitable. "What will you do with death?" I will show you by act through it, what a man is like who follows the will of nature? "What will you do with disease?" I will show its nature, I will be firm, I will be happy, I will not beg the doctor, but I also won't wish to die. What else do you seek? Whatever you give me, I will make it happy, fortunate, honoured, and a thing which any man would seek.

If I think about poverty as I do about disease, and about not having a job, isn't that enough for me? Won't it be an advantage? How could I continue to seek good and bad in these externals?

CHAPTER 75 – AGAINST THOSE WHO COME TO THE PROFESSION OF PHILOSOPHY

They who have learnt a few hypotheses immediately wish to vomit them out, like people whose stomach is diseased with food. First digest the thing, don't vomit: if you don't digest it, the thing becomes truly disgusting, a bad food which is unfit to eat. But instead, after digestion show us the change in your ruling faculty, as athletes show in their shoulders by how they have been exercising and what they have eaten; just like those who have taken up certain arts display what they have learned. The carpenter doesn't come and say, "hear me talk about the carpenter's art"; but having undertaken to build a house, he makes it, and proves that he knows the art. You should also do something like this; eat like a man, drink like a man, dress, marry, have children, be a good citizen, endure abuse, bear unreasonable people, bear with your father, bear with your son, neighbour, and show compassion. Show us these things so we can see that you have in truth learned something from the philosophers. You say, "come and listen to me read commentaries." Go away, and seek somebody else to vomit them on. "You say you will explain the writings of Chrysippus like no other man can: and explain his text most clearly."

Is it, then, for this reason that young men leave their country and their parents, so they can come to this place, and hear you explain words? Shouldn't they return with a capacity to endure, to be active in association with others, free from passion, free from disturbance, prepared with the right things for the journey of life with which they will be able to bear things that happen and derive honour from them? And how can you give them any of these things when you don't possess them? Have you done anything other than employ yourself to resolve sophisticated arguments? "But many men have a school; why shouldn't I have a school as well?" These things aren't done in a careless way; you must find the right time in life, with the right age, and God as a guide. What else are you doing other than revealing the mysteries? You say, "There's a temple in Eleusis, and one here as well. There is a school Eleusis, and I want to make one here as well. Yes, the words can be the same: but how do the things done here differ from those done there?" There is no difference. These things are done both in due place and in due time; and when accompanied with sacrifice and prayers, when a man is first purified, and when he has arranged in his mind the thought that he's going to approach sacred and ancient rites. In this way the mysteries are useful, in this way we come to the notion that all these things were established by the ancients for the instruction and correction of life. But you publish and divulge them out of time, out of place, without sacrifices, without purity; you don't have the garments, or the hair, or the voice, or the age; neither have you purified yourself: but you have committed to your memory the words only, and you say: "the words are sacred by themselves."

You should approach these matters in another way; because it's great, it's mystical, not a common thing, and neither is it given to every man. Not even wisdom perhaps is enough to enable a man to take care of youths: a man must also have a certain willingness and fitness for this purpose, and a certain quality of body, and above all things he must have God to advise him to occupy this position, as God advised Socrates to occupy the place of one who disproves error, Diogenes the office of royalty and criticism, and the office of teaching principles. But you open a doctor's shop, though you have nothing except words: but where and how they should be applied, you don't know neither have you taken any trouble to know it. "See," that man says, "I have lotions for the eyes as well." Do you also have the power of using them? Do you know both when and how they will do good, and to who they will do good? Why do you take such excessive risk in things of the greatest importance? Why are you careless? Why do you undertake a thing that is in no way fit for you? Leave it to those who are able to do it, and to do it well. Don't bring disgrace on philosophy through your own acts, and don't be one of those who load it with a bad reputation.

If theories please you, sit and analyse them by yourself; but don't say you're a philosopher, or allow another person to say it to you; but say: "He's mistaken, because my desires aren't different from what they were before, my activity hasn't changed, and neither has my use of appearances altered at all from my former condition." This is what you should think and say about yourself, if not, you act as a hazard.

CHAPTER 76 – ABOUT CYNICISM

When one of his pupils asked Epictetus, as he was a person who appeared to be in favour of Cynism, what kind of person a Cynic should be and what was the notion of it, we will inquire, said Epictetus, when we have time: but I have a lot to say to you about the men who without God attempt such great matters, making them hateful to God, and have no other purpose than to act indecently in public. Because in any well-managed house no man says to himself, "I should be the manager of this house." If he does, the master turns around and, seeing him giving orders, drags him out and beats him. And it's the same in this great city; because here also there is a master of the house who gives all the orders.

"If you are the sun; you make the year and seasons, make the fruits grow and nourish them, and warm the bodies of men properly: go, and travel around, and administer these things." "If you are a calf; when a lion appears, do what is necessary: if you don't, you will suffer." "If you are a bull: advance and fight, because this is your nature." "You can lead the army." "You can fight in single combat."

Are you thinking about this carefully? It's not what it seems to you. "I wear a cape now and I will wear it then: I sleep hard now, and I will sleep hard then: I will take in a little bag a stick, and if I see any man plucking the hair out of his body, I will beat him, or if he has altered his hair, or if he walks about wearing purple." If you imagine yourself to be like this, keep far away from cynicism: don't approach it: it's not for you. But if you understand what I just said, and think you're fit for cynicism, consider what a great thing you will undertake.

Firstly, in things which relate to you, you must not be in any respect like what you do now: you must not blame God or other men: you must take away desire altogether, you must transfer avoidance only to the things which are within the power of the will: you must not feel anger, resentment, envy or pity; a girl must not appear pretty to you, you can't love reputation, or be pleased with a cake. Because you should know that the rest of men put up walls around them and darkness when they do these things, and they have many methods of concealment. A man shuts the door, and places himself inside: if someone appears outside, he doesn't feel peace. But the Cynic instead of all these things uses modesty as his protection: if he doesn't, he would be indecent and naked under the open sky. This is his house, and his door: this is his darkness. Because he shouldn't wish to hide anything that he does: and if he does, he's gone, he's lost the character of a Cynic, of a man who lives under the open sky, of a free man: he's begun to fear something external, he's begun require concealment, but he cannot have concealment when he chooses. Because where can he hide himself and how? And if by chance this public instructor is detected, this teacher, what kind of things will he have to suffer? When a man fears these things, is it possible for him to be bold with his whole soul to oversee men? It can't be: it's impossible.

So firstly, you must make your ruling faculty pure, and live life like this as well. "So I need to work on my understanding, like carpenters work on wood; and learn the right use of appearances. But the body is nothing to me: the parts of it are nothing to me. Death? Let it come whenever it wants. Can any man eject me from the world? He can't. But wherever I go, the sun, the moon, the stars, dreams and signs are there, and I can converse with God."

If he's prepared, the true Cynic can't be satisfied with this; and he must know that he's sent as a messenger from God to men about good and bad things, to show them that they are lost and are seeking the substance of good and evil where they won't find it, because where it is, they never think of.

In fact, the Cynic is a spy of the things which are good for men and which are evil, and it is his duty to examine carefully and to report truly, and not to be struck with terror and begin pointing out as enemies those who are not enemies, neither should he be in any other way disturbed by appearances or confused.

It is his duty, to be able to say, with a loud voice, if the occasion arises: "Men, where are you hurrying to, what are you doing, fools? Like blind people you are walking up and down: you are taking another road, and have left the correct road that you seek for prosperity and happiness. And if someone shows you where it is, you don't believe him." Why do you seek it externally? Or in the body? It's not there. If you doubt, look at Myro, look at Ophellius and their possessions? It's not there. If you don't believe me, look at Croesus: look at those who are now rich, and the sorrow their life is filled with. Can you find it in power? It's not there. If it is, those who have been diplomats must be happy; but they're not. Who should we believe in these matters? You people who from the outside see their affairs and are dazzled by an appearance, or the men themselves? What do they say? Hear them when they moan, when they grieve, when because they became diplomats, the glory and splendor they wanted now makes them sadder and in great danger. Can it be found in royal power? It's not there: if it were, Nero would have been happy, but he wasn't. While others were sleeping what is he doing? "From his head, he ripped out his hair." And what did he say? "I am confused and Disturbed," and "my heart is beating out of my chest."

Fool, if none of these things cause happiness, what's the matter with you? That part of you that has been neglected and is corrupted, the part with which we desire, with which we avoid, with which we move toward and move away from things. How neglected? You don't know the nature of good for which you are made by nature and the nature of evil; and what's your own, and what belongs to others; and when anything that belongs to others goes badly, you say, "poor me." Such a disordered ruling faculty, alone neglected and uncared for. What are you then? In truth, a shepherd: because you cry like shepherds do, when a wolf has carried off one of their sheep: and those who are governed by you are sheep. Why did you come here? Was your desire in any danger? Was your aversion? Was your movement? Was your avoidance of things? "No; but the wife of my brother was taken." Wasn't it a great gain to be deprived of an adulterous wife?

Where is the good, if it's not in these things? If you chose to truly seek it, you would have found it inside yourselves; you wouldn't be wandering, or seeking what belongs to others as if it were your own. Turn your thoughts inwards: observe the preconceptions which you have. What kind of a thing do you imagine good to be? "That which flows easily, that which is happy, that which is not impeded." And don't you also imagine it to be great and to be valuable? Don't you imagine it to be free from harm? How can you seek that which flows easily, and that which isn't impeded? In that which serves or in that which is free? "In that which is free." Do you possess the body, then, free or is it in a subservient condition? "We don't know." Don't you not know it becomes a slave of fever, of a tyrant, of fire, of iron, of everything which is stronger? Yes, it's a slave." How, then, is it possible that anything which belongs to the body can be free from hindrance? Do you possess something which is free? Who can compel you to agree with things which appear false? "No one." And who can compel you not to agree with things which appear true? "No one." By this, then, you see that there is something in you which is naturally free. "How is it possible that a man who has nothing, who is naked and homeless, can possess a life that flows easily?" See, God has sent a man to show you that it's possible. "Look at me, I have no house, no possessions, and I sleep on the ground; I have no wife and no children, only the earth and sky, and one robe. And what do I want? Do I have sorrow? Do I fear? Am I not free? When did any of you see me failing in the object of my desire? Or falling into that which I should avoid? Did I ever blame God or other men? Did I ever accuse any man? Did any of you ever see me with an upset face? And how do I meet those who are afraid? Don't I treat them like fools? And who, when he sees me, doesn't think that I am his king or master?"

This is the language of the Cynics, this is their character, this is their purpose. You say "no": but their characteristic is a slim wallet: and the devouring of all that you give them, or storing it up, and correcting those who they meet. Can you see being able to undertake such a great business? First take a mirror: look at your shoulders; observe your legs. You are going to be enrolled as a warrior in the Olympic games. In the Olympic games a man is not permitted to be conquered, but first he must be disgraced in the sight of the whole world, next he must be whipped as well: and before being whipped, he must suffer thirst and heat, and swallow a lot of dust.

Reflect more carefully, know yourself, consult God, without God attempt nothing; because if he advises you to do something, be assured that he intends for you to become great or to receive a downfall so you learn.

When a man is suffering, doesn't he call God? Isn't he convinced that, whatever he suffers, it's God who is testing him? When Hercules was exercising he didn't think that he was suffering, and without hesitation he attempted to execute all that he could. So, is he who has trained for a contest and exercised by God going to be angry? Diogenes says to the people who pass by when he has a cold, "why don't you stay? Would a man with a cold accuse God as if God were treating him unfairly, because what could he really accuse him of? And what would he say about his poverty, about death, about pain? How would he compare his own happiness to that of a Great King? It's better to think that there's no comparison between them. Because where there is worry, grief, fears and desires not satisfied, aversions of things which you can't be avoided, envy and jealousy, how can a road to happiness be found there?

When the young man asked, if when a Cynic is sick, and a friend asks him to come to his house and be taken care of in his sickness, should the Cynic accept the invitation, he replied: And where will you find, I ask, a Cynic's friend? Because the man who invites him should be such a cynic that he's worthy of being called a Cynic's friend. He should be a partner in the Cynic's life, and a worthy minister, if he intends to be considered worthy of a Cynic's friendship. Do you think that, if a man comes to a Cynic and salutes him, he's the Cynic's friend, and that the Cynic will think he's worthy to enter a Cynic's house?

A young man once said, "should marriage and the procreation of children be the primary duty of a Cynic?" If you gave me a community of wise men, perhaps no man would apply themselves to this practice. However, if we suppose that a man does, nothing would prevent him from marrying and having children; because his wife would be like himself, and his father-in-law another like himself, and his children will be brought up like himself. But in the present state of things which is like that of an army placed in order for battle, isn't it better that the Cynic should without any distraction be focused on the administration of God only, and be able to go about among men, not tied down to the common duties of mankind, or entangled in the ordinary relations of life, which if he neglects, he wouldn't be able to maintain the character of an honourable and good man? And if he accommodates them he will lose the character of the messenger of God. Because, consider he has a duty to do something for his father-in-law, something to the other family members of his wife, and something for his wife also. He's also required to look after the sickness of his own family, and providing them support. He must provide heating and water for the child so the child can be washed, a bed, a cup: and increase the furniture of the house. This is not to mention his other occupations and distractions. Where would that king be, he who devotes himself to the public interest.

The people's guardian, so full of care. Whose duty it is to look after others, the married and those who have children; to see who uses their wife well, and who abuses her; who argues; what family looks like when it is well managed, and what it shouldn't be like? He's like a doctor, he says to someone, "you have a fever," to another, "you have a headache": he says to others, "Abstain from food"; or "Eat." How can he have time for all of this if he is tied to the duties of the common life? Consider how this would be bringing the Cynic down, how we would take his royalty from him. "Yes, but Crates had a wife." You are speaking of a circumstance which arose from love and of a woman who was another Crates. But we are talking about ordinary marriages and those which aren't free from distractions, and we don't find marriage in this state of the world a thing which is especially suited to the Cynic.

The Cynic is the father of all men; the men are his sons, the women are his daughters: he carefully visits all of them, and he cares for all. Do you think that it's disrespect that he lectures those who he meets? He does it as a father, as a brother, and through the minister and father of all, God.

It is necessary for a man like this exercise? All that is required is that he shows by his body that his simple and frugal way of living in the open air doesn't injure the body. "See," he says, "I'm the proof of this, and my body is as well." This is what Diogenes used to do. He used to go out fresh-looking, and many people noticed his personal appearance. He shouldn't appear dirty, but his very roughness should be clean and attractive.

There should be as well, belonging to the Cynic much natural grace and sharpness; and if not, he's stupid, and nothing else; he must have these qualities ready to match all circumstances that might happen.

The Cynic's ruling faculty must be purer than the sun; and, if it isn't, he must be a cunning man with no principles, because while he's entangled in some vice he will accuse others. To kings and tyrants their guards give them the power of criticizing others, and make them able to punish those who do wrong although they are themselves bad; but to a Cynic instead of guards it is the conscience which gives this power. When he knows that he's cared for and worked hard for mankind, has slept pure, and sleep has made him purer, and that he thought whatever he has thought as a friend of God, as a minister, as a participator of the power of God, and that on all occasions he is ready to say lead me, God, to my destiny; and also, "If it pleases Gods, let it be"; why shouldn't he have the confidence to speak freely to his own brothers, to his children, in a word to the public? For this reason, he's not a troublemaker with others when he is overseeing human affairs, but he's looking after his own affairs. If that's not true, you could say also that a general is a nuisance, when he inspects his soldiers, examines them, watches them and punishes the disorderly. But if, while you have an unclean conscience you are poking your nose into the affairs of others"; what right do you have? Who are you? Are you the bull of the herd, or the queen of the bees? Show me how you acquired your supremacy, like they have from nature.

The Cynic should also have the power of endurance to seem insensitive to the common man and a stone: no man insults him, no man strikes him, no man offends him, but he gives his body so that any man can do whatever they want with it. He keeps in mind that the inferior must be overpowered by the superior in that in which he is inferior; and the body is inferior to many, the weaker to the stronger. He never then descends into such a contest in which he can be overpowered; but he immediately withdraws from things which belong to others, he doesn't claim things which are subservient. Where there is will and the use of appearances, there you will see how many eyes he has, and you will say, "most men are blind compared to him." Is his behavior ever rushed, his movement impulsive, does he fail to acquire his desire, does he turn to that which he wants to avoid, is his purpose ever unaccomplished, does he ever find fault, is he ever humiliated, is he ever envious? To these things he directs all his attention and energy; and to everything else he sleeps. All is peace; there is no robber who can take away his will, no tyrant. But what about his body? I say there is.

If you are deliberating about this. I urge you to defer the matter, and first consider your preparation for it. Remember what Hector said to Andromache, "Retire, go into the house: war is the work of men. But specifically, 'it's mine.'" So, he was conscious of his own credentials.

CHAPTER 77 – TO THOSE WHO READ AND DISCUSS FOR THE SAKE OF GOSSIP

First say to yourself, who do you want to be: then act accordingly. Those who follow specific exercises first determine what they want to be, then do what is necessary. If a man is a runner for recreation, there's a certain kind of diet, walking and other exercise required: but if a man is a runner in a stadium, all these things are different. And you will find this in the arts as well. If you're a carpenter, you will have to learn specific things: if you're a metal worker, again specific things. So, for everything we do, if we refer to no end, we will do it for no purpose; and if we refer it to the wrong end, we will miss the mark. In addition, there's a general end or purpose, and a particular purpose. First of all, we must act as a man. What is comprehended by this? We shouldn't be like a sheep, gentle, or mischievous like a wild beast. But the character of a man can be referenced to each person's mode of life and his will. The piano player acts as a piano player, the carpenter as a carpenter, the philosopher as a philosopher, the mathematician as a mathematician. When you say, "Come and hear me speak": first of all, be careful that you are not doing this without a purpose; then, if you have discovered that you are doing this with reference to a purpose, consider if it's the right purpose. Do you want to do good or be praised? "To me what's the value of praise from a crowd?" It has no value to a musician, so far as he's a musician. Do you want to be useful? Tell me, can a man do anything useful for others, if hasn't received something useful himself? No, because neither can a man do anything useful in the carpenter's art, unless he's a carpenter; or in the shoemaker's art, unless he's a shoemaker.

Do you want to know then if you have anything to offer? What are your opinions, philosopher? What is the thing which desire promises? The movement toward an object. What does aversion promise? Not to move in the direction of that which you wish to avoid. Well; do we fulfill these promises? Tell me the truth; because if you lie, I will tell you. Recently when your hearers did not give you applause, you went away humbled. And also, quite recently, when you were praised, you went and said to all, "What did you think of me?"

So, can you tell me that in desire and in aversion you are acting according to nature? Go away and try to persuade somebody else. Didn't you praise a certain person contrary to your opinion? And didn't you flatter a certain person who was the son of a senator? Would you like your own children to be like that too? "I hope not." Why then did you praise and flatter him? "He is an ingenuous youth and listens well to discourses." How is this? "He admires me." You have stated your proof. What do you think? Don't these very people secretly despise you? So, when there is a man who's conscious that he does no good and doesn't even think of it, finds a philosopher who says, "You have a great natural talent, and you have an honest and respectable disposition," what else do you think he says other than this, "This man is in need of me?" Or tell me what act that indicates, what kind of great mind has he shown? Observe your student; he's been in your company a long time; he's listened to your talks, he's heard you read; has he become more modest? Has he begun to reflect on himself? Can he detect his bad state? Has he removed self-conceit? Is he looking for a person to teach him? "Yes." A man who will teach him to live? No, you fool, but how to talk; because this is what he admires in you. Listen and hear what he says: "This man writes with perfect art, much better than Dion." However, this is another thing. Does he say, "This man is modest, faithful, free from disturbance?" and even if he did say it, I would ask him, "Since this man is faithful, tell me what this faithful man is." And if he couldn't tell me, I would add this, "First understand what you say, then speak."

You, then, who are in a dilemma and seeking applause, do you intend to be useful to others? "Today many more attended my talk." "Yes, many; maybe five hundred." "That is nothing; it could be a thousand." "Dion never had so many hearers." "How could he?" "And they understood what he said beautifully." "Fine speech can even move a stone." See, these are the words of a philosopher. This is the disposition of a man who will do good to others; here is a man who has listened to talks, who has read what is written about

Socrates. You appear to have been reading these incorrectly, because if you read them like you should, you wouldn't focus on applause, but you would have been looking at these words: "Anytus and Meletus are able to kill me, but they cannot harm me": and "I am always of such a disposition as to pay regard to nothing of my own except to the reason which on inquiry seems to me the best." Therefore, whoever heard Socrates say, "I know something and I teach"; but he used to send different people to different teachers. They used to come to him and ask to be introduced to philosophy by him; and he would take them and recommend them to whoever knew best.

Why should I hear you? Do you want to show me that you can put words together cleverly? You put them together, and what good will it do you? "Praise me." What do you mean by praise? "Say I'm admirable and wonderful." Well, If, praise belongs to whatever the philosophers call good, what do I have to praise in you? If it's good to speak well, teach me, and will praise you. "Can a man listen to these things without pleasure?" I hope not. Hear what Socrates says, "It wouldn't be right for a man of my age, to appear before you like a young man composing letters." "Like a young man," he says. Because in truth this small art is an elegant thing, to select words, and to put them together, and to come forward and gracefully read them or to speak, and while reading to say, "There are not many who can do this."

Does a philosopher invite people to hear him? As the sun draws men to it, or as food does, does not the philosopher also draw to him those who will receive benefit? What doctor would invite a man to be treated by him? However, I am now hearing that even doctors in Rome are inviting patients, but when I lived there, the doctors were invited. "I invite you to come and hear that things are in a bad state for you, and that you are taking care of everything except that which you should take care of, and that you are ignorant of the good and the bad and are unfortunate and unhappy." A fine kind of invitation: and yet if the words of the philosopher don't produce this effect on you, you die, and so does the speaker. Rufus used to say: "If you have time to praise me, I'm speaking with no purpose."

The philosopher's school, is a surgery: you shouldn't leave it with pleasure, but with pain. Because you're not in sound health when they enter. Someone has a dislocated shoulder, another has an abscess, a third has a headache. Would I sit there and speak about little thoughts and exclamations so you can praise me and go away, one with his shoulder in the same condition in which he entered, another with his abscess, and a third with his head still aching just as it was? Is this why men should leave home, their parents, their friends and property, so they can call you, "Wonderful?" when you are stating your exclamations. Did Socrates do this?

Isn't there a better style? To be able to show people the struggle in which they are engaged, and that they think so much more about other things, than what they really wish for. Because they want the things which lead to happiness, but they look for them in the wrong place. In order that this can be done, a thousand seats must be placed and men must be invited to listen, and you must take the podium in a fine robe or cloak and describe the death of Achilles. Stop, I ask you, not to spoil good words and good acts. Nothing can have more power than when the speaker shows to the hearers that he also has a need for them. But tell me who when he hears you reading is anxious about himself or reflects on himself? Or when he leaves says, "The philosopher struck me well: I shouldn't do these things anymore." But don't your hearers say to some people, "He spoke finely"; Is this listening to a philosopher?

CHAPTER 78 – WE SHOULDN'T BE MOVED BY A DESIRE FOR THINGS WHICH AREN'T IN OUR POWER

Don't let something in another which is contrary to nature appear evil to you: because you're not formed to be depressed with others or to be unhappy with others, but to be happy with them. If a man is unhappy, remember that his unhappiness is his own fault: because God made all men to be happy and free from worry. For this purpose, he's given to them some things which belong to them, and other things which are not: which are subject to hindrance, compulsion and deficiency. These things are not a man's own: but the things which are not subject to hindrance are his.

"But," you say, "I have parted from someone, and he's upset." Why did he consider as his own that which belongs to another? Why, when he looked at you, didn't he realise that you are mortal, that it's natural for you to part from him at some point? Therefore, he suffers the consequences of his own foolishness. Why does this bother you? Is it because you haven't thought of this as well? Like a fool, you've enjoyed all the things in which you took pleasure, as if you would always enjoy them: places, people and conversation; and now you sit and cry because you don't see the same people and don't live in the same place. You deserve to be like birds, which have the power of flying wherever, changing their nests, and crossing the seas without crying or regretting their former condition. "Yes, but this happens to them because they are irrational creatures." Was reason, then, given to us by God for the purpose of unhappiness and misery, so we can live our lives feeling unhappy and crying? Should no one ever live abroad and remain rooted like plants; and, if any of our friends go abroad, should we sit and cry; and, on the contrary, when they return, should we dance and clap our hands like children?

Shouldn't we now remember what we've heard from the philosophers? Didn't we listen to them as if they were jugglers instead: they tell us that this world is one city, and the substance out of which it has been formed is one, and that there must be a certain period, and that some things must give way to others, that some must be dissolved, and others take their place; some to remain in the same place, and others move; and that all things are full of friendship, first from God, and then of men who by nature are made to be of one family; and some must be with one another, and others must be separated, rejoicing with those who are with them, and not crying for those who are removed from them; and man in addition to having a noble character and having a dislike of all things which are not in the power of his will, also possesses this: not to be rooted or to be fixed to the earth, but to go at different times to different places, sometimes from the urgency of certain occasions, and at others merely for the sake of seeing.

This is how it was for Ulysses, who saw many men from different places, and learned their ways. And earlier than this, Hercules was fortunate enough to visit a populated city, seeing men's bad deeds and their good rules of law: removing and clearing the lawless, and introducing in its place good rules of law. And yet how many friends do you think he gained while travelling? He also got married, when it seemed like the right time, and had children, and left them without crying or regretting leaving them as orphans; because he knew that no man is an orphan; because it's our father God, who takes care of all men, always and continuously. To Hercules, this wasn't just a concept, he thought that God was his own father, and he called him as such, and looked to him when he was doing anything. Therefore, he was able to live happily in all places.

It's not possible for happiness to exist if there is a desire for what is not present to come. That which is happy must have all its desires met, must resemble a person who is filled with food, and must not be thirsty or hungry. "But Ulysses felt strong desire for his wife and cried as he sat on a rock." If Ulysses really cried, what else was he than an unhappy man? And what good man is unhappy? In truth, the world must be badly administered if God doesn't allow people to be happy like himself. But these things are not right to think of: and if Ulysses did cry, he wasn't a good man. Because who is good if he doesn't know who he is? And who knows what he is, if he forgets that things which have been made are perishable, and

236

that it's not possible for one human being to be with another always? To desire, things which are impossible is to have a mindless character and is foolish: this is what strangers to God do, they fight against God in the only way they can, through their opinions.

"But my mother cries when she doesn't see me." Why hasn't she learned these principles? I don't say this, like you shouldn't take care to avoid her tears, but I say that people shouldn't desire what is not their own. The sorrow of another is another's sorrow: but my sorrow is my own. I, then, will stop my own sorrow in every way, because it's in my power: and the sorrow of another I will endeavor to stop as much as I can; but I won't attempt to do it in every way; because if I do, I would be fighting against God, I would be opposing and placing myself against him in the administration of the universe; and the penalty for this fighting against God and of this disobedience not only will the children of my children pay, but so will I, through the day and night, frightened by dreams, disturbed by every piece of news, and having my tranquility depend on the words of others.

Some people have arrived from Rome. "I only hope that there's no harm." But what harm can happen to you, when you are not there? Someone has come from Hellas: "I hope there's no harm." To act like this, means there is misfortune for you everywhere. Isn't it enough for you to be unfortunate where you are, do you have to be so even beyond sea, and due to the report of letters? Is this the way in which your affairs can be in a state of security? "suppose my friends have died in places that are far away from me." What have they suffered from other than that which is the condition of mortals? How do you desire to live to an old age, and at the same time not to see the death of any person who you love? Don't you know that in the course of a long time many and various kinds of things must happen; that a fever could overpower someone, a robber another, and a third a tyrant? This is the condition of things around us, the world consists of: cold and heat, and unsuitable ways of living, journeys by land, voyages by sea, winds, and various circumstances which surround us, which can destroy one man, banish another, throw one into the embassy and another into an army. Go on, sit down worried about all of these things, crying, unhappy, unfortunate, dependent on another for happiness.

Is this what you heard when you were with the philosophers? Did you learn this? Don't you know that human life is warfare? That one man must keep watch, another must act as a spy, and a third must fight? It's not possible that everything can be in one place, and it's not better for it to be so. But you, neglecting to do the commands of the general, complain when anything harder than usual is imposed on you, and you don't observe what you make the army become as far as it is in your power; that if all men imitate you, no man would dig the trench, no man would build the wall, or keep watch, or expose himself to danger. All of them would appear to be useless for the purposes of an army.

If you went as a sailor, and were ordered to climb the mast, you would refuse; if to run to the head of the ship, you would refuse; so, what master of a ship would put up with you? Wouldn't he have thrown you overboard as a useless person, as a bad example to the other sailors?

Every man's life is a kind of warfare, and it is long and diversified. You must observe the duty of a soldier and do everything at the command of the general; and if it's possible, anticipating what his wishes are.

You are in the great office of command, but you are always acting like a politician. Don't you know that a man like this must give little attention to the affairs of his household, and is away from home, either as a governor, being governed, serving in war or acting as a judge? So, are you telling me that you wish, like a plant, to be fixed to the same places and to be rooted? "Yes, because it's comfortable." Who says it isn't? But soup is pleasant, and a pretty woman is pleasant. And what else do those who value pleasure say? Don't you see what type of men do this? That it is the language of Epicureans. While you're doing what they do and holding their opinions, can you tell us the words of Zeno and Socrates? Can't you throw away, as far as you can, the things which belong to others with which you decorate yourself, although they don't suit you at all? Because what else should anyone desire than to sleep without disturbance and free from compulsion. But these people, when they have woken in the morning to wash their face, write and read what they choose, and then talk about some insignificant matter being praised by their friends, then they go for a walk, and after having walked a little they bathe, and then eat and sleep. Sleeping excessively seems to be the fashion of these men.

What's your way of passing time? You, who admire the truth of Socrates and Diogenes. What do you want to do in Athens? The same, or something else? Why do you call yourself a Stoic? Those who falsely call themselves Roman citizens, are severely punished; and should those, who falsely claim to be a Stoic, such a great and respected name, get off unpunished? Perhaps the divine law, which is strong and inevitable, allocates the severest punishments for those who commit the greatest crimes? What does this law say? "Let a man who pretends to be things which he is not be a conceited man: let a man who disobeys the divine administration be dishonorable; let him suffer grief, let him be envious; and in other words, let him be unhappy and cry."

"Should I pay attention to these people? Go to their doors?" If this was required for the sake of the country, or for mankind, why wouldn't you go? You aren't ashamed to go to a shoemaker, when you need shoes, or to the farmer, when you want lettuces; so, are you ashamed to go to the rich when you want something? "Yes, because I have no admiration for a shoemaker." And I don't want to flatter the rich. "Why then, would I go?" Remember that you go to the shoemaker, to the seller of vegetables, who have no power in anything great. You go to buy lettuces: they cost a fortune, but there is no talent to make them. So, is it worth going to the rich man's door? He may have valuable things to talk about, but you must also kiss his hand and flatter him with praise. Forget that, it's not worth it: it's not profitable to me, to the state or to my friends, to do that.

Don't you know that a good man does nothing for the sake of appearances, but for the sake of doing the right thing? "What advantage does this bring to the man who has done right?" "Is there a reward?" Do you seek a greater reward than doing what is good? At Olympia people wish to be crowned at the games but it seems insignificant and worthless to be good and happy?

It's your duty to undertake the work of a man, do you still want a nurse and a mum to run to, and foolish women around you who cry and make you effeminate? Will you stop being a foolish child? Don't you know that a man who acts like a child, the older he is, the more ridiculous it is?

In Athens didn't you visit anyone? "Of course, I visited any man that I wanted to." So here as well you should be ready to see anyone you want to: but only visit if you go without mean intentions, desire or with aversion, and your affairs are well managed. But this doesn't depend on going or not, but it depends on what's within, it's basis is found in your opinions. When you have learned not to value things which are external, and not dependent on the will, and to consider that none of them are your own, but that these things are yours: to exercise judgment well, to form opinions, to move toward an object, to desire, to turn away from flattery and meanness.

Why do you long for the places to which you are accustomed to? Wait for little while and you will find new places familiar: but if you have a dishonorable nature, when you leave, again you will cry.

"How can I be more affectionate?" By having a noble disposition, and by being happy. Because it's not reasonable to be mean-spirited, or to put yourself down, or depend on another for happiness, or even to blame God or other men. I encourage you, become an affectionate person by observing these rules. But if through this affection, you are going to be a slave to another, there's no profit in it for you.

What prevents you from loving a person subject to mortality, and may leave you one day? Didn't Socrates love his children? He did; but he was a free man, and remembered that he must first be a friend to God. For this reason, he dishonored nothing which was opposed to being a good man. But we are fully equipped with every excuse for being dishonorable, some blame a child, some a mother, and others: their friends. But it's not fit for us to be unhappy due to any person, but to be happy with God who has made us to be like this.

Didn't Diogenes love? He was a lover of all mankind and in general he willingly undertook work and bodily suffering. He did love mankind, but how? He became a minister of God, at the same time caring for men, and being also subject to God. For this reason, the whole earth was his country, and in no particular place when he was taken prisoner did he regret. He even became familiar with pirates and tried to improve them. This is the freedom he acquired. For this reason, he used to say, "Ever since I have been made free, I haven't been a slave." How did Antisthenes make him free? This is what he says: "Antisthenes taught me what is my own, and what isn't; possessions are not my own, friends, or reputation, or familiar places; all these belong to others." What then is your own? "The use of appearances. This has been shown to me, that I possess it free from hindrance, and from compulsion, no person can put an obstacle in my way, no person can force me to use appearances other than how I wish." Who then, has any power over me? Philip, Alexander or the Great King? How would they have this power? Because if a man is going to be overpowered by a man, he must have long before be overpowered by external things. If, then, pleasure is not able to subdue a man, or pain, or fame, or wealth, but he is able, when he chooses, to dispose of his body in a moment's notice and depart from life, whose slave can he be? But if he dwelt with pleasure in Athens, and was overpowered by this manner of life, his affairs would have been at every man's command; the stronger would have had the power of making him sad. How do you think Diogenes would have flattered the pirates so they would sell him to some Athenian, that after some time he would see the beautiful Piraeus, the Long Walls and the Acropolis? In what condition would see him? As a captive and as a slave? "Not at all: I would see him as a free man." Tell me, how would you be free? Some person has caught you, and takes you away from your home and says, "You're my slave, because it's in my power to hinder you from living as you want, it's in my power to treat you gently, and to humble you: whenever I choose, but on the contrary, you're cheerful and happily go to Athens." What would you say to the man who treats you as a slave? What methods do you have of finding someone who will rescue you from slavery? Or maybe you can't even look him in the face, without pleading to be set free? You go gladly to prison, in a rush, arriving before those who take you there.

I'm asking you, are you unwilling to live in Rome and desire to live in Hellas? When the time comes for you to die, will you also moan and cry, because you won't see Athens again? Have you gone abroad for this? Was this the reason you've gone to find some person from who you might receive benefit? What benefit? That you are able to solve hypothetical arguments? Is this the reason you leave your brother, country, friends, and your family, so you might return after you had learned these things? Didn't you go abroad to obtain constancy of mind, freedom from worry, to be secure from harm, never to complain about any person, accuse no one, and so you may maintain your relative position without being impeded? But no, you've gone for hypothetical arguments: if you like, take a place alongside the physics. What harm has philosophy done to you? How has Chrysippus injured you, perhaps you could prove by your acts that his work is useless? Wasn't the evil which was in you enough, the evil which was the cause of your pain and crying before you went abroad? Have you added more to the list? And if on your journey you gain more friends, you'll have more causes for crying; and the if start to have a strong affection for another country. Why, then, do you live to surround yourself with sorrows upon sorrows which cause your unhappiness? I ask you, do you call this affection? What affection! If it's a good thing, it causes no evil: if it's bad, I have nothing to do with it. I am formed by nature for my own good: I am not formed for my own evil.

What's the discipline for this purpose? First of all, the highest and the principal, and that which stands as it were at the entrance, is this; when you are delighted with anything, be delighted but be aware that it can be taken away. Treat it like a pot, or glass cup, that, when it has been broken, you can remember what it was and are not troubled. In the same way: if you kiss your own child before they leave and don't have awareness the potential for not seeing him or her again; check this tendency like those who stand behind men in their triumphs and remind them that they are mortal. Do you remind yourself that those who you love are mortal, and that what you love is not your own: it has been given to you for the present, not that it won't be taken from you, and neither has it been given to you forever? It is given like a an orange or a bunch of grapes at the appointed season of the year. But if you hope for these things in winter, you're a fool. So, if you wish for your son or friend when it's not possible, you must know that you are wishing for a orange in winter. Because just like there are no oranges in winter, every event which happens in universe can be taken away according to its nature. And when you are delighted with something, hold in your mind the opposite appearance. What harm is it while you are kissing your child to say internally, "Tomorrow you might die"; and when saying goodbye to a friend, "Tomorrow you will go away and I might never see you again"? "But these are words." And some prayers are also bad; but because they're useful, I don't care about that; let them be useful. Cowardice is a word of bad, and meanness of spirit, and sorrow, and grief and shamelessness. These words are of bad: and yet we shouldn't hesitate to say them in order to protect ourselves against these things. Are you telling me that a name which is significant to any natural thing is evil? Are the falling leaves bad, and for raisins to be made from grapes? Because all of these things are changes from a former state into other states; not a destruction, but a certain fixed path and administration. The same is going away from home, this is a small change, and death, a greater change, not from the state which it now is to that which it is not, but to that which it is not now. "Should I no longer exist then?" You will not exist, but you'll be something else, of which the world has a need for: because you also came into existence not when you chose, but when the world required you.

Therefore the wise and good man, remembering who he is and where he came from, and by who he was produced, is attentive only to this, how he may fill his place with due regularity and obediently to God. "Do you still wish me to exist? I will continue to exist as free, as noble in nature, as you wish for me to exist: because you have made me free from hindrance in that which is my own. But if you have no further need of me? I'll thank you; as so far I have remained for your sake, and for the sake of no one else, and now in obedience to you I'll depart." "How do you depart?" Again, I say, as you please, as free, as your servant, as one who has known your commands and your prohibitions. And so long as I stay in your service, who do you want me to be? A prince or a private man, a senator or a common person, a soldier or a general, a teacher or a master of a family? Whatever place and position you assign to me, as Socrates says, "I will die ten thousand times rather than desert my post." And where to you want me to be? In Rome or Athens? If you send me to a place where there are no means for men to live according to nature, I won't depart in disobedience to you, but as if you were giving me the signal to retreat: I won't leave you, my intention is to perceive that you have no need for me there. But if I find the means to live according to nature, I won't seek another place than that which I'm in, or other men than those who I am among.

Let these thoughts be in mind night and day: these you should write, these you should read: these you should talk to yourself, and to other people. Ask a man, "can you help me for this purpose?" And, go to another and to another. Then if anything that is said is contrary to your wish, this reflection first will immediately relieve you, that it's not unexpected. Because it's a great thing in all cases to say, "I knew that I had a son who is mortal." Because you will also say, "I knew that I'm mortal, I knew that I may leave my home, I knew that I may be ejected from it, I knew that I may be led to prison." Then if you turn around, and look at yourself, and seek the place from which comes that which has happened, you will recollect that it comes from the place of things which are out of the power of the will, and of things which are not your own. "What is it to me then?" Then, you will ask, and this is the main thing: "And who is it that sent it?" The leader, or the general, the state, the law of the state. Give it me then, because I must always obey the law in everything. Then, when the appearance brings pain to you, because it's not in your power to prevent this, fight against it with reason, conquer it: don't allow it to gain strength or to lead you to the consequences by raising images such as it pleases. If you're Gyara, don't imagine living in Rome, and how many pleasures there are waiting for any man who lives there: but fix your mind on this matter, how a man who lives in Gyara should live in Gyara like a man of courage. And if you are in Rome, don't imagine what the life in Athens is like, but think only of the life in Rome.

Then in the place of all other pleasures substitute this, being conscious that you are obeying God, not only in word but in-deed, you are performing the acts of a wise and good man. Because what a thing it is for a man to be able to say to himself, "They are discussing what I am doing in the schools; they are sitting there and talking about my virtues, inquiring about me and praising me; and this is what God wanted for me. That I receive from myself a confirmation, that I know if God has a soldier such as he should have, a citizen such as he should have, and that He has chosen me from the rest of mankind as a witness of the things which are independent of the will: 'Can you see you fear without reason, that you foolishly desire what you desire: don't seek good in external things; seek it in yourselves: if you don't, you won't find it.' For this purpose, God leads me at one time here, and at another time there, shows me poor men, without authority, and sick; sends me to Gyara, leads me into prison, not because He hates me, far from him to do such a thing, because who hates the best of his servants? Or because He doesn't care for me, because He doesn't neglect even the smallest things;' but He does this for the purpose of exercising me and making use of me as a witness to others. Being appointed to such a service, do I still care about the place which I'm in, or who I'm with, or what men say about me? Don't I entirely direct my thoughts to God, to His instructions and commands?"

Having these things always in mind, and exercising them by yourself, and keeping them ready, you'll never be in need of someone to comfort you and strengthen you. Because it's not shameful to have nothing to eat, but it is not to have reason sufficient for keeping away fear and sorrow. But if you gain freedom from sorrow and fear, would there be any tyrant for you? Or would any appointment to the offices at court cause you pain? Or would those who become named to certain functions by God, cause you pain? Don't make a proud display of it, or boast of it; but show it by your acts; and if no man perceives it, be satisfied that you yourself are in a happy and healthy state.

CHAPTER 79 – TO THOSE WHO FALL OFF FROM THEIR PURPOSE

Think of the things which you have mastered and those which you haven't; and how you feel happy when you recall to your memory the ones which are secured and have a pain over the ones which you haven't secured; and if it's possible, recover the things in which you have failed. Because we shouldn't shrink when we are engaged in the greatest combat, but we must even take blows. Because the combat before us is not in wrestling, in which both the successful and the unsuccessful can both receive merit, but the combat discussed is for good fortune and happiness. So, even if temporarily we have withdrawn from the contest in this sense, no man can stop us from renewing the combat again, and we aren't bound to wait for another four years for the Olympic games to come again; but as soon as you have recovered and restored yourself, and employ the same zeal, you can renew the combat again; and if again you leave it, you can again renew it; and if you finally you gain the victory, you are like the man who has never renounced the combat. However, don't, through habit of doing the same thing, begin to do it with pleasure and forget it's seriousness, because this is what bad athletes do, after being conquered, they run away.

"The sight of a beautiful young woman distracts me. Well, haven't I been overpowered before? And when you were overpowered by the young woman, didn't you come away unharmed? Why, then, do you talk about what you did before? You should, I think, remembering what you did, abstain from the same faults. In the case of your faults, what is the pain, what is the punishment; because when have you previously been accustomed to stop yourself doing evil acts? Suffering then, of the character who is trying to correct the faults, is useful to us, whether we choose it or not.

CHAPTER 80 – TO THOSE WHO FEAR TO BE IN NEED

What fugitive ever died of hunger? But you are afraid that you will lack necessary things, and can't sleep because of this. Fool, are you that blind, and don't see the road which the want of necessary things leads to? "Well, where does it lead?" To the same place to which a fever leads, or a stone that falls on you, to death. Haven't you often said this yourself to your companions? Haven't you read much on this subject, and written much about it? And how often have you boasted that you didn't fear death?

"Yes: but my wife and children will also suffer from hunger." Well then, does their hunger lead to any other place? Isn't it the same destination for them as well? Don't you choose, then, to look at death full of boldness against every want and deficiency, to that place to which both the richest and those who have held the highest offices, and kings themselves and tyrants must go to? What beggar did you ever see who wasn't an old man, and even in extreme old age? Chilled by the cold day and night, and lying on the ground, eating only what is absolutely necessary they seem to be immortal. Can't you write? Can't you teach children? Can't you be a watchman at another person's door? "But it's shameful to take a job like that." First learn what things are shameful, and then tell us that you are a philosopher: but at present don't, even if any other man calls you a philosopher, allow it.

Are the acts of others shameful to you, those of which you are not the cause, that which has come to you by accident, like a headache, like a fever? If your parents were poor, and left their property to others, and if while they live, they didn't help you at all, is that shameful to you? Is this what you've learned from the philosophers? Didn't you ever hear that the thing which is shameful should be blamed, and that which is blamable is worthy of blame? Who do you blame for an act which is not his own, which he didn't do himself? Did you make your father like he is, or is it in your power to improve him? Is this power given to you? Well then, should you wish for things which aren't given to you, or to be ashamed if you don't obtain them? And have you also been accustomed while you were studying philosophy to look to others and to hope for nothing from yourself? Cry then and moan and eat with fear that you might not have any food tomorrow. So live, and continue to live, you who have approached philosophy and have disgraced its theories as far as you can by showing them to be useless and unprofitable to those who learn them; you who have never sought constancy, freedom from distress, and from passion: you who have not sought any true teacher for the sake of this, but many for the sake of hypothetical arguments; you who have never thoroughly examined any of these appearances by yourself, "Am I able to bear, or am I not able to bear? What remains for me to do?" But as if all your affairs were well and secure, you have been resting on the third topic, that of things being unchanged, in order that you may possess unchanged - what? cowardice, mean spirit, the admiration of the rich, desire without attaining any end, and avoidance which fails? About security in these things you have been anxious.

Shouldn't you have gained something in addition from reason and, then, to have protected this securely? And who did you ever see building a fortress and not encircling it with a wall? And what doorkeeper is placed with no door to watch? But you practice in order to be able to prove what? You practice so you are not tossed about like a ship at sea by hypothetical arguments, and tossed about from what? Show me first what you hold, what you measure, or what you weigh; and show me the scales; and how long will you go on measuring? Shouldn't you demonstrate those things which make men happy, which make things go on for them in the way they wish, and why we shouldn't blame no man, accuse no man, and we should yield to the administration of the universe? Show me these. "See, I show them: I will resolve hypothetical arguments for you." This is the measure, fool; but it is not the thing being measured. Therefore, you are now paying the penalty for what you neglected, philosophy: you tremble, you lie awake, you advise people; and if your deliberations are not likely to please all, you think that you have deliberated incorrectly. Then you fear hunger: but it's not hunger that you fear, you're afraid that you won't have a cook, that you will not have another person to purchase ornaments for the table, a third person to take off your shoes, a fourth to dress you, and others to massage you. You're afraid of this, that you might not be able to lead the life of a sick man. So, learn the life of those who are in good health, how labourers, how those live who are genuine philosophers; how Socrates lived, who had a wife and children; and how Diogenes lived. If you choose to have these things, you will have them everywhere, and you will live in full confidence. Confiding in what? In that alone in which a man can confide, in that which is secure, in that which is not subject to hindrance, in that which cannot be taken away, that is, in your own will. And why have you made yourself so useless and good for nothing that no man will choose to invite you into his house, no man would care for you? Because if a utensil was useful and was found abroad, every man who found it would take it and think that they've gained something; but no man will take you, and every man will consider you a loss. Why do you choose to live any longer, when you are what you are?

Does any good man fear that he will fail to have food? It doesn't even happen to the blind, why would it happen to a good man? Does God neglect the things that He has established, His ministers, His witnesses, who alone He employs as examples to the uninstructed, both that He exists, and administers the whole, and does not neglect human affairs, and that to a good man there is no evil either when he is living or when he is dead? So, what does it mean when He doesn't supply him with food? What else does He do, than like a good general, He has given me the signal to retreat? I obey, I follow, agreeing with the words of the Commander, praising, His acts: because I came when it pleased Him, and I will leave when it pleases Him; and while I lived, it was my duty to praise God both by myself, and to each person individually. He doesn't supply me with many things, or with abundance, He doesn't want me to live luxuriously; because neither did He supply Hercules who was his own son; and Hercules obeyed orders, worked hard, and was exercised. And when Ulysses was shipwrecked, did the need of necessary things humiliate him, did it break his spirit? How did he go to the virgins to ask for necessities, to beg for that which is considered most shameful? As a lion bred in the mountains trusting in his strength. Relying on what? Not on reputation, or on wealth, or on the power of the magistrate, but on his own strength, that is, on his opinions about the things which are in our power and those which are not. Because these are the only things which make men free, which make them escape from worry, which raise the head of those who are depressed, which make them look with steady eyes on the rich and on tyrants. And this was the gift given to the philosopher. But you will not take this seriously, but instead you worry about your garments and silver pots. Unhappy man, haven't you wasted your time until now?

"What if I get sick?" You'll be sick in a way as you should to be. "Who will take care of me?" God; and your friends. "I'll have to lie down on a hard bed." But you will lie down like a man. "I won't have a convenient room." You will be sick in an inconvenient room. "Who will provide for me the necessary food?" Those who provide for others also. "And what will be the end of the sickness? Anything other than death?" Do you then consider that death is the main evil to man or that the main indicator of a weak spirit and of cowardice is not death, but rather the fear of death? Against this fear I advise you to exercise yourself: let all your reasoning, your exercises, and reading work on this; and you will know that only real men are made free.

CHAPTER 81 – ABOUT FREEDOM

A man is free if he lives as he wants to; when he is not subject to compulsion, hindrance, or force; when his movements to action are not impeded, and whose desires attain their purpose, without falling into that which he wants to avoid. Who, chooses to live in error? No man. Who chooses to live deceived, liable to mistakes, unfair, unrestrained, discontented, and mean? No man. So, no bad man lives as he wants to; neither is he, then, free. And who chooses to live in sorrow, fear, envy, pity, desiring and failing in his desires, attempting to avoid something and falling into it? No one. So, do we find any bad men free from sorrow, free from fear, who doesn't fall into that which he wants to avoid, and doesn't obtain that which he wants? Not one; so, then we don't find any bad man free.

Let's say your ancestors were as free as possible, what's that to you? What if they were fearless, and you a coward; if they had the power of self-restraint, and you are not able to exercise it.

Now consider in the case of animals, how we use the notion of liberty. Men tame lions, and feed them, who could say that this lion is free? Isn't it true that the more he lives in comfort, the more he's in a slavish condition? and who if he had perception and reason would want to be like the lion in this case?

Take birds for example, once they are caught and are kept in a cage, how much do they suffer when they attempt to escape? Some of them die from hunger rather than submit to such a kind of life. They desire their natural freedom so much, and to be independent and free from hindrance. What harm is there in this for you? "What do you say? I'm formed by nature to go where I choose, to live in the open air, to sing when I choose, 'what harm is it to you?' For this reason, we say that animals are only free if they aren't captured, but, as soon as they are caught, their only escape from captivity is by death. So Diogenes says that there is one way to freedom, and that is to die content: and he writes to the Persian king, "You can't enslave the state any more than you can enslave fishes." "How is that? Can't I catch them?" "If you catch them," says Diogenes, "they will immediately leave you, as fishes do; because if you catch a fish, it dies; and if these men that are caught they'll die, and what use will they be to you?" These are the words of a free man who had carefully examined this, and naturally discovered it. But if you look for it in a different place from where it is, you'll never find it.

A slave wishes to be set free immediately. Why? Because he imagines that up until now, not having obtained this, he's hindered and unfortunate. "If I were to be set free, immediately I'll be happy, I can speak to everyone as an equal and, like them, I go where I choose." Then he's set free; and having no place where he can eat, he looks for some man to flatter, someone with will provide for him: then he works with his body and endures the most painful work; and if find this, he falls into a slavery much worse than his former slavery; or even if he becomes rich, being a man without any knowledge of what is good, he falls in love with some girl, and in his happiness cries and desires to be a slave again. He says, "What evil did I really suffer in my state of slavery? I was clothed, supplied with shoes, fed, and looked after in sickness; and I only did a few simple services. But now look what things I suffer, being a slave of many instead of one. But however," he says, "if I can acquire money, then I'll live prosperously and happily." First, in order to acquire these things, he submits to that which he is worthy of; then, when he has acquired them, it is again all the same. Then he says, "if I'm engaged in military service, I'll be free from all evil." He obtains military service. He suffers as much as a flogged slave, and nevertheless he asks for a second service and a third. After this, when he has put the finishing touch on his career and is become a senator, then he becomes a slave by entering into the assembly, then he serves the finer and most splendid slavery - not to be a fool, but to learn what Socrates taught: the nature of each thing that exists, and that a man should not recklessly adapt preconceptions to the things which are. Because this is the cause of all men's evils, not being able to adapt their general preconceptions to things. But we have different opinions. One man thinks that he's sick: however, this is not so, the fact is, he doesn't adapt his preconceptions correctly. Another man thinks that he's poor; but all of this is one and only one thing, not knowing how to adapt preconceptions. Because who hasn't got preconceptions of what's bad, what's hurtful, what should be avoided, and what should be guarded against? One preconception is not unacceptable to another, only where it comes to the matter of adaptation. What is evil, if it can be both hurtful, and something which can be avoided? He answers, "Not to be Caesar's friend." He's far from the mark, he has missed the adaptation, he's embarrassed, he seeks things which aren't at all relevant to the matter; because when he's succeeded in being Caesar's friend, he's failed in finding what was looking for.

What is that every man seeks? To live secure, to be happy, to do whatever he wants, not to be hindered, or compelled into action. When he becomes the friend of Caesar, is he free from hindrance? Free from compulsion, is he tranquil, is he happy? Who should be ask? What more trustworthy witness do we have than a man who became Caesar's friend? Tell us when did you sleep more quietly, now or before you became Caesar's friend? Immediately you hear the answer, "Stop, don't mock me: you know not what miseries I've suffered, sleep doesn't come to me, Ceasar is already awake." So when did you enjoy more pleasure, now or before? Hear what he says about this also. He says that if he's not invited somewhere, he feels pain: and if he is invited, he acts like a slave with his master, all the while being anxious that he doesn't say or do anything foolish. And what do you think he's afraid of; more than being treated as a slave? Can he expect anything good? No, but such a great man, Caesar's friend, is afraid that he might lose his head. And when did you bathe free from trouble, and exercise more quietly? Which kind of life did you prefer? Your present or your former life? I can swear that no man is so stupid or so ignorant of truth not to cry over his misfortunes the closer his friendship to Caesar becomes.

Neither those who are called kings live as they choose, or the friends of kings, so, who can we call free? Seek, and you will find; because you have the aid from nature to discover the truth. But if you aren't able to discover it by yourself, listen to those who have made the inquiry. What do they say? Does freedom seem to be a good thing to you? "The greatest good." Is it possible, then, that he who obtains the greatest good can be unhappy? "No." So, when you see those who are unhappy, unfortunate, and crying, can you confidently declare that they are not free. "I can."

OK, so in addition, answer this question for me as well: Does freedom seem to you to be something great and valuable? "How couldn't it be?" Is it possible, then, for a man once obtaining anything, so great and valuable to be mean? "It's not possible." When, then, you see any man subject to another, or flattering him contrary to his own opinion, confidently affirm that this man is also not free. Do you think that freedom is a thing which is independent and self-governing? "Certainly." Whenever then this is in the power of another to hinder and compel, you can declare that this man is not free as well. And if you hear a man saying to himself, "I'm such a fool, look how much I suffer," call him a slave. And if you see him crying, complaining, and unhappy, call him a slave. But if he doesn't do this kind of thing, don't say he's free, first learn his opinions, whether they are subject to compulsion, or may produce hindrance; and if you find this to be the case, call him a slave. Treat him as if he's gone on holiday: like his true master is away from home: and soon he will return. "Who will return?" Whoever has in himself the power over anything which is desired by men, either to give it to him or to take it away? "Do we therefore have many masters?" We have: because we have circumstances as masters prior to our present masters; and there are many of these circumstances. Therefore, it must be out of necessity that those who have the power over any of these circumstances are our masters. Because no man fears Caesar himself, but he fears death, banishment, deprivation of his property, prison, and disgrace. And no man loves Caesar, unless Caesar is a person of great merit, but he loves wealth, and the office. When we love, and hate, and fear these things, it must be that those who have the power over them must be our masters. Therefore, we adore them like gods; because we think that what possesses the power of giving us the greatest advantages in life is divine. Then we wrongly assume that a person has the power of giving the greatest advantages; therefore, he is something divine. Because if we wrongly assume a certain person has the power of giving the greatest advantages, it is a necessary consequence that the conclusion from these premises must be false. What, then, is that which makes a man free from hindrance and makes him his own master? Because wealth doesn't do it, neither a position in the office, or royal power; but there is something else which must be discovered. What then is that which, when we write, makes us free from hindrance and unimpeded? "The knowledge of the art of writing." What, is it in playing the guitar? "The science of playing the guitar." Therefore, in life as well, it's the science of life. You have, then, heard in a general way: but examine this in the several parts as well. Is it possible that he who desires any of the things which depend on others can be free from hindrance? "No." Is it possible for him to be unimpeded? "No." Therefore, he can't be free. Consider then: whether we have nothing which is in our own power, or whether we have all things, or whether some things are in our power, and others in the power of others. "What do you mean?" When you want the body to be whole, is it in your power or not? "It's not in my power." When you want it to be healthy? " That's not in my power either." When you want to be handsome? "This isn't either." Life or death? "Not in my power." Your body, then, is another's, subject to every man who is stronger than you? "It is." What about your estate, is it in your power to have it when you want, and as long as you want? "No." And your clothes? "No." And your house? "No." And your horses? "Not one of these things." And if you hope for your children to live, or your wife, or your brother, or your friends, is it in your power? "No, this isn't in my power."

Do you have you anything which is in your own power, which depends on yourself only and cannot be taken from you? "I don't know." Look at this then, and examine. Is any man able to make you believe what you know to be false? "No." In this matter then, you are free from hindrance and obstruction. "Yes." Well; and can a man encourage you to desire or move toward that which you don't choose? "He can, because he might threaten me with death, so he would compel me to desire and move toward it." If, death doesn't bother you, would you still pay him any attention? "No." Is, then, the act of not caring about death your own? "It is." Isn't it then, your own act to desire to move toward something or not? "It's my own act." But to desire to move away from something, whose act is that? This is also your act. "So, if I attempt to walk, and another man tries to hinder me." What part does he hinder? Your desire to walk? "No: my body." Yes, as he would do with a stone. "Yes; but I can't walk because of that." And who said that walking is your own act and is free from hindrance? Because I said this only was free from hindrance, the desire to move: but where there is need of your body and its co-operation, you have heard many times that this is not your own. "OK." Who can compel you to desire what you don't wish for? "No one." And to propose, or intend, or in short to make use of the appearances which present themselves, can anyone compel you? "No: but he can hinder me from obtaining what I desire." If you desire anything which is your own, and one of the things which can't be hindered, how can he hinder you? "He can't." Who, then, told you that he who desires the things which belong to another is free from hindrance? "So, I shouldn't desire health?" Not at all, and nothing else which belongs to another: because what's not in your power to acquire or to keep when you please, is something which belongs to another. Keep, then, far from these type of things, not just what you can hold in your hands, but even in your desires. If you don't, you have surrendered yourself as a slave; you have subjected your neck, if you admire anything not your own power. "Isn't my hand my own?" It is a part of your own body; but it is by nature, subject to hindrance, compulsion, and the slave of everything which is stronger.

When you have prepared, and practiced this discipline, to distinguish that which belongs to another from that which is your own, the things which are subject to hindrance from those which are not, to consider the things which are free from hindrance to concern yourself, and those which are not free not to concern you, to keep your desire steadily fixed to the things which do concern you, and turn away from the things which don't; would you still fear any man? "No one." Because what would you be afraid of? About the things which are your own, in which consists the nature of good and evil? And who has power over these things? Who can take them away? Who can impede them? No man can, no more than he can impede God. But will you be afraid about your body and your possessions, about things which are not yours, about things which don't concern you? And what else have you been studying from the beginning than to distinguish between your own and not your own, the things which are in your power and not in your power, the things subject to hindrance and those which aren't? And why have you come to the philosophers? Was it to be unfortunate and unhappy? You have come to be without fear and disturbance. And what is grief to you? Because fear comes from what you expect, but grief from that which is present. What more will you desire? For things which are within the power of the will, as being good and present, you have a proper and regulated desire: but the things which are not in the power of the will you do not desire, and so you do not allow any place to that which is irrational, and impatient, and above measure.

When you are moving toward these things, what man can be formidable to you? Because what does a man have who is formidable to another, either when you see him or speak to him or, finally, are conversant with him? Nothing more than one horse has with respect to another, or one dog to another, or one bee to another. Things, indeed, are formidable to every man; and when any man is able to offer these things to another or to take them away, then he too becomes formidable.

I have never been hindered in my will, or compelled to that which I didn't will. And how is that possible? I have placed my movements toward action in obedience to God. If it's His will that I have fever? It's my will also. If it's His will that I should move toward something? It's my will also. If it's His will that I obtain something? It's my will also. If he doesn't will? I don't either. Who then, is still able to hinder me contrary to my own judgement, or to compel me? No more than he can hinder or compel God.

A traveler has heard that the road is occupied by robbers; he doesn't want to travel the road alone, so he waits for the companionship on the road either of an ambassador, or a public official, and when he travels with them he goes along the road safely. This is how the wise man acts.

There are many robbers, tyrants, storms, difficulties and losses of things which mean something to us. "Is there any place to take refuge? How can a man pass along without being attacked by robbers? What company should he wait for so he can pass in safety? Who should he attach himself to? To what person generally? To the rich man, to the man of high ranking? What use is that to me? A man like that once stripped of his wealth or rank moans and cries. What if the companion turns against me and becomes the robber, what should I do? I'll be 'a friend of Caesar': when I am Caesar's friend no man will do me wrong. Firstly, so I can become well-known, what things do I have to endure and suffer? How often and by how many people must I be robbed? If I become Caesar's friend, he's also mortal. And if Caesar due to any circumstance becomes my enemy, where is it best for me to hide? In the desert? But even there I could get a fever from the heat? What would be best then? Isn't it possible to find a safe companion, a faithful one, strong, and secure against all surprises?" Therefore, if a man considers and perceives that if he attaches himself to God, he will make all journeys in safety.

"How can you understand 'attaching yourself to God'?" In this sense, that whatever God wills, a man should also will; and whatever God doesn't will, a man shouldn't will. How, can this he done? In what other way than by examining the movements of God and his administration What has he given to me as my own and in my own power? What has he reserved for himself? The things he has given to me are in the power of the will: He has put them in my power free from impediment and hindrance. How was He able to make the body free from hindrance? And accordingly, He has subjected to the rest, possessions, household things, house, wife and children subject to impediment. Why, then, do I fight against God? Why do I want what he doesn't want for me? Why do I want to have what isn't granted to me? How should I direct my will? In the way in which it was given. He who has given it takes things away from me. Why do I resist? I know it's foolish to fight against one who is stronger, but I even more so, it would be unfair. How did I have things when I came into the world? My father gave them to me. And who gave them to him? And who made the sun? And who made the fruits on the earth? And the seasons? And who made the connection of men with one another?

Then after receiving everything from another and even yourself, are you angry and blame the Giver if he takes anything away from you? Who are you, and for what purpose did you come into the world? Didn't He bring you here, didn't He show you the light, didn't he give you perception and reason? Didn't He create you subject to death, and as one to live on the earth with a little flesh, and to observe His administration, and to join with Him in the spectacle and this festival for a short time? Will you not, then, as long as you have been permitted, after seeing the spectacle and the seriousness, when he allows you to be here, admire Him and thank Him for what you've seen and heard? "No; but I would still enjoy the feast." Leave like a grateful and modest man; make room for others: others must be born as well, as you were, and being born they must have a place, and houses and necessary things. And if the first don't leave, what happens? Why are you insatiable? Why aren't you content? "Yes, but I would have my children and my wife to stay for." What, are they yours? Don't they belong to the Giver? Won't you give up what belongs to Him? "Why, then, did He bring me into the world under these conditions," If the conditions don't suit you, leave! He doesn't need a spectator who isn't satisfied. He wants those to join in the festival, those who take part in the chorus, to create a grand applause. But those who don't take part, He will see absent from the great assembly and won't like it; because they don't behave as they should and take their place properly, but instead they cry, and find fault with God, fortune, their companions; not seeing what opportunity they had. And their own powers, which they received for the power of magnanimity, generosity and a manly spirit, and what we are now discussing, freedom. "For what purpose, have I received these things? To use them. "How long;" As long as He who gave them chooses. "What if I find other things necessary to me?" Don't attach yourself to them and they won't be necessary: Don't say to yourself that they're necessary, and then they are not necessary.

This you should study from the morning to evening, beginning, with the smallest things and those most liable to damage, with a pot, a cup. Then proceed to a dog, a horse, to a small estate of land: then to yourself, your body, the parts of your body, to your friends. Look all around and remove these things from you. Purge your opinions so that nothing of these things which are not your own sticks to you, that you become attached to nothing and no one, so that nothing gives you pain when you are separated from it; and say, while you are doing this daily exercise, that you aren't philosophizing, but you are practising freedom: because this is really freedom. Due to this freedom Diogenes said that he could no longer be enslaved by any man. For this reason, when he was taken prisoner, how did he behave to the pirates? Did he call any of them his master? Did he seek a master? When he was sold, how did he behave to the purchaser? Immediately he disputed with him. So, in every matter, it is absolutely necessary that he who has a skill must be superior to the man who doesn't possess it. So, whoever possesses the science of life, what else can he be than his own master? Who is the master of the ship? "The man who governs the helm."

Can any man do what is unfair without suffering for it. No, when anything is in a condition contrary to its nature it suffers. Is it a man's nature to bite, kick, put people in prison, to cut off heads? No; but to do good, to co-operate with others, to wish them well. At that time, then, he would be in bad condition, whether you choose to admit it or not, when he is acting foolishly.

Let's summarise the things which have been agreed on. The man who is not under restraint is free, and for who things are exactly in the state in which he wishes them to be; but he who can be restrained or compelled or hindered, or thrown into any circumstance against his will, is a slave. But who is free from restraint? He who desires nothing that belongs to others. And what are the things which belong to others? Those which are not in our power either to have or not have, or to have a certain kind or in a certain manner. Therefore, the body belongs to another, the parts of the body belong to another, possessions belongs to another. If, then, you are attached to any of these things as your own, you will pay the penalty which is appropriate for him to pay who desires that which belongs to another. This road leads to freedom, that is the only way of escaping from slavery, to be able to say at with your whole:

Lead me God, to my Destiny.
The way which you want me to go.

But what do you say? The tyrant calls you, for you to say something which don't want to. Would you say it or not? Answer me. "Let me think." Have you thought? When you were in school, what did you think about? Didn't you study the things which are good and bad, and the things which are neither? "I did." What was your opinion? "That fair and honourable acts were good; and that unfair and disgraceful acts were bad." Is life a good thing? "No." Is death a bad thing? "No." Is prison? "No." What did you think about mean and faithless words and betrayal of a friend and flattery of a tyrant? "That they are bad." Well then, you're not thinking, neither have you considered or deliberated. What is there to think about: is it whether it's right for me, when I have it in my power, to secure for myself the greatest of good things, and not to secure for myself the greatest evils? A fine thought indeed, and necessary, and one that demands a lot of deliberation. But such an inquiry is never made. If you really imagined that dishonourable things were bad and honourable things were good, and that all other things were neither good or bad, you would not even have to think about this, or come near it; but immediately you would have been able to distinguish by your predetermined understanding just as you use your vision for seeing. When do you think that black things are white, that heavy things are light, and do not comprehend the evidence given to you by the senses? So how can you now say that you are considering whether things which are neither good or bad should be avoided more than things which are bad?

Keep yourself strong and fit for the uses of life by being exercised in action. "And how does this relate to freedom?" Like this: whether you choose to be rich or not. "And how is this possible when you say, "I can't do this: it's not in my power." Why isn't it in your power? Did you tell me you're free "But Aprulla has hindered me." Tell the truth then fool, don't run away, or deny, or say someone else has granted your freedom, when we have so much evidence that you are a slave.

When a man is compelled by love to do something which opposes his opinion, and at the same time sees the better option, but doesn't have the strength to follow it, we might consider that he has a worthy excuse as he is being held by a violent divine power. But who could forgive you, you admire honours, you kiss the hands of other people, you are not even the slave of free men. Then you talk to me as if you are.

Someone might say, "are you free?" I pray to God to be free; but I'm not able to face my masters, I still value my body, I value the preservation of it although I don't possess it. But I can tell you who is a free man, so you can find a good example. Diogenes was free. How was he free? Not because he was born free, but because he freed himself, because he removed all forms of slavery, and it wasn't possible for any man to approach him, and no man possessed a way to enslave him. He had no attachments. If you took his property, he would rather let it go and it be yours than follow you for it: if you held his leg, he would have let his leg go; if you took his body, then he would let go; his friends and country, just the same. Because he knew where they came from, and from who, and on what conditions. His true parent, God, and his real country he would never let go of, and he wouldn't' yielded them to any man in obedience to them or to their orders, and no other man would have died for this more readily. He never used to question events in life, because he remembered that everything which is done comes from there and is done on behalf of that country and is commanded by him who administers it. Therefore, this is what Diogenes himself says and writes: "For this reason," he says, "Diogenes, it is in your power to speak with the King of the Persians and with Archidamus the king of the Lacedaemonians, however you want to." Why does he say that it's in his power? "Because he didn't consider the body to be his own, because he wanted nothing, because law was everything to him, and nothing else is." These were the things which allowed him to be free.

You might think that I'm showing you an example of a man who is a solitary person, who has no wife or children, or country, or friends, which draw him in various directions. Take Socrates then, and observe that he had a wife and children, but he didn't consider them as his own; he had a country, as long as it was fit for him to have one, and the same for friends, but he treated all of them without attachment. For this reason, he was the first to go out as a soldier, when it was necessary; and in war he exposed himself to danger most unsparingly, and when he was sent by the tyrants to take over Leon, he didn't deliberate about the matter, because he thought that would be a weak action, and he knew that if he must die, then that's what is destined for him. What difference would that make to him? Because he intended to preserve something else, not his body, but his faithfulness, and his honourable character. These are things which couldn't be attacked.

So, when he was obliged to speak in defence of his life, did he behave like a man who had children or a wife? No, he behaved like a man who had neither. And what did he do when he drank the poison, and when he had the power of escaping from prison, and when Crito said to him, "Escape for the sake of your children," what did Socrates say? Did he consider the power of escape as an unexpected gain? Not at all: he considered what was fit and proper; but the rest he didn't even look at or take into consideration. Because he didn't choose, he said, to save his body, but to save that which is increased and saved by doing what is fair, and is impaired and destroyed by doing what is unfair. Socrates wouldn't save his life by doing a bad act; he refused to obey the tyrants, he who spoke in such a manner about virtue and right behaviour. It isn't possible to save a man's life by bad acts, he was saved by dying, not by running away.

The good actor also preserves his character by stopping when he should stop, better than when he goes on acting beyond his time. What should all the children of Socrates do? "If," said Socrates, "I leave, wouldn't there be a man to take care of them?" But the usual philosophers would have defended themselves by saying, "My life should be saved because I will be useful to many men." But, if we made our escape by slipping through a small hole, how in that case would we have been useful to any man? Wouldn't the philosophers be a better example, and more useful to them by dying when they should, and how they should? Socrates is now dead, and is no less useful to men, and in fact, what is even more useful, is the remembrance of what he did and said when he was alive.

Think of these things, these opinions, these words: look at these as examples, if you want to be free, only desire things according to their worth. For the sake of that which is called "freedom," some hang themselves, others throw themselves down wells, and sometimes even whole cities have vanished: won't you for the sake of the true, unassailable and secure freedom give back to God when He demands the things which He has given? Wont you, as Plato says, study, not only to die, but to endure torture, exile, and, in a word, to give up everything which isn't your own? If you won't, you'll be a slave among slaves, even if you make a high rank in the city; and if you make your way into the Palace, you will still be a slave; and you will feel, that perhaps philosophers say words which are contrary to common opinion, but these words are not contrary to reason. Because you will know by experience that the words are true, and that there is no profit from the things which are valued and eagerly sought, by those who have obtained them; and by those who haven't. There is an imaginary act, that when these things come, all that is good will come with them; but, when they come, the bad feelings are the same, the restlessness, the desire for things which are not in the present; because freedom is acquired not by the possession of things which are desired, but by removing the desire. And you will find this is true, if you have worked for those things, you've transferred your labour for those things and nothing has changed; so, be vigilant for acquiring opinions which will make you free; pay the philosopher to teach you, instead of the rich old man: go to the philosopher: you won't disgrace yourself by being seen in the school; you won't leave empty or without profit, if you go to the philosopher as you should, and if you are unsure, try at least: a trial is not disgraceful.

CHAPTER 82 – ON FAMILIAR INTIMACY

This issue is highly important: don't be so close to anyone that you begin to act as they do. If you don't follow this rule, you will ruin yourself. But if the thought arises in your mind. "I'll seem rude to him, and he won't have good feelings towards me," remember that nothing is done without a cost. It's not possible for a man to change if he does the same acts that he used to do. Choose, then, which of these paths you will take, to be loved by those who formerly loved you, being the same as your former self; or, being superior, not to be loved the same as you were before. If this is better, go for it, and don't let other considerations draw you in a different direction. Because no man is able to make progress, when he is wavering between opposing ideas, so, if you prefer this, choose to focus on this only, to work on this only, give up everything else. But if you won't do this, your wavering will produce both of the following results: you won't improve as you should, or be loved as you formerly were. Because before, by desiring the things which were worth nothing, you pleased your friends. But you can't excel in both at the same time, and it's necessary that as far as you take one road, you will fall short in the other. You can't, when you no longer drink with those who you used to drink with, be agreeable to them as you were before. Choose, then, whether you will be a hard drinker and pleasant to your former associates or a sober man and disagreeable to them. You can't, when you no longer sing with those who you used to sing with, be equally loved by them. Choose, then, in this matter also which path you will take. Because if it's better to be modest and orderly than to be praised, give up the rest, renounce it, turn away from it, have nothing to do with men like that. But if this behavior doesn't please you, turn completely toward the bad: become an adulterer, and act accordingly, and you will get what you wish for. But characters which are so different can't be mingled: you can't act like both. If you intend to be like Thersites, you must have a hunchback and be bald: if Agamemnon, you must be tall and handsome, and love those who follow you.

CHAPTER 83 – WHAT WE SHOULD EXCHANGE

Keep this thought in mind, when you lose anything external, what do you acquire in place of it; and if it's worth more, never say, "I've lost something"; neither if you gained a horse in place of an donkey, or an donkey in place of a sheep, or a good action in place of money, or in place of useless conversation you gained tranquillity, or in place of vulgar speech you gained modesty. If you remember this, you'll always maintain your character as you should. It doesn't need much to have a true loss and overturn all, basically a small deviation from reason. For the captain of a ship to lose control, has to act in a different way that he does when he steers correctly: if he turns it a little toward the wind, it's lost; if he doesn't do this purposely, but has been neglecting his duty, the ship is lost. Something of the kind happens in this case also: if you day dream, everything you collected until now is gone. Therefore, watch for appearances of things, and watch over them; because that which you have to preserve is no small matter: it is modesty, faithfulness and constancy, freedom from the affects, a state of mind undisturbed, freedom from fear, tranquillity, in a word, "liberty." What will you sell these things for? Consider what's the value of the things which you'll obtain in exchange for these. "Won't I obtain anything for these things?" If you do, consider what you'll receive. "I possess decency, he possesses a place in office: he possesses a ranking, I possess modesty. I don't praise anyone when it is not deserved: I won't stand for what I shouldn't; because I'm free, and a friend of God, and so I obey Him willingly. I shouldn't claim anything else, neither my body or possessions, or in fact, anything. Because He doesn't allow me to claim them: because if He had, He would have made them good for me; but He hasn't, and for this reason I can't disobey his commands." Preserve that which is your own good in everything; and to every other thing, as it is permitted, and behave consistently with reason in respect to them, content with this only. If you don't, you'll be unfortunate, you will fall into bad things, you'll be hindered and impeded. These are the laws which have been sent from God; these are the orders. A man should be a messenger of these laws, and these laws he should obey: not the laws of Masurius and Cassius.

CHAPTER 84 – THOSE WHO WANT A TRANQUIL LIFE

Remember that not only the desire of power and riches subjects us to others, but even the desire of tranquillity, leisure, travelling and learning does. To speak plainly, whatever the external thing is, the value which we set on it places us in subjection to it. What, then, is the difference between desiring, to be a senator or not desiring to be one; what is the difference between desiring power or being content without it; what is the difference between saying, "I'm unhappy, I have nothing to do, but I have time to read my books"; or saying, "I'm happy, I have no time for reading"? Power is external and independent of the will, and so is a book. For what purpose do you choose to read? Tell me. Because if you only direct your purpose to being amused or learning something, you are fool and incapable of enduring hard work. But if you refer reading for its proper purpose, what else could there be than a tranquil and happy life? But if reading doesn't secure for you a happy and tranquil life, what's the use of it? But it does secure that," the man replies, "and for that reason I'm angry that I haven't gained it yet."

What is this tranquil and happy life? A tranquil and happy life contains nothing more than the continuity of freedom from obstacles. Now I'm asked to do something: I go, with the purpose of observing the actions I take, whilst acting with modesty, steadiness, without desire and aversion to things external; and then I can talk to men, so they say, how they've been moved; and this isn't done with any bad disposition, or so I can blame or ridicule something, but I turn to myself, and ask if I also have the same faults. "How can I stop making them?" I used to act incorrectly, but now I don't: thanks to God.

When you have done these things and have thought about them, have you done a worse act than when you have read a thousand verses written by many? Because when you eat, you're unhappy that you aren't reading? Aren't you satisfied with eating according to what you have learned by reading, and the same with bathing and exercise? Why, then, don't you act consistently in all things, both when you approach Caesar and when you approach any person? If you maintain yourself free from worry, free from alarm, and steady; if you look rather at the things which are done and happen than look at yourself; if you don't envy those who are preferred before you; if surrounding circumstances don't strike you with fear or admiration, what do you want? Books? For what purpose? Because isn't this preparation for life? And isn't life itself made up of other things than this? This is just as if an athlete should cry when he enters the stadium, because he's not being exercised outside of it. It was for this purpose that he used to practice exercise; does he seeks those things when the time of action comes? This is just as if when coming to an agreement on appearances, some of which can be comprehended, and some which can't, we shouldn't distinguish between them but should read what has been written about comprehension.

What's the reason of this? The reason is that we have never read for this purpose, we have never written for this purpose, so that we may in our actions use in a way conformable to nature the appearances presented to us; but we dismiss this, in learning what is said, and in being able to explain it to others, in resolving the syllogism, and in handling the hypothetical theories. For this reason, what we study alone is the impediment. Do you want all the things which are not in your power? Be prevented then, be hindered, fail in your purpose. But if we read what is written about action, not that we may see what is said about action, but that we may act well: if we read what is said about desire and aversion, in order that we may neither fall in our desires, or fall into that which we try to avoid: if we read what is said about duty, in order that, remembering the relations, we may do nothing irrationally or contrary to these relations; we should not be angry in being hindered by our reading, but we should be satisfied with doing. "Today I've read many verses, I have written many"; but, "Today I have adjusted my actions as taught by the philosophers; I haven't had desire; I have used avoidance only with respect to things which are within the power of my will; I have not been afraid of any person, I haven't been overcome by another; I have exercised my patience, my abstinence and my cooperation with others"; and so, we should thank God for what we should thank Him for.

A man is afraid that he won't have power: you should be afraid that you will. Don't do so, my man; but as you ridicule the one who is afraid that he, won't have power, ridicule yourself as well. Because it makes no difference whether you are thirsty like a man who has a fever, or have a fear of water like a man who's mad. How will you be able to say as Socrates did, "If it pleases God, let it be"? Do you think that Socrates, if he was eager to spend his leisure time in Lyceum or in the Academy and to speak daily with the young men, would have so easily gone into military expeditions and so often as he did; wouldn't he have moaned and cried about it? He would have said, "What a fool I am, why am I miserable here, when I could be sunbathing in Lyceum?" Is it your business to sunbathe? Isn't it your business to be happy, to be free from hindrance, free from impediment? Would he still have been Socrates, if he cried in this way: how would he have been able to write Paeans in prison?

In short, remember this, that whatever you prize which is beyond your will, that's how far you destroy your will. But these things are not in the power of the will, not only power, but also leisure. "So, do I have to live in this turmoil?" Why do you say "turmoil?" "I mean among many men." Well what is the hardship? "Vinegar is sharp; honey disturbs my habit of the body. I don't like vegetables." So also, "I don't like leisure; it is a desert: I don't like a crowd; it's confusion." But if circumstances make it necessary for you to live alone or with a few, it is what it is, use the experience as you should: talk with yourself, exercise the appearances, work on your preconceptions. If you fall into a crowd, call it a celebration of games: try to enjoy the festival with other men. Because what's a more pleasant sight for a man who loves mankind than a number of men? We see with pleasure herds of horses or sheep: we are delighted when we see many ships: so who upset when he sees many men? "But they deafen me with their cries." Then your hearing is impeded. What is this to you? Has your power of making the use of appearances been hindered? Who prevents you from using, according to nature, inclination to a thing and aversion from it; and movement toward a thing and movement away from it? What turmoil is able to do this?

Do you only bear in mind the general rules: "What is mine, what is not mine; what is given to me; what does God want me to do? What does He not want me to do?" Before he want you to have leisure time, to talk with yourself, to write about these things, to read, to hear, to prepare yourself. You had sufficient time for this. Now He says: "Come to the contest; show us what you've learned, how you've practiced the athletic art. How long did you exercise for? Now's the opportunity for you to learn whether you are an athlete worthy of victory, or one of those who are easily defeated." Why are you angry? No contest is without confusion. There are many who exercise themselves for the contests, many who seek those who can train them, many masters, and many spectators. "But my wish is to live quietly." Cry then, and moan as you deserve to do. Because what is a greater punishment to the untrained man than this, and to him who disobeys the divine commands: to be cry, to envy, and in a word, to be disappointed and to be unhappy? Wouldn't you like to release yourself from these things? "And can I do that?" Haven't you heard that you should remove desire entirely, apply aversion to those things only which are within your power, that you should give up everything, body, property, fame, books, turmoil and power? Because whatever way you turn, you are a slave, you are subjected, you are hindered, you are compelled, you are entirely in the power of others. But keep these words in mind,

Lead me God to my destiny.

Is it your will that I go to Rome? I will go to Rome. To Athens? I will go to Athens. To prison? I will go to prison.

If you say, "When should a man go to Athens?" you are lost. If you desire to go, if it's not accomplished, you'll be unhappy; and if it's accomplished, you'll be vain, since you are elated at things at which you sought; and on the other hand, if you are impeded, it makes you a fool because you encounter that which you want to avoid. Give these things up. "Athens is a good place." But happiness is much better; and to be free from passion, free from disturbance, because your affairs don't depend on any man. "There is turmoil in Rome." But happiness is the parallel for all troublesome things. If, then, the time comes for these things, why don't you stop seeking to avoid them? What purpose is there to avoid carrying a burden like a donkey, and to be beaten with a stick? Do you realise you must always be a slave to a man who has it in his power to affect you, and to impede you, you must serve him as an evil genius.

There is only one way to happiness, and let this rule close by, in the morning, during the day and at night; the rule is not to look toward things which are out of the power of our will, to think that nothing is our own, to give up all things to the Divinity, to Fortune; to make them the administrators of these things, as God as designed it; for a man to watch only that which is his own, that which cannot be hindered; and when we read, to refer our reading to this only, and our writing and our listening. For this reason, I can't call the man industrious, if I hear that he reads and writes only; and even if a man adds that he reads all night, I can't say it, if he doesn't know what he should refer his reading to. Neither would you say that a man is industrious if stays awake for a girl. And if he does it for reputation, I say that he's a lover of reputation. And if he does it for money, I say that he's a lover of money, not a lover of work; and if he does it through love of learning, I say that he's a lover of learning. But if he refers his work to his own ruling power, that he may keep it in a state conformable to nature and pass his life in that state, then, and only then, would I say that he is industrious.

I never commend a man for the things which are common to all, but on what his opinions are; because these are the things which belong to each man, which make his actions good or bad. Remembering these rules, rejoice in that which is present, and be content with the things which come in at the right time. If you see anything which you have learned and inquired about occurring, to you the course of your life, be delighted. If you have put aside a bad disposition and removed a bad habit; if you've lost the bad temper, obscene words, impulsiveness, laziness; if you are not compelled by what you formerly were, and not in the same state as you once were, you can celebrate a daily festival, today because you have behaved well in one act, and tomorrow because you have behaved well in another. Is there a greater reason than this for sacrificing what is not in your power? These things come to you from yourself and from God. Remember who gives you these things and for what purpose. If you treasure these thoughts, do you think it makes a difference where you will be happy, or where you will please God? Isn't God equally distant from all places? Can't He see from all places alike what is going on?

CHAPTER 85 – AGAINST THOSE WHO ARGUE

A wise man doesn't fight with any person, and he doesn't allow another to, as much as he can prevent it. And an example of this and other things we see in the life of Socrates, who not only always avoided fights, but wouldn't even allow others to argue. He settled many arguements; he tolerated his wife, and his son who attempted to go against him and his teachings. Because he always remembered that no man has in his power another man's ruling principle. He wished, therefore for nothing else than that which was his own. And what is this? Not that any other man acts according to nature; because that is something which belongs to another; but while others are doing their own acts, however they choose to, he won't be affected and will always be in a state conformable to nature. Because this is the objective always set by a wise man. Is it to be the commander of an army? No: but if he were, his objective would still be to maintain his own ruling principle. Is it to marry? No; but if he gets married, his objective is still to be in a state conformable to nature. But if hoped for his son not to do wrong, or his wife, he would wish for what belongs to another. So, his objective is not to seek that which belongs to another; but he instructs himself to learn what things are a man's own and what belongs to another.

How then could there be any fighting if a man has this opinion? Don't those who fight expect that which comes from the bad to be worse and more severe than what actually happens? And don't they see the bad actions they do as a gain? "Some person has insulted you." Great, thank him for not striking you. "But he struck me as well." Great, thank that he didn't wound you "But he wounded me as well." Great, thank that he didn't kill you. Did he not learn in school that man is a tame animal, that men love one another, that an act of injustice does great harm to the man who does it. If he hasn't learnt this and has no concept of it, why should we expect him not to follow that which seems to benefit him "Your neighbour has thrown stones." Have you done anything wrong? "But the things in the house have been broken." Are you one of the utensils? No; you're a free power of will. How should you answer to this? Be like them and throw more stones in return? But if you consider what is right for a man, examine your mind, see what faculties you came into the world with. Do you have the temperament of a wild beast, do you have the nature for revenge and to injure? When is a horse worthless? When it's been deprived of his natural faculties; not when it can't crow like a rooster, but when it can't run. When is a dog worthless? Not when it can't fly, but when it can't track its target. Doesn't it follow then, that a man is also unhappy, not because he can't strangle lions or reach a certain status, because he didn't come into the world in possession of powers from nature for this purpose, but because he's lost his morality and his loyalty? People should meet and cry for this poor man, for the misfortunes which he has fallen into; not to cry because a man has been born or has died, but because it has happened to him in his lifetime to have lost the things which are his own, not that which he received from his father, not his land and house, because none of these things is a man's own, all of them belong to others, and at different times are given to different people by those who have them in their power: but I mean the things which belong to him as a man, the marks in his mind with which he came into the world, marks like we seek on coins, and if we find them, we approve of the coins, and if we don't find the marks, we reject them. What is the stamp of his opinions? "It is gentleness, a sociable disposition, a tolerant temper, a character of mutual affection." If he has these qualities. I accept them: I consider this man a citizen, I accept him as my neighbour, a companion on my travels. Check that he doesn't have the stamp of Nero. Is he passionate, is he full of resentment, is he fault-finding? If he was angry would he attack those who come his way? How could we call this person a man? Is he judged only by the exterior? If that were the case, say that we had a wax formation, green which looked like an apple, and had the smell of an apple. The external wouldn't be enough, we need to know what is inside the skin: so, the nose and eyes aren't enough to recognise a man, he must have the opinions of a man as well. If we find a man who doesn't listen to reason, who doesn't know when he is disproven: he's a fool: if we find in another man his sense of shame has become dead: he's good for nothing, he should be called anything other than a man. Another man seeks someone who he can fight, this man is not a sheep or a donkey, but some kind of wild beast.

Wouldn't I be despised by people who know me? How could anyone who knows you despise a man who is gentle and modest? Perhaps you mean by those who don't know you? And what is that to you? No artist cares about the opinion of those who know nothing about his art. "But they might become more hostile toward me because of this." Why do you say "me"? Can any man damage your will, or prevent you from using in a natural way the appearances which are presented to you, "No he can't." Why, then, are you disturbed and why do you choose to show fear? And why don't you claim that you are at peace with all men whatever they do, and laugh at those who think they can harm you? "These fools," you say, "don't know who I am or where my good or my evil exists, because they have no access to the things which are mine."

This like when those, who have a strong city and army, mock those who try to take it; "Look at the trouble these men are going through, for nothing: our wall is secure, we have food for a long time, and many other resources." These are the things which make a city strong: but nothing else than the opinions makes a man's soul impenetrable. In reality, what wall is so tall, or what body so hard, or what possession so safe, or what honour so free from assault? All things everywhere are perishable, easily taken by assault, and, if any man in any way is attached to them, he must be disturbed, expect what is bad, he must fear, cry, find his desires disappointed, and fall into things which he wants to avoid. So, wouldn't we choose to make secure the only method of safety which is offered to us, wouldn't we choose to withdraw ourselves from that which is perishable, and to work hard toward the things, which are imperishable and by nature free; and wouldn't we remember that no man can hurt another or does good to another, but that a man's opinion about each thing is that which hurts him, is that which upsets him; this is fighting, this is civil conflict, this is war? That which made Eteocles and Polynices enemies, was nothing more than the difference in opinion they had about royal power and exile; one believed it was extremely evil, the other believed it to be the greatest good.

The nature of every man is to seek the good, to avoid the bad; to consider him who deprives us of good and involves us in evil an enemy, even if he's like a brother, or a son, or a father. Because nothing is more like us than the good: however, the whole world is full of enemies who try to encourage what's bad. But if the will is in a state as it should be, there is only good; and if the will, is in a state that it shouldn't be, there is only evil.

Where can we find conflict? About what? About the things which don't concern us. Conflict with who? With the ignorant, the unhappy, and with those who are deceived about the important things. Remembering this Socrates was able to manage his own house and endured a very bad-tempered wife and a foolish son. How did she show her bad temper? She poured water on his head, threw the cake on the floor and stepped on it. What is this to me? Well, my business is the same; no one can change my will; because this power of being free is given by God to every man. These opinions make love in a house, harmony in a city, peace among nations, and gratitude to God; they make a man cheerful toward externals and things which belong to others, and about things which are of no value.

Of course, we are able to read and write these things, and to claim them to be good for us, but do we put them into practice? This is what is necessary.

CHAPTER 86 – AGAINST THOSE WHO CRY

"I'm upset," one man says, "because everyone feels sorry for me." Is it the fact people feel sorry for you which concerns you or those who feel sorry for you? Is it in your power to stop this? "It's in my power, if I show them that I don't need them to feel sorry for me." So, are you in a condition which makes people feel sorry for you or not? "I don't think I am: but these people don't feel sorry for me for things which they should, I mean, for my faults; they feel sorry for me for my poverty, for not having an honourable job, for disease and things like this." Therefore, are you prepared to convince them that none of these things is evil, and that it's possible for a man who's poor and has no job to be happy; or to show display yourself as a rich man with power? The latter, belongs to a man who is boastful, silly and good for nothing. And consider what things are required to support the act. You will need servants, and silver jewellery, and to display this in public, and to show that you are a man honoured by many, and prepared to try and appear to be more handsome than you are. This spectacle you must create, if you choose to take the second path so people won't feel sorry for you. But the first path is impracticable and long, to attempt the something which God hasn't been able to do, to convince all men which things are good and bad. Is this power given to you? The only thing given to you, is to convince yourself; and you haven't even done that yet. So I ask you, are you able to persuade other men? Who has lived with you, as long as you have lived with yourself? Who has more power to convince you than you do to convince yourself; and who is closer to you than you are to yourself? How, then, haven't you already convinced yourself to learn? Aren't things upside down at the moment? Is this what you've been serious about doing, to learn to be free from grief, free from disturbance, not to be shamed, and to be free? Haven't you heard that there's only one way which leads to this, to give up the things which don't depend on the will, to withdraw from them, and to admit that they belong to others? For example, another man has an opinion about you, what is that? "It's something independent of the will." Then isn't it nothing to you? "It's nothing." So then, would you be angry about that and disturbed, haven't you created firm beliefs about good and evil?

Won't you forget about others, and be your own teacher, and a student of yourself? "The rest of men can consider whether it's in their interest to live their lives in a state opposing nature: but to me no man is closer than myself. What is the meaning of this, that I have listened to the words of philosophers and I agree with them, but in fact I am no way much different? Am I stupid? And yet, in all other things that I've chosen, I haven't been found to be stupid: I learned letters quickly, and to wrestle, and geometry, and to resolve complex arguments. Hasn't reason convinced me? Which is strange because there is nothing else which I have from the beginning approved and chosen: and now I read about these things, hear about them, write about them; and have so far discovered no reason stronger than this. So, what causes this deficiency? Have the opposing opinions not been removed from me? Have the notions not been applied in action, but like armour once set aside becomes rusted and won't fit me? I don't find myself satisfied with general reading or writing, but I love philosophy. However, the necessary teachings which show how a man can become free from grief, fear, passion, and hindrance, these I don't apply or practice. Then I care about what other people will say or think about me, whether they notice me, and whether I appear happy."

Fool, can't you see what you're saying about yourself? What do you appear to yourself to be? In your opinions, in your desires, in your aversions from things, in your movements, in your preparation, in your designs, and in other acts suitable to a man? Do you really worry yourself about this, whether others feel sorry for you? "Yes." And you're upset about that? Isn't a man who is upset a person to feel sorry for? "Yes." So how aren't you felt sorry for as you should be? Because by the act that you feel about people feeling sorry for you, you make yourself deserving of it. What does Antisthenes say? Haven't you heard? "It's a royal thing, to do right and be spoken bad about." My head is clear, but people think that I have the headache. What do I care? I am free from fever, and people sympathize with me as if I had a fever, they say: "Poor man,

I can see you've had a fever for a long time." I reply: "It's true I've been ill for a long time, what will happen to me?" "Whatever God wants": and at the same time, I secretly laugh at these people. So, what would I do in this case also? I'm poor, but I have the right opinion about poverty. Why, then, would I care if they feel sorry for me about my poverty? I'm not in power; but others are: and I have the opinion which I should have about power. Let them feel sorry for me; but I'm not hungry or thirsty, neither am I suffering from a cold; but because they're hungry or thirsty they think that I am too. What should I do for them? Should I go and say: "Don't be mistaken, men, I am very well, I'm not upset about poverty, and don't desire power, or anything else other than right opinions. These I have free from restraint, I care about nothing at all." What nonsense talk is this? How do I possess right opinions when I am not content with being what I am, and am uneasy about what I'm supposed to be?

"But," you say, "others will acquire more in life and be preferred to me." Well, what is more reasonable than for those who have worked toward anything to have more of that which they have worked for? They have worked for power, you have worked on your opinions; and they have worked for wealth, you for the proper use of appearances. See if they have more than you in the things which you have worked for, and which they neglect; if they agree better than you with respect to the natural rules of things; if they are less disappointed than you in their desires; if they fall less into things which they want to avoid than you; if in their intentions, if in the things which they propose to themselves, if in their purposes, if in their motions toward an object they take a better aim; if they better observe proper behavior, as men, as sons, as parents, and so on as to the other names by which we express the relations of life. But if they exercise power, and you don't, won't you tell yourself the truth, that you do nothing for the sake of this, and they do? Since I care about the right opinions, is it more reasonable for me to have power." Yes, in the matter of which you care about, in opinions. But in a matter in which they have cared more than you, give way to them. The case is just the same as if, because you have the right opinions, you thought that when using a bow and arrow you should hit the mark better than an archer. If that's what you expect give up your pursuit of the right opinions and work toward the things you want to acquire; and then cry, if you don't succeed; because you deserve to cry. Now you say you're busy with other things, that you are looking after other things, but it must be said that no other acts will help you to obtain what you need. He who wakes in the morning seeks who he should talk to, who he should send a gift to, how he can be helpful. When he prays, he prays about these things; and when he sacrifices, he sacrifices for these things. The saying of Pythagoras goes:

A lazy man should not sleep, he should contemplate instead. "Where have I failed myself?" "What have I done?" Anything like a free man, anything like a noble-minded man? And if he can't recall anything like this, he should blame himself. If you truly care about nothing else except the proper use of appearances, as soon as you wake in the morning you should reflect, "What do I want in order to be free from passion, and free from worry? What am I? Am I body, a piece of property? I am none of these? If not, what am I? I am a rational animal. What is required of me?" Reflect on your acts. "Where have I failed in the acts which create happiness? What have I done which is either unfriendly or unsocial? What have I not done in regards to these things, and what should I have done?"

There is such a great difference in desires, actions, wishes, would you still expect to share with others the things which they have worked for, and you haven't? Would you still be surprised if they feel sorry for you, and would you be angry? They aren't angry if you feel sorry for them. Why? Because they are convinced that they have that which is good, and you aren't convinced. For this reason, you are not satisfied with what is your own, and you desire what they have: but they are satisfied with what they have, and don't desire what is yours: therefore, if you were really convinced with respect to what's good, you will see you possess it and they have missed it, and you wouldn't care one bit what they say about you.

CHAPTER 87 - ON FREEDOM FROM FEAR

What makes a tyrant formidable? "The guards," you say, "and their swords." So, why if you bought a young boy to the tyrant when he is with his guards, is he not afraid; is it because the child doesn't understand these things? If a man understands what guards are and that they have swords, and goes to the tyrant because he wants to die would he be afraid of the guards? "No, because he wants the thing which makes the guards feared." If, a man doesn't want to die but doesn't care to live, is indifferent and only wants what is allowed for him, approaches the tyrant, what would stop him from approaching the tyrant without fear? "Nothing." If then, a man has the same opinion about his property as the man who I have just mentioned does about his body; and also about his wife and children, and is not affected by whether he possesses them or not, like children who are playing with shells only care about the play not worrying about the shells, he too has set no value on the materials, but values the pleasure that he has with them and the livelihood, what tyrant is then formidable to him, even with guards and swords?

So, isn't it possible for a man to be inclined toward these things through habit, and isn't it possible that a man can learn from reason and from demonstration that God has made all the things in the universe and the universe itself completely free from hindrance and perfect, and that the parts of it are for the use of the whole? All other animals are incapable of comprehending the administration of it; but the rational animal, man, has faculties for the consideration of these things: understanding if it's a part, and what kind of a part it is, and that its right for the parts to be secondary to the whole. And besides this being naturally noble, magnanimous and free, man sees in the things which surround him that some are free from hindrance and in his power, and the other things are subject to hindrance and in the power of others; that the things which are free from hindrance are in the power of the will; and those which are subject to hindrance are the things which are not in the power of the will. And, for this reason, if he thinks that his good and his interest be in these things only which are free from hindrance and in his own power, he will be free, prosperous, happy, free from harm, magnanimous, thankful to God for all things; and in no way finding fault with any of the things which have not been put in his power, or blaming any of them. But if he thinks that his good and his interest are in externals and in things which are not in the power of his will, he must out of necessity be hindered, impeded, be a slave to those who have the power over things which he admires and fears; and he must out of necessity be ungodly because he thinks that he is harmed by God, and he must be unfair because he always claims more than belongs to him; and he must out of necessity be hopeless and shameful.

What impedes a man, who has clearly separated these things, from living with a light heart and bearing with the restraints, quietly expecting everything which can happen, and enduring that which has already happened? "What if you have to bear poverty?" You will already know what poverty is and would have found someone who can act the part of a poor man. "What if you possess power?" Have the power, and also the trouble of it. "Banishment?" Wherever I have to go, there I will be well; because I am here as well, it's not because of the place that I'm well, but because of my opinions which I take with me: because no man can deprive me of them; my opinions are mine and they can't he taken from me, and I am satisfied while I have them, wherever I may be and whatever I'm doing. "But now it's time to die." Why do you say "to die"? Don't make it a tragedy, but speak of it as it is: it's now time for my body to be dissolved into the things out of which it was composed. And what's difficult here? Is it that I perish and am absorbed by universe? What new and amazing thing is going to happen? Is it because of this that a tyrant is formidable? Is it because of this reason that the guards appear to have swords which are large and sharp? Say to others: I have considered these things; and no man has power over me. I have been made free; I know His commands; no man can lead me as a slave. I am granted my freedom from the true giver of freedom; and selected the true judge. Are you the master of my body? What is that to me? Are you the master of my property? What is that to me? Are you the master of my exile?

Well, from all of these things and from my body I will leave whenever you like. Try to display your power and you will see how far it goes.

After this who can I fear? Those who grant access to the theatre? What can they do? Shut me out? If they know I want to enter, let them shut me out. "Why, would I even go to the doors?" Because, unless someone allows me to go in, I wouldn't even go, and am always content with whatever happens; because I think that what God chooses for me is better than what I choose. I'll attach myself as a minister and follower to Him; I have the same movements as He does, I have the same desires; in a word, I have the same will. There is no shutting out for me. Some try to force their way in. Why don't I force my way in? Because I know that nothing good is distributed within to those who enter. And when I hear that a man is called fortunate because he's honoured by Caesar, I say, "What does he receive?" A province. Does he receive the right opinions as he should? He receives a place in the office. Does he also obtain the power of using his office well? Why would I strive to enter? A man scatters dried figs and nuts: the children take them and fight with each another; men don't, because they think that is a small matter. But if a man threw shells, even the children wouldn't take them. Provinces are distributed: let children look at that. Money is distributed: let children look at that. Offices are distributed: let children scramble for them, let them be shut out, beaten, and kiss the hands of the giver: but to me these are only dried figs and nuts. What If you fail to receive them, while Caesar is scattering them about, don't be bothered: if a dried fig comes your way, take it and eat it; if you even value the fig. And if this va;ue is high, you'll compliment those have them, however a dried fig isn't worth the trouble.

You show me the swords of the guards and say: "Can you see how big they are, and how sharp." What, then, do these big and sharp swords do? "They kill." And what can a fever do? "The same." So, should I wonder about these things and worship them, and live as slave to them? I hope this won't happen: but when I've learned that everything which has come into existence must also leave it,

288

that the universe may not stand still or be impeded, I no longer consider it any difference whether a fever does it, or a soldier. But if a man must make a comparison between these things, I know that the soldier will do it with less trouble, and quicker. When I don't fear anything which a tyrant can do to me, or desire anything which he can give, why would I still look toward him with wonder? Why would I be confused? Why would I fear the guards? Why would I be happy if he spoke to me in a friendly way, and why would I go and tell others how he spoke to me? Is he Socrates, is he Diogenes, does his praise offer me proof of what I am? Am I eager to imitate his morals? So why would I play this game, and go to him, and serve him just so he doesn't kill me. If he asked me, "Go and bring eon of Salamis to me," I would say to him, "Find someone else, because I'm not playing." "Take him away." He says, and I follow; this part of the play. "But your head will be taken off." Well, does the tyrant's head always remain where it is, and the heads of those who obey him? "But you won't even be buried" These things are intimidating to children and fools. But if a man has attended a philosopher's school and still doesn't know what he is, then he deserves to be full of fear and to flatter these people; if he hasn't learned yet that he is not his body, but he is that which makes use of the parts of the body and controls them and follows the appearances of things.

This talk teaches us to give it up the body and property, to give up children, parents, brothers, to withdraw and to give up everything; and to make an exception for the opinions, which God has decided to be the true property of every man.

If you are superior and stronger, I give way to you: on the other hand, where I'm superior, you yield to me; because I've studied this, and you haven't. Did you study to live in houses with floors made from various stones, having servants cater to you, and how you'll wear fine clothing. Do I seek any of these things? Have you studied of opinions and your own rational faculty? Do you know the parts its composed of, how they are brought together, how they are connected, what powers it has, and what type? Why are you angry, if another, who has studied this, has the advantage over you in these things? "These things are the greatest." And who stops you from studying these things and looking after them? And who has a better stock of books than the people here to assist you? All you need to do, is at last place your focus on your ruling faculty: consider what it is that you possess, and where it came from, this which understand things, tests them, and selects and rejects. But if you only bother to study the externals you will possess them like other men do; but you're ruling faculty will be neglected and in a bad state.

CHAPTER 88 – AGAINST THOSE WHO RUSH

Don't praise or blame a man due to the things which are common to all, and don't declare he possess a skill or lack of skill; and you will be free from malice. "That man eats too quickly." So, is he doing wrong? Of course not. So, what does he do? He eats quickly. Are all things done well? Not at all: but the acts which follow from the right opinions are done well; and those which follow from bad opinions are done ill. So, don't, until you know the opinion which makes a man do something, praise or blame the act. But an opinion is not easily discovered by viewing people. "That man is a carpenter." Why? "Because he uses a saw." So? "That man is a musician because he sings." What does that signify? "That man is a philosopher. Because he wears a cloak and has long hair." For this reason, if a man sees a philosopher acting indecently, immediately he says, "See what the philosopher is doing." Because if this is the preconceived notion of a philosopher and what he claims to be, to wear a cloak and have long hair, men would be right in that case; but if we say a philosopher is someone who keeps himself free from faults, why wouldn't we rather, take from him the name of philosopher? Because we do this in the case of all other arts. When a man sees another handling a saw incorrectly, he doesn't say, "Look how badly carpenters do their work"; but he says the opposite, "This man is not a carpenter, because he uses a saw very badly." In the same way if a man hears another singing badly, he doesn't say, "Look how badly musicians sing"; but rather, "This man isn't a musician." But it is in the matter of philosophy only that people do this. When they see a man acting contrary to the profession of a philosopher, they don't take away his title, they assume him to be a philosopher, and from his acts of behaving indecently they conclude that there is no use in philosophy.

What is the reason of this? Because we attach value to the notion of a carpenter, and to that of a musician, and to the notion of other artisans in a similar way, but not to a philosopher. What other kind of art has a name derived from a hair style; without referring to its theories and material? What is the material of a philosopher? Is it a cloak? No, it is reason. What is his objective? is it to wear a cloak? No, but to possess reason in its right state. What are his theories? Are they about the what way a beard can look great or how long hair should look? No, it's to know the elements of reason, what each of them is, and how they are fitted together, and what follows them. Instead of just looking at what he claims to be and when he acts in an opposing manner blame the art, you should first study what the art is.

To begin with some start to study what is common to all philosophers: and as soon as they have a cloak and a beard, they say, "I'm a philosopher." But no man would say, "I'm a musician," just because he bought a guitar and a plectrum. But this style of appearance has become synonymous with the philosopher, and for this reason, Euphrates used to say, "For a long time I strove to be a philosopher without people knowing it; and this," he said, "was useful to me: because first I knew that when I did anything well, I didn't do it for the sake of the spectators, but for the sake of myself: I ate well for the sake of myself; I had my face well composed and my walk: all for myself and for God. Then, as I struggled alone, alone I was in danger: in no respect through me, if I did anything bad or wrong, was philosophy endangered; or did I injure anyone by doing anything wrong as a philosopher. For this reason, those who didn't know my purpose used to wonder how it was that, while I spoke and lived with philosophers, I was not a philosopher myself. And what harm was there in this, for me not to be known as a philosopher by my appearance over my actions?" See how I eat, how I drink, how I sleep, how I co-operate, how I manage desire, how I manage aversion, how I maintain the relations, those which are natural or those which are acquired, how I am free from confusion, how I am free from hindrance. Judge of me from this, if you can. But if you are so deaf and blind that you can't conceive what a good builder is, unless you see the cap on his head, what is the harm in not being recognized by such a foolish judge?

Socrates wasn't known to be a philosopher by most people; and they used to come to him and ask to be introduced to philosophers. Was he angry? And did he say, "Don't you think I'm a philosopher?" No, but he would take them and introduce them to others, being satisfied not being thought to be a philosopher, he wasn't annoyed: because he knew he was a philosopher. What is the work of an honourable and good man? To have many students? Not at all. Those who are interested in that will do that. Is it to carefully examine difficult theories? No, others will do that as well. So, what I do? Wherever there is no hurt to yourself, or advantage over others. "If any man can damage me," he says, "I'm not doing this: if I am waiting for another man to do good to me, I'm not doing this.

You can see others say, "I'm free from passion and disturbance," but without being ignorant, notice really, they are uneasy and disturbed by things with no value. You should learn to truly say I am free from all worry."

You will be honoured with the magic wand from God, and be able to say, "You see, men, you seek happiness and tranquillity where it can't be found, I am sent to you by God as an example. I who have no property, or house, or wife, or children, not even a bed, or coat, or household utensils; and see how healthy I am: try me, and if you see that I am free from worries, hear my remedies and how I've been cured." Whose work is this? The work of God, through the man who God judges worthy to deliver this service, where he can give a demonstration of true virtue:

His beautiful face.

He wipes a tear.

And not only this, he neither desires or seeks anything, no place or amusement, like children who seek holidays; always fortified by modesty as others are fortified by walls, doors and doorkeepers.

But now, being inclined toward philosophy, like those who have a bad stomach are drawn to foods which soothe. They let their hair grow, they wear a cloak, they show their bare shoulders, they argue with those who they meet; and if they see a man in a thick winter coat, they argue with him. Fools, first exercise yourself in winter weather: first strive not to be known as a philosopher: be a philosopher for yourself for a little while. Fruit grows like this: the seed must be buried for some time, hidden, then it grows slowly so it may come to fruition. If it has only sprouted, it is not complete, its imperfect. Such a poor plant you are: you have developed the blossom too early; and the cold weather will ruin you. What do the farmers say about seeds when the warm weather is too early? They are afraid that the seeds will thrive too early, and then a single frosty day will destroy them and show them that they are too fast. Don't you also consider, my man: that you have shot out too soon, you have hurried toward a fame before the right season: you think that you are something, a fool among fools: you will be caught by the frost, and although you have been frost-bitten at the root, your upper parts appear to have blossomed a little, and for this reason you think you're alive and flourishing. Allow us to ripen in the natural way: why should we force this? Let the root grow, then acquire the first joint, then the second, and then the third: in this way, then, the fruit will naturally force itself out, even if I didn't choose it to. Because, who full of such great principles doesn't perceive his own power and move toward the corresponding acts? A bull is not ignorant of his own nature and his power, when a wild beast shows itself, it doesn't wait for someone to persuade him to appear. So, if I have the power of a good man, should I wait for you to prepare for me my own acts? At present if you don't possess them, why do you want to appear as if you do? Develop properly.

CHAPTER 89 - ABOUT A PERSON WHO HAS BECOME SHAMEFUL

When you see another man who possess a power, make it clear that you have no desire for power; when you see a rich man, contemplate what you possess in place of riches: because if you possess nothing in place of them, you'll feel miserable; but if you have no desire for riches, you already know that you possess more than this man possesses and what is worth much more. Another man has a beautiful woman: you have the satisfaction of not desiring a beautiful wife. Do you think these things are insignificant? How much would these people give, these very men who are rich and in possession of power, and live with beautiful women, to be able to despise riches and power and these women who they love and enjoy? Don't you see how thirsty a man is who has a fever? His thirst is much greater than a man who is in good health: because he is satisfied with a glass of water; but the sick man, is only satisfied for a short time, then he vomits, and becomes thirstier. There is a desire for riches and to possess riches, desire of power and to possess power, desire for a beautiful woman and to sleep with her: to this is added jealousy, fear of being deprived of the things which you love, indecent words, indecent thoughts and unseemly acts.

"And what do I lose?" you will say. My man, you were modest, and aren't any more. Have you lost nothing? Instead of Socrates and Diogenes, you admire the man who is able to corrupt and seduce most women. You want to appear handsome although you aren't. You like to display clothes so you can attract women; and you imagine that you are happy. But formerly you didn't think of these thing, there used to be decent talk, a worthy man, and a generous start. Therefore, you slept like a man, walked like a man, wore manly clothes, and used to talk like a good man; then you ask, "I have lost nothing?" Do men lose nothing more than money? Isn't their modesty lost? Isn't their decent behaviour lost? Has a man who has lost these things sustained no loss? Perhaps you think that none of these things is a loss. But there was a time when you considered this to be the only loss and damage a man could sustain, and you were anxious that no man could corrupt you.

Well, notice you are disturbed by these words and actions by nobody but by yourself. Fight with yourself, restore yourself to decency, to modesty, to freedom. If any man ever said to you, that someone can force me to be an adulterer, to wear fine clothes, and to wear perfume, wouldn't you killed the man who claimed he could corrupt me? Now, won't you help yourself? How much easier is it to help yourself? There is no need to kill any man, or to put him in chains, its only necessary for you to speak to yourself, the self which can be easily persuaded by you, the self which no man has more power of persuasion than yourself. First of all, condemn what you're doing, and then, when you have condemned it, change the bad spirit.

What do the wrestling coaches do? Has the boy fallen? "Get up," they say, "wrestle again until you are strong." You have to do the same: be well assured that nothing is more malleable than the human soul. You must exercise the will, and then it's done, it's set right: as on the other hand, if you sleep on this, it's lost: because from within comes your downfall and from within comes your help. What greater good can you seek than this? From a shameless man, you will become a modest man, from a disorderly man, you will become an orderly man, from a faithless man, you will become a faithful man, from a man of uncontrolled habits to a sober man. If you seek anything more than this, continue doing what you are doing: not even God can now help you.

CHAPTER 90 – WHAT THINGS WE SHOULD VALUE AND WHAT WE SHOULDN'T

All difficulties men face are about external things, their helplessness is about the external. "What should I do, how will it be, how will it turn out, will this happen, will that happen?" All of this is due to the words of those who are turning themselves toward things which are not within the power of the will. Because who says, "How can I avoid agreeing with anything which is false? How can I never turn away from the truth?" If a man has a good disposition, and is anxious about these things, I will remind him: "Why are you anxious? These things are in your own power: be assured: don't be impulsive in agreeing before you apply the natural rule." On the other side, if a man is anxious about desire, that he might not obtain that which he wants, and with respect to avoidance of things, that he might end up falling into that which he wants to avoid, I would hug him, because he is ignoring the things which others panic about, and their fears, and engagements his thoughts toward his own affairs and his own condition. Then I would say to him: "If you don't choose to desire that which you can fail to obtain or attempt to avoid that which you can fall into, desire nothing which belongs to others, or try to avoid any of the things which are not in your power. If you do not observe this rule, you will fall in your desires and fall into that which you want to avoid. What is the difficulty here? Where is there room for the words, 'How will it be?' and 'How will it turn out?' and, 'Will this happen or that happen?'

Isn't that which will happen independent of the will? "Yes." And the nature of good and of evil, isn't it in the things which are within the power of the will? "Yes." Is it in your power, then, to consider according to nature everything which happens? Can any man hinder you? "No man." So, don't say anymore, "How will it be?" Because however it may be, you will handle it well, and the result will be fortunate. What would Hercules have been if he had said, "How can I avoid a lion or vicious men?" What would you care? If a great lion appeared, you will fight a greater fight: if bad men appear, you relieve the earth of the bad. "Suppose, that similarly you lost your wife." You can still die a good man, doing noble acts. We know certainly we die, so, in the meantime a man should be found doing something worthy with his life. What do you want to be doing, when you are found dead? I would like to be found doing something which belongs to a man, beneficent, suitable to the general interest, noble. But if I can't be found doing these great things, I would be found doing at least that which I cannot be hindered from doing, that which is permitted me to do, correcting myself, cultivating the faculty which makes use of appearances, working toward freedom, interpreting the relations of life; if I succeed, also touching on the third topic, safely forming judgements about things. If death surprises me when I'm busy working on these things, it's enough for me if I can stretch out my hands to God and say:

"The perception I have received from God for seeing his administration and following it, I have not neglected: I haven't dishonoured you with my acts: look how I've used my perceptions, look how I've used my preconceptions: have I ever blamed you? Have I been discontent with anything that happens, or wished it to be different? Have I desired to disobey you? You, that has given me life, I thank you for what you have given me: so long as I have used the things which are mine, I am content; take them back and put them wherever you choose; because all that was mine was what you gave to me." Isn't it not enough to depart in this state of mind, and what life is better and more fit than that of a man who is in this state of mind? And what other man can be this happy?

So, this may be done, a man doesn't' receive small things, and these things which can be lost are not small. You can't wish to be an officer and at the same time have these things, and to be eager to have land and these things as well. Because, if you wish for anything which belongs to another, that which is your own is lost. This is the nature of it: nothing is given or possessed for nothing. Why do people wonder about this? If you wish to be an officer, you must stay awake, run around, kiss hands, tire yourself to exhaustion at other men's orders, say and do many things unworthy of a free man, send gifts to many, and daily presents to some. And what is gained by this? A little money. If you don't agree on this, tell someone to show me what there is besides this.

In order to secure freedom from passion, tranquillity, to sleep well when you sleep, to be really awake when you're awake, to fear nothing, to be anxious about nothing, would you spend nothing and give no work? But if anything belonging to you is lost while you are busy being an officer, or someone else obtains what you should have obtained, would you immediately be angry at what has happened? Will you not take into account on the other side what you received, and what it cost you? Do you expect to have for nothing the things which are great? And, how can you? You can't have the external things and your own ruling faculty: and if you want the externals, give it up. If you don't, you won't have either the externals or the will, and you'll be drawn in different directions toward both. Why don't you straightway, after considering where your good and your evil is, say, "Both of them are in my power? No man can deprive me of the good, or involve me in the bad against my will. Why don't I sleep well? Because all that I have is safe. In regards to the things which belong to others, I'll let someone else focus on those. Who am I to wish to possess them in some way or another? Is the power of selecting them given to me? Has any person made me the distributer of them? The things which I have power over are enough for me: I should manage them as well as I can: and all the rest, whoever possess them may choose."

When a man keeps these things in mind, does he stay awake and move back and forward? What does he want, and what does he regret? When did he believe that any of his friends were immortal, and when didn't he realise that a friend could pass away tomorrow? "Yes," he says, "but I thought that he would live longer than me and bring up my son." You would be a fool for that reason, as you were thinking of what was uncertain. Why, then, don't you blame yourself, and sit crying like girls do?

CHAPTER 91 – ABOUT PURITY

Some people raise a question whether the social feeling is contained in the nature of man; and yet I think that these same people would have no doubt that a love of purity is certainly contained in it, and that, if man is distinguished from other animals by anything, he is distinguished by this. When we see any other animal cleaning itself, we are accustomed to act with surprise, and to add that the animal is acting like a man: and, on the other hand, if a man blames an animal for being dirty, straightway as if we were making an excuse for it, we say, of course the animal is not a human. So, we suppose that there is something superior in the man, and that we receive it from God. Because, since God by his nature is pure and free from corruption, men who approach reason, cling to purity and to a love of purity. But since it is impossible that man's nature can be completely pure being mixed of different materials, reason is applied, as far as it is possible, and reason endeavours to make the human nature: love.

The first, then, and highest purity is that which is in the soul; and we say the same of impurity. Now you could not discover the impurity of the soul as you could discover that of the body: but in regards to the soul, what else could you find in it other than that which makes it impure in respect to the acts which are its own? The acts of the soul are movement toward an object or movement from it, desire, aversion, preparation, design and belief. What is it about these acts which make the soul filthy and impure? Nothing else than its own bad judgements. Consequently, the impurity of the soul is the soul's bad opinions; and the purification of the soul is planting in it the proper opinions. A soul is pure if it has the proper opinions, because the soul alone in its acts is free from worry and pollution.

We should work toward something like this in the body as well, as much as we can. It's impossible for the nose not to run when man has a disturbance in his body. If, a man decides to taste what is body is trying to expel, he is not doing the act of a man. It was impossible for a man's feet not to become muddy and dirty when he passes through a field. For this reason, nature has made water and hands. It was impossible that an impurity wouldn't remain in the teeth from eating: for this reason, the soul says, wash the teeth. Why? To be a man and not a wild animal. It was impossible that the sweat which covers the body and saturates the clothes would not need to be cleaned. For this reason, water, hands, and towels were made necessary for cleaning the body. Won't you wash your body or make it clean? "Why?" he replies. I will tell you again, so you can do the acts of a man. If you think that you deserve to stink. So be it: you deserve to stink. Do you think that those who sit next to you, those who dine at the table with you, those who kiss you deserve the same? Either go into a desert, where you deserve to go, or live by yourself, and smell yourself. Because its only you who should enjoy your own impurities. But when you are in a city, don't behave so inconsiderately and foolishly, what character do you think that belongs to? If nature gave you a horse, would you neglected to clean him? And now think that you have been intrusted with your own body just like a horse; wash it, and take care that no one turns away from it, that no one gets out of the way for it. Who doesn't avoid a dirty man, a stinking man, a man whose skin is foul, more than he avoids a man who has deceived him?

"But Socrates didn't wash often." Yes, but his body was clean: and the most beautiful and the most noble loved him, and desired to sit next to him. It wasn't in his power to use a bath or to wash himself, if he could have, he would have; and yet the rare use he got had an effect. If you don't choose to wash with warm water, wash with cold.

Aristophanes says that Socrates stole clothes from the shop. But anyone who has written about Socrates say the opposite and give evidence in his favour; they say that he was pleasant, not only to hear, but also to see. On the other hand, they write the same about Diogenes. But we shouldn't only focus on the appearance of the body and deter from what else is required from a philosopher; a philosopher should also show himself as cheerful and tranquil. Even if he happened to be without a home, he would live happily as if he were born rich. He can then refer to the body, and say look at my body and see that it is not injured by a hard way of living."

I prefer a young man, who is making his first movements toward philosophy, come to me with his hair carefully cut than with it dirty and rough, because I can see in him a certain notion of beauty and a desire of that which is beautiful. It is only necessary to show him, and to say: "Young man, you seek beauty, and that's ok, but you must know then, that it grows in the part of you where you have the rational faculty: seek it where you have the movements toward and the movements from things, where you have the desire toward, and the aversion from things: because this is what you have in yourself which is superior; but the body belongs to the earth: why do you focus on it, this is not the correct purpose. If you learn nothing else, you will learn from time that the body is nothing." But if a man comes to me covered in filth, dirty, with a moustache down to his knees, what can I say to him? He has no notion of beauty, could I change him and say "Beauty is inside, not in your appearance?" What would you suggest I tell him, that beauty consists not in being covered with dirt, but that it lies in the rational part? Has he any desire of beauty? Has he any concept of it in his mind? Go and talk to a pig, and tell it not to roll in the mud.

For this reason, the words of Xenocrates touched Polemon; because he was a lover of beauty, because he started, having in him a certain motivation toward the love of beauty, but he looked for it in the wrong place. Nature hasn't made even the animals which live with man dirty. Does a horse ever roll in the mud or a well-bred dog? But the pig, the dirty geese, worms and spiders do, which are preferred to be kept furthest away from humans. Should you, then, being a man, choose not to be a man, but carry yourself as a worm, or a spider? Wouldn't you wash yourself? Wouldn't you remove the dirt from your body? Wouldn't you keep clean so those who you know have pleasure to be with you? Would you go into the temples in this state, where it's not permitted to spit, smelling so foul? Am I telling you to overdress yourself, and wear perfume? Far from it; only to be what you are by nature, the rational faculty, the opinions, the actions; but in regards to the body, as far as purity in concerned, only not to offend others.

CHAPTER 92 – ABOUT ATTENTION

When you have diverted your attention for a short time, don't imagine that you'll recover it whenever you choose; let this thought be in mind, that the consequence of the fault committed today your affairs will be in a worse condition tomorrow. That is the first thing, and but what causes the most trouble, is that the habit of not attending to your priorities is formed in you; then a habit of deferring your attention. And continually from time to time you push away, by deferring it, the happiness of life, proper behaviour, being and living conformably to nature. If, then, the procrastination of attention is profitable to you, the complete omission of attention would be more profitable; but if it's not profitable, why wouldn't you maintain constant attention? "Today I choose to play." Well then, shouldn't you play with attention? "I choose to sing." What hinders you from doing that with attention? Is there any part of life which attention does not extend to? Would you do worse by using attention and better by not using attention? And what other things in life are done better by those who don't use attention? Does a man carving wood do better when he doesn't apply attention? Does the captain of a ship manage it better by being inattentive? Don't you see that, when you let your mind loose, it's no longer in your power to use it, either in regards to modesty, or moderation: then you'll do everything that comes into your mind which appeals to your inclinations.

What things should I pay attention to? Firstly, to the general principles and to have them in mind, and without them not to sleep, not to wake up, not to drink, not to eat, not to speak to men; understand that no man is master of another man's will, and that in the will alone we find the good and the bad. No man, then, has the power to create in me any good or to involve me in any evil, but I myself have power over myself in these things. When, I have secured these things, why would I be disturbed about external things? What tyrant is formidable, what disease, what poverty, what offense? "I haven't pleased someone." Is he my work? "No." Why would I trouble myself about him then? "But he's supposed to be someone." Let him think about that; and those who think so as well. But I know who I should please, who I should obey, God. He has given me my will in obedience to myself alone, and has given me rules for the right use of it; and when I follow these rules, I don't care if any man says anything else: in an argument, I don't care about no man. Why would I let those who disagree with me bother me? What is the cause of this disturbance? Nothing else than a lack of discipline in this matter. Because all knowledge despises ignorance and the ignorant; and not only the sciences, but even the arts. Consult any shoemaker you want, and disagrees with many in regards to his own work.

First, then, we should have in mind, and keep the soul directed to this, to pursue nothing external, and nothing which belongs to others, but to do as He who has given us the power asks for; that we should pursue the things which are in the power of the will, and anything else if it is permitted. Next to this we should remember who we are, direct our attention toward the character of this: what will be the consequence of our actions; whether our associates will despise us, whether we should despise them; when to cheer, and who to ridicule; and on what occasion to comply and with someone; and finally, in complying how to maintain our own character. But wherever you have deviated from any of these rules, there is damage immediately, not from anything external, but from the action itself.

Is it possible to be free from faults? It's not possible; but it's possible to direct your efforts incessantly to being faultless. Because we must be content that, if we never lose this attention we will escape at least a few errors. But now when you say, "Tomorrow I'll begin," you must be told that you are saying this, "Today I will be shameless, disregardful of time and place; it will be in the power of others to give me pain; today I will be passionate and envious." Look at how many evil things you are permitting yourself to do. If it's good to use attention tomorrow, how much better is it to use it today? If tomorrow it's in your interest to be attentive, it is ever better today. The things which you may be able to do so tomorrow, you might not be able to defer it again for a third day.

CHAPTER 93 – AGAINST THOSE WHO DISCUSS THEIR AFFAIRS

When a man has talked to us about his own affairs, how inclined are we to divulge our own secrets? Firstly, it seems unfair for a man to have listened to the affairs of another, and not communicate his affairs in return. Men often say, "I've told you my affairs, do you have anything to discuss? In addition, we have the opinion that we can safely trust him who has already told us his own affairs; because the notion arises in our mind that this man could never divulge our affairs because he would be careful not to divulge his own. This is the way those who are not cautious are caught by the soldiers in Rome. A soldier sits next to a man in casual clothing and begins to speak bad about Caesar; then the man, as if he had received a promise not to divulge his opinions, says what he thinks, and then he's carried off in chains.

Something like this happens to us generally. Now as this man has confidently trusted his affairs to me, should I do that as well to any man I meet? No. When I hear, I keep my silence, because if I decide to talk; and he goes and tells all men what he's heard; then I hear what's been done, and if I was a man like him, seek revenge, I divulge what he's told me: this disturb myself and others. But if I remember that no man can injure another, and that every man's acts injure and profit him only, I am secure, and won't do anything like him, but I would suffer whatever I do through my own talk.

"True: but it's unfair when you've heard the secrets of someone and you communicate nothing to him." Do I ask for secrets? Did you decide to speak about your affairs on certain terms, that you in return must hear mine? If you like to divulge, and think that anyone you meet are friends, do you expect me to be like you as well? So why, do you expect me to be so careless? It's the same as if I had a glass which is water-tight, and you have one with a hole in it, and you come and put your wine in my glass, and then you complain that I didn't pour my wine in yours. Because you have a glass with a hole in it. How is there any equality here? You entrusted your affairs, to a man who is faithful and modest, to a man who thinks that his own actions alone are injurious and useful, and that nothing external is. Would you like me to tell you mine, to offer them to a man who has dishonoured his own faculty of will? Is this equality? Show to me that you are faithful, modest, and steady: show me that you have friendly opinions; show that your glass has no hole in it; and you will see that won't wait for you to trust me with your affairs, but I would come to you and ask you to hear mine. Because who doesn't choose to make use of a good container? Who doesn't value a caring and faithful adviser? Who wouldn't willingly accept a man who is ready to tolerate a share in the difficulty of the circumstances, and by this very act ease the burden by taking a part in it.

"True: but I trust you; you don't trust me." Firstly, you don't even trust me, you just like to divulge, and for this reason you can't hold anything; because, if it's true that you trust me, trust your affairs to me; but now, whenever you see a man, you sit next to him and say: "Brother, I have no friend more caring than you; can I tell you, my problems." And you do this to people you don't even know. But if you really trust me, it is plain that you trust me because I am faithful and modest, not because I have told my affairs to you. Allow me, then, to have the same opinion about you. Show me that, if one man tells his affairs to another, he who tells them is faithful and modest. Because if this were so, I would go and tell my affairs to every man, if that would make me faithful and modest. But the thing is, this is not so. If, then, you see a man who focused on things which are not dependent on his will, you must know that this man has ten thousand people to compel and hinder him. You must remember, then, among general principles that secret discourses require loyalty and corresponding opinions. But where can we find these? If you can't answer that question, let someone point out to me a man who can say: "I care only about the things which are my own, the things which are not subject to hindrance, the things which are by nature free." This I view to be the nature of the good: and let all other the things be as they are intended; these I don't concern myself with.

END

For more adapted classics by James Harris please visit:

www.JamesHarris.world